S0-DOR-387

IN THE LABYRINTHS OF LANGUAGE:
A Mathematician's Journey

IN THE LABYRINTHS
OF LANGUAGE:
A Mathematician's Journey

by V. V. NALIMOV

Edited by ROBERT G. COLODNY

PHILADELPHIA

Published by

iSi PRESS™

A Division of the Institute
for Scientific Information®
3501 Market St., University City Science Center, Philadelphia, PA 19104 U.S.A.

© 1974 Vsesojuznoje Agentstvo Po
Avtorskim Pravam

© 1981 ISI Press

ISBN 0-89495-007X

Library of Congress Cataloging in Publication Data

Nalimov, Vasiliĭ Vasil'evich.
  In the labyrinths of language.

  Translation of Veroi͡atnostnai͡a model'i͡azyka.
  Includes bibliography and index.
  1. Language and languages. 2. Linguistic models.
3. Semiotics. I. Colodny, Robert Garland. II. Title.
P106.N313 1981   401'.41   80-39783

All rights reserved. No part of this publication may be reproduced, stored in a retrieval
system, or transmitted, in any form or by any means, including electronic, mechanical,
photographic, or magnetic, without prior written permission of the publisher.

Printed in the United States of America

To the memory
of A. A. Solonovich, Russian mathematician
and philosopher.

Contents

Foreword

It is a pleasure to express my sincere gratitude to V. I. Agol, A. G. Volkov, V. I. Dubrovskii, E. M. Dumanis, V. V. Fedorov, S. M. Raiskyi, S. K. Shaumyan, and O. V. Shimelfenik for a stimulating discussion of the manuscript during its preparation. My hope is that their criticism has eliminated some grosser imperfections of the book. None but the author is responsible for the errors which still remain.

This version slightly differs from the book *Probabilistic Model of Language* published in Russian.

Introduction to English Edition

> . . . Without a hoard of culturally accumulated knowledge, the
> frontal cortex, which only evolved as a memory bank for cultural
> tradition, would remain empty. The same applies to its most impor-
> tant parts, the language area, without which there would be no
> logical or abstract thought, but which on the other hand could not
> function unless the cultural tradition provided it with a vocabulary
> developed over thousands of years of history.
>
> KONRAD LORENZ
> *Behind the Mirror,* p. 190

Looking back on his marvelously creative years, Albert Einstein ex-
claimed ". . . the eternal mystery of the world is its comprehensibility."
One might add to this the observation that the eternal mystery of the
history of human culture is the capacity of human beings to capture so
many aspects of the world by means of man-made symbols, including
that extraordinary artifact — language!

The self-consciousness of man as a thinking and creative creature is, in
all ages, reflected in the uninterrupted effort to probe the mystery of
creativity and cognition by a deeper understanding of the structure and
nature of language. From the time of the early Sumerian cuneiform tab-
lets to the epoch of computer languages, this quest has continued.

Philosophy as we have it now would be a shriveled and useless husk if
we could imagine its corpus stripped of all of the debates concerning the
use and interpretation of language. It might even be said that the vitality
of the culture of any epoch is indexed by the concern given to the problem of communication in all its modes and forms.

When the semitic Akkadians overran ancient Sumer in the third millenium B.C., the problem of compiling multilingual dictionaries first appeared and was solved. And when within the first multi-faceted scientific culture—the Babylonian—thinkers became aware of the problem of equivalence of words and things, these ancient scribes attempted to solve the problem by seeking the clue to ontological classification by grouping together the denotative words according to their intrinsic written patterns. Thus were born the first encyclopedias, and the first *tractatus* on language.

One of the features of modern investigation of the language problem is the recognition that ordinary language—be it written or spoken—is only one member of a class of coherent symbolic communication systems. In his 1674 treatise, *On the Method of Universality*, Leibniz, the greatest of polymaths, wrote:

> That is the aim of that great science which I am used to calling Characteristic, of which what we call Algebra, or Analysis, is only a very small branch, since it is that Characteristic which gives words to languages, letters to words, numbers to Arithmetic, notes to Music. It teaches us how to fix our reasoning, and to require it to leave, as it were, visible traces on the paper of a notebook for inspection at leisure. Finally, it enables us to reason with economy, by substituting characters in the place of things in order to relieve the imagination. . . .

It seems reasonable to believe that only when our great contemporaries unravelled some of the mysteries of the brain and its links with the external world were insights into the nature of language able to advance very far beyond speculations and genial intuitions. In 1935, Anton Pavlov, the Russian physiologist, stated what was to become a major *leit motif* on the linkage of standard linguistics to emerging neurophysiology.

> The developing animal world on reaching the phase of man acquired an exceptional supplement to the mechanism of nervous activity. To an animal, reality is signaled almost exclusively merely by the stimulations—and the traces they leave in the cerebral hemispheres—conveyed directly to the special cells of the visual, auditory, and other receptors of the organism. This is what we likewise possess in the form of impressions, sensations, and conceptions of the environment, both of the general natural environment and of our social environment, with the exception of words—visible and audible. This *first system of signalling reality* is the same in our case as in the case of animals. But words have built up a *second system of signalling reality*, which is only peculiar to us, being a signal of the primary signals. The numerous stimulations by word have, on the one hand, removed us from reality, a fact we should constantly remember so as not to misinterpret our attitude toward reality. On the other hand, *it was nothing other than words which has made us human*, but this, of

course, cannot be discussed here in greater detail. However, it is beyond doubt that the essential laws governing the work of the first system of signalling necessarily regulate the second system as well, because it is work done by the same nervous tissue.[1]

It is clear that there is now a division of labor between those who concentrate on the biological basis of the language capacity or potential and those who are primarily concerned with those aspects of language which can be analyzed at the logical-philosophical level.

Yet for those who are concerned with the unity of the world as object of cognition and who postulate that the searching mind is embedded in nature, these divisions are for analytical convenience only.

V. V. Nalimov, whose work is now to be introduced to the English-speaking world, is such a scholar. His childhood was spent against the background of war, revolution, and civil war. As a young man, trained in the sciences, he worked in high-vacuum physics during the early Five Year Plans. His work at that time also involved studies of the photoelectric effect and quantum electrodynamics. During the tragic years of the Second World War, he was attached to the laboratories of a large metallurgical plant and was a member of the board that directed the geological surveys of the USSR. In 1957, he returned to Moscow to participate in the All Union Institute of Scientific Information of the Academy of Science. For more than a decade, he has been chief of the Laboratory of Mathematical Experiment of Moscow State University. Long a professor of statistics, Nalimov was led to examine in depth the philosophical implications of the penetration of the probabilistic mode into the foundations of the exact sciences. These investigations led him to the foundational problems of science and the languages in which experimental results and inferences were expressed. The corollary was the relation between hypotheses and verification, particularly when the data supporting a theory were of a statistical nature. He knows thoroughly the texts of Popper, Gödel, Black, inter alia. In more recent years, his interest and work have expanded to include the more general relations of science, culture, and society, and to look closely at the diversity of human cultures of past and present.

In the pages that follow, a vast range of informational systems and modes of human communication are examined. The core problem is the intelligibility of communication under conditions of uncertainty. Here, analogy with the general problem of statistical inference has a great heuristic value.

---

[1] This paragraph was brought to my attention by Morris Coleman's extraordinary paper, "On Consciousness, Language and Cognition, Three Studies in Materialism" (American Institute for Marxist Studies, 1978).

Nalimov constructs a semantic scale of languages. Mathematics stands at one extreme of the "hard" languages, and abstract painting and Hindu metaphysics are at the extreme of "soft" languages. In between is a rather amorphous zone where is found the language of ordinary human discourse. Physics, poetry, philosophy, painting are assigned their relative places on this scale, and this procedure permits Nalimov to present a synoptic vision of human culture, a vision that illuminates significant chapters in cultural evolution. Not the least of these includes the evolving meanings of the crucial words: language and statistics.

As a mathematician, Nalimov has a professional's insight of the extraordinary role of mathematics in human culture, and his trenchant critiques of the precise limitations of the use of mathematics will be of permanent value.

He is not afraid to stand at the frontier of our knowledge (or our ignorance), particularly where the problems of language, cognition, and consciousness meet. Here, no doctrinaire answers are given, but a set of fascinating possibilities are sketched out.

It has long been recognized that the first step in advancing human knowledge is to pose challenging questions. In this sense Nalimov's work will be of permanent interest to Western scholars.

ROBERT G. COLODNY
University of Pittsburgh

Introduction to Russian Edition

Recently, our notion of language has become much broader. Nowadays language is being studied not only by traditionally minded linguists but also by representatives of other fields of knowledge which seem to be quite independent from one another: philosophers, logicians, mathematicians, biologists, representatives of cybernetics, and art critics. At the latest Congress of Philosophy (the XIV Congress in Vienna in 1968), 41 reports were devoted to the problem of language, which is 12.4% of the total number of the reports presented at the Congress. [A brief critical account of these reports may be found in the paper by Kopnin (1971).] One of the well-known Western philosophical trends, the British school of linguistic philosophy, considers the study of language to be the principal task of philosophy.

The great interest of philosophers in language problems can be easily explained: the study of language is a way of studying thinking. It seems reasonable to believe that epistemology may be turned from a theoretical-speculative subject into a natural science if language is made an object of study. Then it will become possible in epistemology to discuss hypotheses in comparison with actually observed phenomena, as is the case in other natural sciences. When an experiment is performed, it will be possible to express the results of some observations regarding language in quantitative terms, and hypotheses will be verifiable.

True, all this must be paid for: in such an approach the profoundness in problem formulation which is characteristic of classical epistemology is lost. The same, however, happened in physics: classical physics was to a significant degree purely metrological (i.e., based on measurements and their interpretation) and remained far from philosophical analysis.

Modern physics, with such sections as quantum mechanics and the
theory of relativity, looks quite different. Here, philosophical problems
are already touched upon, but, again, they are no longer so profound as
they used to be in traditional philosophy. Reading even very serious basic
papers of modern physics, we still do not learn anything about the
general philosophical state of mind of their authors. The same happens
when we read papers of philosophers about language.

If one accepts an altogether naïve, from our standpoint, thesis that
human languages adequately reflect the outer world, it will follow immediately that, if we succeed in constructing a *universal grammar*, we
shall have a real opportunity to answer the eternal ontological questions
— to understand the way the world around us is built. Such a universal
grammar should, of course, embrace both the sense classification of
meaningful words ("morphology") and the rules of correct ordering of
words into phrases ("syntax"); in addition, it should be built so as to
make it possible to abstract from the unique qualities of separate
languages. Such a grammar, if at all possible to construct, could be called
philosophical grammar (Black, 1962).

The study of scientific language has acquired quite a specific significance for the philosophers who began to study the analysis of scientific
thinking. Science has become an object of investigation, and a new trend
of thought has matured: *philosophy of science*. Here again, it was necessary to begin by studying the language of science. This approach has
opened the possibility of tracing the logic of constructing judgments in
science, the rules of inference and verification of scientific statements.
One of the most popular recent schools of thought on the philosophy of
science in the West, *logical positivism*, has even declared that the principal task of philosophy is a logical analysis of scientific languages.

The profound interest of logicians and mathematicians in language
can be easily explained. In verbal behavior, logical constructions are
broadly used; hence, naturally, the idea occurs of the possibility of creating abstract linguistic models given by a calculus. True, here another
problem emerges, that of relationships between logic and mathematics.
While according to the thesis of Frege–Russell mathematics is part of
logic, according to the notions of mathematicians–intuitionists, on the
contrary, logic is part of mathematics. I do not, at present, consider it
necessary to dwell upon this opposition. Another problem is important
for us: to emphasize the deep inner links between logic and mathematics
which allow the comparison of the logical structure of language with
mathematical models.

Mathematicians have also come across purely applied problems of a
linguistic character: first among these is the construction of algorithms

for machine translation of a text from one natural language into another and the construction of artificial languages to permit a dialogue between a human being and a computer. Finally, the broadly expanding process of the mathematization of science, which has penetrated even in the fields of knowledge which had traditionally been developing outside the sphere of mathematical structure, has shown that mathematics itself can play the role of language. In any case, the interest of mathematicians in the study of language is not limited to the range of problems encompassed by *mathematical linguistics.* The subject being already too broad, it can be divided, after Bar-Hillel (1962), into *statistical linguistics,* which considers the frequency analysis of sign systems, and *structural linguistics*, which is engaged in constructing abstract models of language.

The study of language is also one of the main tasks for specialists in cybernetics. The objects of study in cybernetics are self-organized systems, specific organisms formed from a set of things unified by a system of control. Control is effectuated by means of transmitting and processing signals. Control structure is a structure of the system language. Cybernetics may study both live systems (biological organisms and their combinations, such as communities of people and their separate groups) and inanimate objects: automata artificially created by people and naturally evolved systems. Finally, mixed systems are studied, such as the biosphere, where an informational interaction takes place between live and inanimate objects. From the standpoint of cybernetics, science can also be regarded as a self-organized system which behaves as a living organism: in the process of its development, essentially new and previously unpredictable ideas arise which further undergo a complex evolution. These ideas are created and developed as a result of an informational interaction of scientists which is carried out in a special scientific language that differs from everyday language. For this reason the study of scientific language is of special interest to those who deal with the methodology and history of science, even if they are not under the influence of the ideas of logical positivism. And if we wish to speak of information science, a new field of knowledge that attempts to comprehend and improve the system of scientific communications, the development of theoretical concepts is possible only if we thoroughly understand the mode of functioning of the language of scientific interrelations.

I believe that biology, too, deals to a great extent with a problem of language. The problems of a biochemical code or, more broadly, the problems of molecular interactions in a living cell, the problems of genetics and eugenics, of evolution, and the quite old problems of classification and systematization, a concept of the biosphere as a large organism and connected with this a problem of large-scale ecology, all this can be formulated in terms of the science of language if biology is viewed from a broad cybernetic position.

The study of art can be regarded as the teaching of a language for communication in the emotional sphere of life. We may speak of the language of abstract painting, of the language of music, and of that of rhythm in poetry, and we can carry on quite serious investigations in these directions.

Again, we owe such a broad view of language to cybernetics. Its profound philosophical significance lies in the fact that it probably for the first time in European science has proposed an altogether unique approach: studying systems as "organisms" instead of the traditional studying of separate phenomena occurring in the systems. I have already mentioned that a system is composed of things that are united in a certain control structure; then another object of study, the language, appears. But in such a broad approach to language, a notion of language proper is gradually being lost. In any case, the definitions of language which linguists of the traditional school have been attempting to formulate seem very naïve nowadays. However, in certain cases the peculiarity of the problem formulation requires the narrowing of the concept of language. This happened, for example, in a quite new approach to linguistics connected with the name of Chomsky. Here, the concept of language is again narrowed since this approach deals with the study of the universal grammar of a natural language as an inborn human structure.

The purpose of this book is to attempt to find out what language is. In an effort to formulate the criteria determining those sign systems which I would like to regard as a language, I analyze language functions, describe hierarchical structures of language and its dimensions, and consider various approaches to the classification of languages. Classification is one of the steps in a logical analysis of complex systems. Arranging phenomena according to a definite but arbitrarily chosen scheme gives a view of the system in a special way, allowing us to see clearly what has earlier remained shaded. Thus, for example, in constructing a semantic scale of languages, I try to view the whole variety of language systems with the eyes of those who ascribe a particular significance to the probabilistic structure of language. In order to perform all these tasks, I consider a wide range of languages: abstract languages of mathematics, everyday and scientific languages, the language of ancient Indian philosophy, the language of molecular interactions, and, finally, the language of abstract painting. The Danish linguist Hjelmslev seems to have been the first to suggest conducting a comparative study of those language structures which are not languages in the traditional meaning of the word; he believed that this would make it possible to single out an elementary language structure without all the complications characteristic of highly developed languages.

From the standpoint of cybernetics, I regard language as an organism in the belief that, having once emerged under the effect of some perhaps incomprehensible forces, it continues to develop, following its own specific line of evolution and sometimes crucially influencing the hierarchically higher systems such as human thinking. The consideration of language as an independent system may be found in the work of many linguists in the pre-cybernetic period, e.g., the German linguists Humboldt and Schleicher and much later the Swiss linguists de Saussure and Bally.

If language is regarded as a living system open to direct observation, I shall have to agree with Shreider (1971), who stated that ". . . mathematical linguistics has a certain chance of becoming a field of knowledge wherein new schemes for the mathematical description of living systems will be conceived."

This book should not be regarded by the reader as a definitive monograph but rather as an attempt to formulate separate judgments of cybernetic linguistics. In presenting my views, I am broadly basing my work upon numerous and versatile publications on the problems of language, but I am not attempting to give a review of all the various scientific conceptions of language. Moreover, I am not trying to subject these conceptions to a critical analysis. The separate statements to which I have taken a fancy are used simply to illustrate my judgments, to strengthen them, and to maintain historical continuity. I believe that even extreme and eccentric statements are of great interest and value. This is just a glance at a complex system from a very special angle. Such an angle allows us to perceive the peculiarities of a given system which remain unnoticed when the system is considered from a broader, more general philosophical point of view. And it seems to me that here we should try to comprehend the way in which various extreme judgments have come to be rather than criticize them. However, sometimes the material is presented in the form of a dialogue with those who thought and wrote much about language. And since it is language which is discussed, it is important not only *what* has been said but also *in what way* it has been said. Hence, the abundance of quotations in the book.

V. V. NALIMOV

Chapter 1

What Language Is

A Collection of Statements About Language

It is good form in the sciences to begin a paper with a review classifying and systematizing the earlier formulated conceptions. However, I cannot do this in the present case. Statements about language are so various and sometimes so contradictory that it seems impossible to place them according to a precise scheme—logically developed in historical perspective. The subject is complicated by the fact that linguistics is the most ancient scholarly branch. Its sources can be found not only in ancient Greece but also in ancient India and the Arab world of the past, and, most importantly, these ancient statements about language retain a peculiar interest; even nowadays, they have not become just a property of the archives of the history of science.

Without attempting to overcome this enormous difficulty, I shall confine myself to quoting, in chronological order, a series of statements about language which I have found most interesting.

Sciences develop in time. They grow as trees do: some of their branches wither and fall off, others spread more luxuriantly, and as the tree grows its lower branches become hidden in the earth—they pass into the domain of history. Linguistics, however, does not follow this pattern of development: this is a mosaic of bright colors in a vast field, and the field turns out to be magical. After new flowers have appeared, the old ones do not fade; they do not lose their brightness and freshness. My collection of statements is but a weak attempt to reflect this bright picture.[1]

---

[1] The collection of statements about language given below was, in its major part, compiled by A. V. Yarkho. If the year of the first edition of the work in which the statement appeared is known, it precedes

1

PLATO (ca. 428–348 B.C.) — the famous ancient Greek philosopher.

> *Socrates.* Then the argument would lead us to infer that names ought
> to be given according to a natural process, and with a proper instru-
> ment, and not at our pleasure. . . . Then, Hermogenes, not every
> man is able to give a name but only a maker of names; and this seems
> to be the legislator, who of all skilled artisans in the world is the
> rarest. . . . Then, as to names: ought not our legislator also know
> how to put the true natural name of each thing into sounds and
> syllables. . . . And we must not misinterpret the fact that different
> legislators will not use the same syllables[2] (Plato, 1953)

T. HOBBES (1588–1679) — an English philosopher, one of the founders of
mechanistic materialism.

> Everyone knows from his own most authentic experience how
> human thoughts are vague and transient and how their repetition is
> random . . . to study philosophy a person must have some sensual
> objects of recollection whereby the thoughts forgotten may again be
> revived in memory and as if be, be fixed in a certain sequence. We
> shall call such objects of recollection marks. . . . If the marks in-
> vented by people for the purpose of developing their thinking cannot
> be communicated to others, all their knowledge will disappear with
> them. . . . For this reason in order to construct and develop the stock
> of philosophical knowledge, symbols are necessary whereby the
> thoughts of one person could be communicated and explained to
> others. As to the symbols or attributes, objects following one
> another serve their function since we have remarked a certain
> regularity in their sequence. . . . Among symbols, some are natural . . .
> others are arbitrary . . . we shall refer here . . . to words in a definite
> combination signifying our thoughts and our spiritual movements. . . .
> If human sounds are connected so that they form symbols of
> thoughts they are called speech, and their separate parts — names.
>
> A name is a word arbitrarily chosen as a mark to arouse in our
> mind thoughts similar to previous ones and at the same time, if it is
> inserted into a sentence and spoken by another person, serving a sign
> of what thoughts the speaker possessed at the moment. . . . I believe
> the names emerged as a result of an arbitrary decision . . . since he
> who watches the way new names arise and old ones disappear every
> day, as various nations use various names and that there is no simi-
> larity or comparison between names and things, he cannot believe
> quite in earnest that names of things come from their nature. . . .

---

the name. The source of the statement which is given in the References at the end of the book appears at
the end of each statement.

   [2] Ivanov (1964) has noted an interesting parallel of the Greek tradition with ancient Indian mythology,
where it is mentioned that the things have been named as the result of the act of creating speech by the
Universal maker. This parallel can be drawn further by including Judaism. In the Old Testament it is also
said that Adam gave names to all living creatures.

Besides, it is not at all necessary that every name be a name of a thing.

As people owe their true knowledge to correct comprehension of words, the foundation of their delusions lies in their wrong com- prehension . . . language is like a cobweb: weak minds cling to the words and get entangled in them, while stronger minds easily break through. (Hobbes, 1658)

1690   J. Locke (1632–1704) – an Englishman of the enlightenment and philosopher, the founder of materialistic sensualism.

Man fitted . . . to make them [articulate sounds] signs of ideas. – Besides articulate sounds . . . it was farther necessary that he [man] should be able to use these sounds as signs of internal concep- tions and to make them stand as marks for the ideas within his own mind; whereby they might be made known to others, and the thought of men's minds be conveyed from one to another . . . It is not enough for the perfection of language that sounds can be made signs of ideas, unless those signs can be so made use of as to compre- hend several particular things: for the multiplication of words would have perplexed their use, had every particular thing need of a distinct name to be signified by. To remedy this inconvenience, language had yet a farther improvement in the use of general terms, whereby one word was made to mark a multitude of particular existences. (Locke, 1665)

1749   D. Hartley (1705–1757) – an English philosopher-materialist, physician, and psychologist.

Since words may be compared to the letters used in algebra, language itself may be termed one species of algebra; and, converse- ly, algebra is nothing more than the language which is peculiarly fitted to explain quantity of all kinds. . . . Now, if every thing relating to language had something analogous to it in algebra, one might hope to explain the difficulties and perplexities attending the theory of language by the corresponding particulars in algebra, where every thing is clear, and acknowledged by all that have made it their study. (Hartley, 1834)

W. von Humboldt (1767–1835) – an outstanding German linguist, the founder of general linguistics.

Language has a certain limit in the completeness of its structure; when it is achieved, neither its organic construction, nor its structure undergo any changes. No language has yet been discovered which would be below the limit of the formed grammatical construction. . . .

Language can emerge in no other way than suddenly and at once, or to be more accurate, language must at every moment of its exis- tence possess everything which makes it an entity. . . .

Language cannot be imagined as something a priori given to hu-

manity since if that were so, it would be perfectly incomprehensible
how man could understand this gift and make it serve himself.

If we attempt to compare this unique human ability with anything
else we shall have to remember animal instincts and call language an
intellectual instinct of the mind. . . .

Attempts were made to replace words of various languages with
generally accepted symbols, as in mathematics, where figures,
numbers and algebraic equations are in one-to-one correspondence
to each other. However, with their help only an insignificant part of
the richness of a thought can be exhausted since, due to their nature,
these symbols are fit only for the concepts formed by abstract construction or purely by mind. . . .

From the mutual interdependence between thought and word it
becomes obvious that languages are not just a means of expressing
the cognized reality, but, in addition, they are a means of cognizing
the previously unknown reality. Their difference is not just that of
sounds and symbols but the difference of outlooks. . . .

Language as a product of the people and its past is something foreign to man, and for this reason man is, on the one hand, tied, but on
the other hand, enriched, strengthened and inspired by the heritage
left in the language by past generations. Being subjective in relation
to the cognized, language is objective in relation to man. (Humboldt,
1843, translated from the Russian)

1851   J. GRIMM (1785–1863) – a German linguist who studied German
languages from the viewpoint of their historical development.

Whatever pictures opened before our eyes in studying the history
of language, you will see everywhere movement, firmness and amazing flexibility, the everlasting urge upwards and declines, perpetual
changeability which has never been allowed to reach completeness;
all this testifies to the fact that language is a human production and
that it is marked with the virtues and defects of our nature. Language
stagnation is unthinkable since everything newly appearing and
forming needs space unnecessary only in a dull existence. Functioning during an immensely long period of time, words have become po-
tent and polished but at the same time they wore out and partially
disappeared due to chance. Like leaves from the trees they fall off
their branches to the ground and are supplanted by new ones; those
which have upheld their existence had changed their appearance and
meaning so often they can hardly be recognized. But in the majority
of cases of losses, new formations spring out almost simultaneously
which compensate for the lost ones . . . (Grimm, 1864, translated
from the Russian)

H. STEINTAHL (1823–1899) – the founder of a psychological trend in linguistics.

Speech is a psychic activity, and, therefore, linguistics is related to
the psychological sciences. . . .

Language in its essence is a product of a community of people. When we call language an instinctive self-consciousness, instinctive outlook and logic, that means that language is self-consciousness, outlook and logic of the popular (folk) spirit. (Steintahl, 1855, translated from the Russian)

1862   A. A. POTEBNYA (1835–1891) — an outstanding Russian linguist with a broad range of interests.

. . . a thought once connected with the word is again called into our mind by the sounds of the word. . . . The thought is reproduced if not in its previous form but so that the second and third reproduction may be even more important for us than the first one. . . .

A notion and a word are related in the following way: a word is a means of creating a notion. . . .

Language is not a means of expressing an existing idea but of creating it . . . it is not a reflection of the formed outlook but an activity forming it. (Potebnya, 1926)

A. SCHLEICHER (1821–1868) — a linguist who approached language from the naturalistic or, in modern terms, precybernetic stance and regarded it as a natural organism.

The life of language does not differ significantly from the lives of other live organisms — plants and animals. Like the latter, it has a period of growth from the simplest structures to more complicated forms, and a period of aging when they go farther and farther from the highest stage of development and their forms suffer damage. (Schleicher, 1869, translated from the Russian)

I. A. BAUDOUIN DE COURTENAY (1845–1929) — a Russian linguist, the founder of the Kazan school of linguistics.

My intention is neither to dwell on the statement that language is an organism, nor to criticize it. I shall only remark that an organism, like inorganic substances, is something tangible and space-like, and on the other hand, something which feeds and multiplies, etc. An organism is always on hand, it exists without interruption from the moment of birth up to the beginning of its decay, called death. Language as a whole exists only *in potentia*.

Words are not bodies or bodily members: they emerge as complexes of meaningful sounds, as meaningful consonances only when a person speaks, and they exist as representations of meaningful consonances in the human mind and consciousness only when one thinks with their help. (Baudouin de Courtenay, 1871)

1872   LEWIS CARROLL (pseudonym of C. Dodgson, 1832–1898) — an English mathematician, the author of the popular books *Alice's Adventures in Wonderland* and *Through the Looking-Glass*.

"My *name* is Alice . . ."

"It's a stupid name enough! . . . What does it mean?"

"*Must* a name mean something?" Alice asked doubtfully.

"Of course it must," Humpty Dumpty said with a short laugh: *my* name means the shape I am — and a good handsome shape it is, too. With a name like yours, you might be any shape, almost."

". . . that shows that there are three hundred and sixty-four days when you might get un-birthday presents . . . and only *one* for birthday presents, you know. There's glory for you!"

"I don't know what you mean by 'glory,' " Alice said.

Humpty Dumpty smiled contemptuously. "Of course you don't — till I tell you. I meant 'there's a nice knock-down argument for you!' "

"But 'glory' doesn't mean 'a nice knock-down argument,' " Alice objected.

"When *I* use a word," Humpty Dumpty said in rather a scornful tone, "it means just what I choose it to mean — neither more nor less."

"The question is," said Alice, "whether you *can* make words mean so many different things."

"The question is," said Humpty Dumpty, "which is to be master — that's all." (Carroll, 1930)

1886   H. PAUL (1846–1921) — a representative of the Young Grammarians; in his papers their views are represented most completely.

From comparing the language organisms of each individual, something average is received, which determines the language norm, or the language usage. This average is naturally established the more accurately more individuals are embraced by observations and the more completely each of them is observed. . . .

Usage, whose description has been almost exclusively the preserve of grammarians, determines the individual language only to a certain extent; much remains not only undetermined by usage, but proves quite opposite to it. . . .

Grammar and logic diverge primarily due to the fact that language formation and usage takes place not on the basis of strictly logical thinking, but as a result of natural and disorderly movement of notions which, depending on natural gifts and education, follows or does not follow the laws of logic. (Paul, 1937, translated from Russian)

A. POTEBNYA (see above)

Language is a form of thought, but such a form which does not occur anywhere but in language. Thus the formality of linguistics is material as compared with that of logic. (Potebnya, 1926)

1894–1895   F. F. FORTUNATOV (1848–1914) — a Russian linguist, the founder of the Moscow school of linguistics.

Language consists of words and words are spoken as symbols for our thinking and for expressing our thoughts and feelings. Separate words of the language in our speech are combined in various ways and become parts of other words; due to this, not only separate words are facts of the language but also words in their combinations and their divisibility into various parts. (Fortunatov, 1897)

I. A. BAUDOUIN DE COURTENAY (see above)

We acknowledge the correctness of Humboldt's statement that "language is a creative organ for thoughts," but it is only with stipulations that we can accept other statements of this thinker, such as "there are no thoughts without language; human thinking is possible only because of language," or that language consists in "continuously repeating spiritual activity aimed at making the voice express thoughts"—we know that thinking is possible without language, and deaf-mutes can never express their thoughts with their voice. In return, we without any stipulation agree with Humboldt's opinion that every language is a kind of Weltanschauung. . . .

Strictly speaking, the term "language" in the sense of something homogeneous and inseparable may be applied only to the individual language. A homogeneous tribal language is but a fiction. (Baudouin de Courtenay, 1907)

1910–1911 *Encyclopaedia Britannica*

Language—the whole body of words and combinations of words as used in common by a nation, people or race, for the purpose of expressing or communicating their thoughts; also, more widely, the power of expressing thought by verbal utterance.

1915 F. DE SAUSSURE (1857–1913)—an outstanding Swiss linguist, the founder of structural linguistics.

1. Language is a well-defined object in the heterogeneous mass of speech facts. It can be localized in the limited segment of the speaking-circuit where an auditory image becomes associated with a concept. It is the social side of speech, outside the individual who can never create nor modify it by himself; it exists only by virtue of a sort of contract signed by the members of a community . . .

2. Language . . . is something that we can study separately. . . .

3. Language is a system of signs in which the only essential thing is the union of meanings and sound-images, and in which both parts of the sign are psychological.

The bond between the signifier and the signified is arbitrary. Since I mean by sign the whole that results from the associating of the signifier with the signified, I can simply say: *the linguistic sign is arbitrary* . . . . This principle dominates all the linguistics of language; its consequences are numberless. (de Saussure, 1959)

1921 B. RUSSELL (1872–1970)—an English philosopher, logician, mathematician, and public figure.

Ordinary speech does not distinguish between identity and close similarity. A word always applies, not only to one particular, but to a group of associated particulars, which are recognized as multiple in common thought or speech.

. . . a host of . . . notions . . . are thought to be profound because they are obscure and confused. . . .

Vagueness and accuracy are important notions, which it is very necessary to understand. Both are a matter of degree. All thinking is vague to some extent, and complete accuracy is a theoretical ideal not practically attainable. . . .

A word is vague when it is in fact applicable to a number of different objects because, in virtue of some common property, they have not appeared, to the person using the word, to be distinct. . . .

A word is not something unique and particular, but a set of occurrences. . . .

The essence of language lies, not in the use of this or that special means of communication, but in the employment of fixed associations (however these may have originated) in order that something now sensible—a spoken word, a picture, a gesture, or what not—may call up the "idea" of something else. Whenever this is done, what is now sensible may be called a "sign" or "symbol," and that of which it is intended to call up the "idea" may be called its "meaning."

. . . To say that a word has a meaning is not to say that those who use the word correctly have ever thought out what the meaning is: the use of the word comes first and the meaning is to be distilled out of it by observation and analysis. . . .

There is no more reason why a person who uses a word correctly should be able to tell what it means than there is why a planet which is moving correctly should know Kepler's laws. (Russell, 1921)

1921 L. WITTGENSTEIN (1889–1951)—an Austrian philosopher and logician, who after 1929 lived in Great Britain. A vivid exposition of the evolution of Wittgenstein's philosophical views on the background of his dramatic life may be found in Bartley (1973).

3.25. There is one and only one complete analysis of the proposition.

3.251. The proposition expresses what it expresses in a definite and clearly specifiable way: the proposition is articulate.

3.26 The name cannot be analyzed further by any definition. It is a primitive sign.

3.262. What does not get expressed in the sign is shown by its application. What the signs conceal, their application declares.

3.263. The meanings of primitive signs can be explained by elucidations. Elucidations are propositions which contain the primitive signs. They can, therefore, only be understood when the meanings of these signs are already known.

3.3 Only the proposition has sense; only in the context of a proposition has a name meaning.

4.002. Man possesses the capacity of constructing languages, in which every sense can be expressed, without having an idea how and what each word means—just as one speaks without knowing how the single sounds are produced.

Colloquial language is a part of the human organism and is not less complicated than it.

From it, it is humanly impossible to gather immediately the logic of language. (Wittgenstein, 1955)

O. E. MANDELSHTAM (1891–1935)—a Russian poet.

A live word does not denote an object but chooses freely, as if for an abode, this or that object notion, thingness, a dear body. And around the thing, a word wanders freely, as a soul around the abandoned but not forgotten body. (Mandelshtam, 1921)

L. BLOOMFIELD (1887–1949)—a representative of the American school of descriptive linguistics which elaborated methods of studying human verbal behavior on the basis of behaviorism.

The totality of utterances that can be made in a speech-community is the *language* of that speech-community. (Bloomfield, 1926)

S. O. KARCEVSKY (1884–1955)—a Russian linguist, the representative of the second generation of the Geneva school, later a member of the Prague circle of functional linguistics.

A sign and its meaning do not completely cover each other. Their boundaries do not coincide in all points. One and the same sign has several functions, one and the same meaning is expressed by several signs. Every sign is potentially a "homonym" and a "synonym" simultaneously, i.e. it is formed by crossing these two rows of thought phenomena.

If signs were fixed and each of them fulfilled only one function, language would become a mere collection of labels. But it is equally impossible to imagine a language with such movable signs that they would not signify anything outside the limit of concrete situations. (Karcevsky, 1929)

Theses of the Prague Circle of Linguistics (translated from the Russian) 1929

Being a product of human activity, language at the same time has a purposeful orientation. The analysis of verbal activity as a means of communication shows that the most common purpose of a speaker revealed most vividly is expression. For this reason one has to approach the linguistical analysis from the functional viewpoint. From this viewpoint *language is a system of expressive means serving some definite purpose.*

A word considered from the functional viewpoint is a *result of nominative linguistic activity* sometimes inseparably connected with syntagmatic activity [generation of syntagmas — word combinations which form a phrase].

E. SAPIR (1884–1939) — an American linguist and anthropologist, one of the authors of the "Sapir–Whorf" hypothesis forming the nucleus of ethnolinguistics.

Language is a purely human and non-instinctive method of communicating ideas, emotions, and desires by means of a system of voluntarily produced symbols. . . .

Language is a fully formed functional system within man's psychic or "spiritual" constitution. We cannot define it as an entity in psychophysical terms alone. . . . The essence of language consists in the assigning of conventional, voluntarily articulated, sounds, or of their equivalents, to the diverse elements of experience. . . .

Most people, asked if they can think without speech, would probably answer, "Yes, but it is not easy for me to do so. Still I know it can be done." Language is but a garment! But what if language is not so much a garment as a prepared road or groove? . . .

Once more, language, as a structure, is on its inner face the mold of thought. . . . There is no more striking general fact about language than its universality . . . we know of no people that is not possessed of a fully developed language. . . .

Our first impulse, no doubt, would have been to define the word as the symbolic, linguistic counterpart of a single concept. We know now that such a definition is impossible. In truth it is impossible to define the word from a functional standpoint at all, for the word may be anything from the expression of a single concept — concrete or abstract or purely relational . . . to the expression of a complete thought. . . . In the latter case the word becomes identical with the sentence. The word is merely a form, a definitely molded entity that takes in as much or as little of the conceptual material of the whole thought as the genius of the language cares to allow. . . .

The word is one of the smallest, completely satisfying bits of isolated "meaning" into which the sentence resolves itself. (Sapir, 1929)

This is the constant interaction between language and experience which excludes language from the lifeless series of such pure and simple symbolic systems as mathematical symbolics or signalling flags. (Sapir, 1933, translated from the Russian)

K. BÜHLER (1879–1963) — a representative of the German school of the psychology of thinking. He regarded language from a psychological standpoint.

Now a brief explanation on the double unity of a word and a sentence. It will never occur to any linguist that there can exist sentences without words, though it sounds no more paradoxical than a suggestion of words existing without sentences. In reality a word and a sentence are two correlative factors in speech construction. The question of what a word is may be satisfactorily answered only by a person who, pronouncing the word, keeps in mind the sentence, and vice versa. . . . A word must be a sound symbol which may be included in the field. When Meillet remarks that it should be grammatically applicable, he formulates the same idea. (Bühler, 1934, translated from the Russian)

L. BLOOMFIELD (see above)

A free form which is not a phrase, is a *word*. A word, then, is a free form which does not consist entirely of (two or more) lesser free forms; in brief, a word is a *minimum free form*. (Bloomfield, 1935)

I. I. MESHANINOV (1883-1967) — a Soviet linguist, the pupil of N. Ya. Marr.

These two principal speech units, a word and a sentence, are inseparably connected. A word does not practically exist outside the sentence. (Meshaninov, 1940).

1940   B. L. WHORF (1897-1941) — an American ethnolinguist, graduated as an engineer–technologist.

Languages have grammars, which are assumed to be merely norms of conventional and social correctness, but the use of language is supposed to be guided not so much by them as by correct, rational, or intelligent thinking . . .

We dissect nature along lines laid down by our native languages. . . . We cut nature up, organise it into concepts, and ascribe significances as we do, largely because we are parties to an agreement to organise it in this way — an agreement that holds throughout our speech community and is codified in the patterns of our language. The argument is, of course, an implicit and unstated one, *but its terms are absolutely obligatory*. (Whorf, 1956)

V. MATHESIUS (1882-1945) — a Czech linguist, the founder of the Prague circle of functional linguistics.

. . . language appears as a complicated system of inseparably connected mutually dependent facts which cannot be referred to independent categories by the most accurate linguistics. (Mathesius, 1942)

1944   *Enclyclopedia Americana*

Language in its broadest sense is any means of expressing thought. The cries of the lower animals are language in so far as they give expression to their state of mind, there is a language of flowers and so on.

C. MORRIS (b. 1901) — an American philosopher; he was the first to formulate clearly basic concepts and principles of a new science, semiotics.

For the term "language" the following five criteria are suggested as those to be embodied in the definition.

First, a language is composed of a plurality of signs. Second, in a language each sign has a signification common to a number of interpreters. Over and above the signification of language signs which is common to members of the interpreter-family, there may of course be differences of signification for individual interpreters, but such differences are not then regarded as linguistic. The fact that a sign is to some degree personal is compatible with the requirement that a language sign be interpersonal, but all that is required is that the signs in a language have some degree of interpersonality.

Third, the signs constituting a language must be comsigns, that is, producible by the members of the interpreter-family and have the same signification to the producers which they have to other interpreters. Comsigns are either activities of the organisms themselves (such as gestures), or the products of such activities (such as sounds, traces left on a material medium, or constructed objects). An odor, for instance, might be interpreted in the same way by a number of organisms in a given situation, and hence be interpersonal, and yet would not be a comsign. Odors would be language signs only if in addition to being interpersonal they were producible by their interpreters.

Fourth, the signs which constitute a language are plurisituational signs, that is signs with a relative constancy of signification in every situation in which a sign of the sign-family in question appears. If the term "odor," for example, signified differently each time the sign occurred it would not be a sign in a language even though at a given occurrence it was interpersonal. A sign in a language is thus a sign-family and not merely a unisituational sign-vehicle.

Fifth, the signs in a language must constitute a system of interconnected signs combinable in some ways and not in others in order to form a variety of complex sign-process.

Uniting these requirements we reach the proposed definition of a language: a language is a set of plurisituational signs with interpersonal significata common to members of an interpreter-family, the signs being producible by members of the interpreter-family and combinable in some ways but not in others to form compound signs. Or more simply, *a language is a set of plurisituational comsigns restricted in the ways in which they may be combined.* If the restriction as to combination be embodied in the word "system," we can say that a language is a system of plurisituational comsigns. And since a sign-family is plurisituational, the simplest foundation would be that *a language is a system of comsign-families.* (Morris, 1946)

R. WELLS (1854–1941) — an American linguist.

De Saussure ascribes . . . to linguistic signs two fundamental properties: they are arbitrary and they are arranged in a line. But he neglects to mention in this place another essential trait . . . to wit that linguistic signs are systematic. . . . "Arbitrary" and "systematic" are the two fundamental properties of signs. (Wells, 1947)

V. SKALIČKA (b. 1909) — A Czech linguist, a member of the Prague circle.

Linguistic theory should be aimed at cognizing language not as an aggregate of non-linguistic (i.e. physical, physiological, psychological, logical and sociological) phenomena, but as a structure closed in itself, as a structure *sui generis*. . . . Hjelmslev does not allow anything which is not a pure relation to enter language. Thus, language, in his opinion, is nothing else but a set of relations which he calls functions. . . .

The linguistics problems are complicated phenomena. If one takes into account the position occupied by language he will see three types of relations and three different problems: 1. First of all, the relation of language to the extralinguistical reality, i.e. a semasiological problem. 2. The relation of language to other languages, i.e. the problem of linguistic differences. 3. The relation of language to its constituents, i.e. the problem of language structure. (Skalička, 1948, translated from the Russian)

1932   C. BALLY (1865-1947) — a representative of the Geneva school, a pupil of F. de Saussure.

Within a system everything is interlinked; this is true of a linguistic system to the same extent as of all other systems. This principle proclaimed by F. de Saussure, preserves its value for us. . . . But it would be utterly wrong if such a general view resulted in presenting language as a symmetrical and harmonic construction. The moment one starts to demount the mechanism, he is seized by the horror of the disorder reigning there, and he asks himself how it can be that so mutually entangled systems of wheels produce such a coordinated motion.

General views of languages are penetrated with many errors, which are sometimes several centuries old and which are supported not only by our ignorance but also, in many instances, by our desire (unconscious or reflective) to conceal or distort the reality. . . . (Bally, 1932)

L. HJELMSLEV (1899-1965) — a Danish linguist, the founder of glossematics (Danish structuralism).

The novel and fruitful in F. de Saussure's work is his understanding language as a pure structure of relations, as a scheme, as something opposite to the random (phonetic, semantic etc.) realization whereby this scheme is presented.

. . . the linguistic sign is bilateral — it possesses a plan of contents and a plan of expression, both sides being able to become the object of a purely structural analysis.

. . . de Saussure understood quite clearly that the structural definition of language should lead to recognizing as languages certain structures hitherto not regarded as such by traditional linguistics, and considering languages regarded as such by traditional linguistics as a kind of language in general.

It would be very interesting to study linguistic structures which are not languages in a traditional meaning of the word with the help of a purely linguistic method first of all because such structures would give us simple samples — patterns revealing the elementary language structure without all the complication typical of a highly developed structure of everyday languages. . . .

A. Sechehaye noted in 1908 that language might be presented as an algebraic expression or geometrical images and that language elements may be expressed in any arbitrary way, if only their individuality be preserved, but not their material character.

Language is an hierarchy, whose every part allows further division into classes determined by mutual relations, so that each of these classes may be dissected into derivatives determined by mutual mutation. (Hjelmslev, 1950–1951, translated from the Russian)

G. A. MILLER (b. 1920) — an American psychologist and linguist, an expert in the theory of verbal behavior.

Verbal behavior is not a simple function of time that makes it possible to predict the behavior exactly from one moment to the next. If a man's words could be predicted in advance, he would not need to speak them. On the other hand, verbal behavior is not like the gambler's dice, nor like the urn full of marbles that the statistician uses to discuss the probability of equally improbable events. It is a function lying somewhere between the completely determined and the completely random — the connections between successive events limit the range of possibilities, but they do not hold the events strictly to a single path. These connections constitute what we call the verbal context. (Miller, 1951, retranslated from the Russian)

W. ENTWISTLE — a British linguist with a broad range of interests.

. . . When we *know* anything we hold the right language about it. . . . There is verbalism in all knowledge and no knowledge without words. . . . Language is an art, and the arts are best defined as languages. . . . Music may perhaps constitute an exception, . . . but the remaining arts are all marked by the intrinsic unlikeness of the signifier and the signified, as between certain lengths of lines on paper and natural distances, or of stone and human flesh. (Entwistle, 1953)

L. WITTGENSTEIN (see above)

23. . . . Here the term "language-*game*" is meant to bring into prominence the fact that the *speaking* of language is part of an activity or of a form of life.

Review the multiplicity of language games in the following examples, and in others:

Giving orders, and obeying them—
Describing appearance of an object, or giving its measurements—
Constructing an object from a description (a drawing)—
Reporting an event—
Speculating about an event—
Forming and testing a hypothesis—
Presenting the results of an experiment in tables and diagrams—
Making up a story; and reading it—
Play-acting—
Singing catches—
Guessing riddles—
Making a joke; telling it—
Solving a problem in practical arithmetic—
Translating from one language into another—
Asking, thinking, cursing, greeting, praying.

31. . . . One can also imagine someone's having learnt the game without ever learning or formulating rules.

43. For a *large* class of cases—though not for all—in which we employ the word "meaning" it can be defined thus: the meaning of a word is its use in the language.

77. . . . In such a difficulty always ask yourself: How did we *learn* the meaning of this word ("good" for instance)? From what sort of examples? in what language-games? Then it will be easier for you to see that the word must have a family of meanings.

108. . . . The question "What is a word really?" is analogous to "What is a piece in chess?"

138. . . . we *understand* the meaning of a word when we hear or say it, we grasp it in a flash, and what we grasp in this way is surely something different from the "use" which is extended in time!

203. Language is a labyrinth of paths. You approach from *one* side and know your way about, you approach the same place from another side and no longer know your way about.

206. . . . The common behaviour of mankind is the system of reference by means of which we interpret an unknown language.

255. The philosopher's treatment of a question is like the treatment of an illness.

329. When I think in language, there aren't "meanings" going through my mind in addition to the verbal expressions; the language is itself the vehicle of thought.

340. One cannot guess how a word functions. One has to *look at* its use and learn from that.

384. You learned the *concept* "pain" when you learned language.

496. Grammar does not tell us how language must be constructed in order to fulfill its purpose, in order to have such-and-such an effect on human beings. It only describes and in no way explains the use of signs. (Wittgenstein, 1953)

N. WIENER (1894–1964) – an American mathematician and physicist, the founder of cybernetics.

> Naturally, no theory of communication can avoid the discussion of language. Language, in fact, is in one sense another name for communication itself, as well as a word used to describe the codes through which communication takes place. . . . What distinguishes human communication from communication of most other animals is (a) the delicacy and complexity of the code used, and (b) the high degree of arbitrariness of this code . . . language is not exclusively an attribute of living beings but one which they may share to a certain degree with the machines man has constructed. (Wiener, 1954)

G. RYLE (b. 1900) – a British philosopher.

> The story of twentieth-century philosophy is very largely the story of this notion of sense or meaning. Meanings (to use a trouble-making plural noun) are what Moore's analyses have been analyses of; meanings are what Russell's logical atoms were atoms of; meanings, in one sense but not in another, were what Russell's "incomplete symbols" were bereft of; meanings are what logical considerations prohibit to the antinomy – generating forms of words on which Frege and Russell had tried to found arithmetic; meanings are what the members of the Vienna Circle proffered a general litmus-paper for; meanings are what the *Tractatus*, with certain qualifications, denies to the would-be propositions both of Formal Logic and of philosophy; and yet meanings are just what, in different ways, philosophy and logic are *ex officio* about. (Ryle, 1956)

G. J. WARNOCK (b. 1923) – a British philosopher.

> I suppose the most immediately striking feature of Logical Positivism was its iconoclasm, its short and apparently lethal way with the ponderous enigmas of metaphysicians. . . . If any one thing is characteristic of contemporary philosophy, it would be precisely the realization that language has *many* uses, ethical, aesthetic, literary, and indeed metaphysical uses among them. There is no tendency to say "You must not (or cannot) say that"; there is a readiness to appraise on its merits whatever may be said and for whatever purpose, provided only that something *is* said and words are not used wildly. (Warnock, 1956)

D. POLE – a British philosopher.

> Wittgenstein's thesis is that a language, like a mathematical system, consists of a complex set of procedures, which may also be appealed to as rules. (Pole, 1958)

A. M. QUINTON (b. 1925) – a British philosopher.

> Where the "Tractatus" saw language as a logically rigid essence concealed behind the contingent surface of everyday discourse, a

skeleton to be excavated by penetrating analysis, in the "Investigations" language is accepted as it actually and observably is, as a living, unsystematic, and polymorphous array of working conventions for a large and not simply classifiable range of human purposes. . . .

The fundamental point of Wittgenstein's new theory of meaning is that the meaning of a word is not any sort of object for which the word stands. . . . To say of a man that he has learned or understands the meaning of a word is simply to say that he has learned or understands how to use it, that he has become party to a certain established social convention. (Quinton, 1966)

1970 Soviet *Philosophical Encyclopaedia* ("Language" by A. Spirkin.

Language is a system of symbols serving the means of human communication, thinking and expression. By means of language the world is cognized; in language the self-consciousness of an individual is objectivized. Language is a specific social means of information storage and transfer, as well as of controlling human behaviour. (*Filosofskaya Entsiklopediya,* 1960–1970)

P. V. KOPNIN (1922–1971)–a Soviet philosopher.

A most general definition of language embracing the so-called ordinary, or natural languages operating with words and sentences, as well as artificial scientific languages with peculiar symbolics, may be formulated as follows: language is a form of existence of knowledge as a system of symbols. Hence the knowledge itself is always viewed as a language. (Kopnin, 1971)

G. V. STEPANOV (b. 1919)–A Soviet linguist.

Semiotics is a science of symbol systems in nature and society.
It stands close to cybernetics which studies the processes of relations and control in a living organism, nature and society.

Semiotics is also close to linguistics, since the latter studies the most complete and perfect system of relations: human language.

H. HESSE (1877–1962)–a German writer, a Nobel-prize winner.

Alphabet

From time to time we take our pen in hand
And scribble symbols on a blank white sheet.
Their meaning is at everyone's command;
It is a game whose rules are nice and neat.

But if a savage or a moon-man came
And found a page, a furrowed runic field.
And curiously studied lines and frame:
How strange would be the world that they revealed.
A magic gallery of oddities.
He would see A and B as man and beast,

As moving tongues or arms or legs or eyes,
Now slow, now rushing, all constraint released,
Like prints of ravens' feet upon the snow.
He'd hop about with them, fly to and fro,
And see a thousand worlds of might-have-been
Hidden within the black and frozen symbols,
Beneath the ornate strokes, the thick and thin.
He'd see the way love burns and anguish trembles,
He'd wonder, laugh, shake with fear and weep
Because beyond this cipher's cross-barred keep
He'd see the world in all its aimless passion,
Diminished, dwarfed, and spellbound in the symbols,
And rigorously marching prisoner-fashion.
He'd think: each sign all others so resembles
That love of life and death, or lust and anguish,
Are simply twins whom no one can distinguish . . .
Until at last the savage with a sound
Of mortal terror lights and stirs a fire,
Chants and beats his brow against the ground
And consecrates the writing to his pyre
Perhaps before his consciousness is drowned
In slumber there will come to him some sense
Of how this world of magic fraudulence,
This horror utterly behind endurance,
Has vanished as if it had never been.
He'll sigh, and smile, and feel all right again.

(Hesse, 1961)

With this wonderful poem by Hesse I am breaking off the collection of statements about language. It certainly cannot replace an essay on the history of linguistics and in no way claims to give a complete and adequate picture of the history of linguistics. I have selected the brightest and most contrasting formulations. Without trying to systematize them in detail, we are still able, though altogether roughly, to trace two principal trends in developing views on language in European thought, going back to ancient culture. One of them is a view of language as a very *hard structure*, in some indubitable way linking the sign with the referent. The second tendency is a view of the language as a *soft structure*[3] so complicated that the rules of ascribing meaningful content to signs or their com-

---

[3] I am using here terminology broadly accepted in the scientific slang of today, which ascribes to the two extreme tendencies in science and technology word combinations borrowed from everyday language: hardware and software. Thus, e.g., in computer technique, everything connected immediately with a machine will be called *hard,* and programs will be called *soft*; in the science of science branches of knowledge with a well-organized system of bibliographic references will be called hard sciences, and those with a disorderly system of references, soft science.

binations do not lend themselves to a clear arrangement, into the logical schemes familiar to European thinking.

The first of these trends clearly manifests itself in the ancient Greek tradition: the word there is *the name of a thing*; thus, sign and meaning prove to be linked in a natural and the only possible way. If we address corresponding sources, this tendency is easily traced in the gnostics who developed the teaching of the mysterious and magic properties of names. To a certain degree it was preserved in the philosophy of the Middle Ages, where the name was considered not as an arbitrary sign but as something symbolically immanent to the named. The reader can easily trace this tendency generated in the ancient world in the statements made about language in modern times, but here stronger statements occur as well: Hartley considered language as a kind of algebra, and we can hardly believe his statements (see above) to refer in fact to the middle of the eighteenth century.

In modern times, as a consequence of scientific development, the concept of a hard language structure has acquired a new interpretation: an opinion has been formulated that this is rather a property of some ideal language, and scientific language seemed destined to become such a language in the first place. Cartesian philosophy demanded that words in the scientific language should possess precise and unambiguous meanings. Leibniz tried to develop an idea of universal symbolics and logical calculus: the rules of operating with these signs. In order not to overload an already lengthy collection, I have not included the statements about language formulated by the representatives of this school.

In modern times, the concept of a hard structure has become peculiarly reflected in the program *of the logical positivists*. This trend of thought was formed in the 1920s almost simultaneously in Austria (the famous philosophical Vienna circle), Germany, Great Britain, and Poland, and to a great extent had exhausted itself already by the 1960s. Its most prominent representatives are Schlick, Carnap (usually considered the leader of the trend), Neurath, and Wittgenstein, as well as Russell in his early papers; Popper, who is well known to everybody interested in the general problems of the philosophy of science, was for a time close to the positivists at some points. A constructive program of the logical positivists was directed at a reconstruction of science, at its formalization. And it is only natural that a central feature of the program was the idea of creating a universal language with ideal terms, which would be clearly understood as distinct from vague terms of speculative constructions. In accordance with this program, the scientific terms were divided into *theoretical* and *non-theoretical*. The latter, in their turn, were divided into *primitive* terms, understandable immediately (without definition) in the process of studying an experiment or a theory, and *precise* ones, to define which necessary and sufficient conditions are given, and the primitive terms of the system are used. Further postulates (rules of correspondence) are introduced, and mixed phrases are created; these contain at least one theoretical and one non-theoretical term and are part of the theory. Theoretical terms are not defined directly; their meaning is given by the theory which links them with well-defined non-theoretical terms. The theory in this system of thought is formed from a set of phrases consisting of non-axioms and theorems. Theoretical texts may contain both mixed phrases and phrases consisting only of theoretical terms; such phrases are subject to testing and serve to support the theory.

Scientists have not apprehended these conceptions which seem very precise. It has proved practically impossible to construct such a logically precise hierarchy of scientific terms; nonetheless, even now attempts are still made to create such a scientific terminology, but this futile activity is carried on outside any general theoretical ideas. Neopositivism has been subjected to sharp criticism by philosophers of various schools (cf., for example, Shvyryov, 1966, and Kozlova, 1972). According to Achinstein (1968), it is almost impossible to divide terms into theoretical and non-theoretical. For example, can one assign the term "temperature" to non-theoretical terms: this is only the change of the height of mercury that we observe in a thermometer. As another example, Achinstein proposes that the notion of King Arthur proves more theoretical that that of "electron," since our knowledge about King Arthur is less experimental than our knowledge of an electron.

The concept of a hard language structure was revived with the effort to achieve machine translation from one language into another. There emerged a temptation to reduce linguistic semantics to logical semantics. Abstract models of natural languages are built consisting of certain initial object–atoms and rules for constructing complex objects from them. A concept of a universal semiotic system is introduced which would be an invariant of the world languages. Such a *genotypical* language not revealed to us by a direct observation is stated to exist objectively (Shaumyan, 1971).

The second trend of linguistic thought is the view that a soft structure of language is not its defect but, on the contrary, the reflection of its variety and inner power. This trend may be easily traced during the whole history of modern time. From the collection presented above, it is readily seen that this idea has been formulated more and more clearly and boldly. It was already formulated quite distinctly by Humboldt; in any case, it was obvious to him that the variety of human thinking could not be expressed with any calculus constructed as a mathematics. Then in Schleicher's papers, we find the statement that the life of language is as complicated as the life of other biological organisms. By and by the idea appeared that the meaning of something said should be sought not in words, names of things, but in phrases built from words. The word began to be interpreted as a symbol linked associatively with a field of meanings. Even utterly heretical statements are made of the arbitrary understanding of a word meaning — as Carroll's Humpty-Dumpty puts it. An especially clear indication of the soft structure of language is found in the papers of representatives of the Geneva school: Bally says that he is seized with horror by the disorder reigning in the language mechanism. Reading the statements of linguists, we cannot but wonder how an opposite conception could develop simultaneously: belief in the possibility of giving language a hard structure. It is curious to note that the criticism of the language program of the neopositivists began from inside: Wittgenstein became the first dissident. His principal early paper, *Tractatus Logico-Philosophicus,* published in 1921, is usually considered to be of a neopositivist trend, and, indeed, the construction of an artificial, logically perfect language in the spirit of Frege–Russell, where symbolics would submit to "*logical* grammar, logical syntax," was broadly discussed. But, as a matter of fact, everything is not so simple with this early paper. It is written in separate, sometimes paradoxical statements, and many of them contain extremely sharp judgments about language that in no way fit the doctrines of logical positivism. In any case, the *Tractatus* has evoked a large number of comments,[4] as if it were not a scholarly paper but a revelation. In his last work, *Philosophical Investigations,*[5] published posthumously, Wittgenstein (1953) proceeds already from a notion of the enormous complexity and confusion of human language. The game model of language is considered by him as an initial, basic model. Thus, Wittgenstein became one of the founders of a new trend of thought, the *British school of linguistic philosophy,* which formulated the concept of a soft language structure more precisely than ever before. Strictly speaking, the formation of this trend should first of all be associated with Moore, a British philosopher who began critical analysis of language from a philosophical standpoint as early as the beginning of our century. Later, we shall return to an examination of the ideas of this philosophical

[4] Some of these comments were of a very caustic character. Thus, Carnap (1959) regards *Tractatus* as a collection of "more or less vague statements which the reader should later acknowledge as pseudophrases and reject." In any case, it is rather common to question the inner inconsistency of *Tractatus* (see, for example, Achinstein, 1968).

[5] This paper, written in German, was published in 1953, two years after the author's death, in two languages: the German original on the left pages and an Engish translation on the right ones. According to Wittgenstein, the book appeared as a result of a 16-year meditation. He himself was not satisfied with the paper, but there was no time for corrections, he wrote. Indeed, in *Philosophical Investigations* we no longer come across those brilliant formulations which are abundant in the *Tractatus*. But in return we find there examples of a refined semantic analysis of separate statements made in our everyday language, which begot numerous subsequent studies in semantics.

school. These two trends, logical positivism and the British analytical school, are often unified under one heading of *analytical philosophy*. The reason for this is not the community of doctrines but that of approaches. This critical analysis of the meaning of judgments acquired in the analysis of philosophical texts a character of iconoclasm. In any case, the philosophy of linguistic analysis is not a clearly formulated conception but an intellectual state in the frame of which there can appear completely uncoordinated and deeply individualized judgments. There is no dominant figure there.

However, the concept of the hard structure has not faded into the background. The famous novel *Das Glasperlenspiel* by Herman Hesse has become a peculiar symbol of the tendency toward the construction of a universal language. In this book, an Order is described, the keeper of a specific universal language, the cryptography of the Game of glass beads. Every sign there is ". . . really all-embracing, every symbol and every combination of symbols leads not somewhere, not to a separate instance, or experiment, or proof, but to the centre, to the most secret mystery of the world, to the basis of all knowledge." The language was, indeed, universal; it contained ". . . a formula of astromathematics, the principle of composing an ancient sonata, a dictum of Confucius and so forth — everything expressed in the language of the Game: in symbols, cyphers, abbreviations and signatures." Language games were played as nation-wide celebrations. There were two types of Game: formal and psychological. "Game formalists directed all their efforts to create out of the components of every game — mathematical, linguistic, musical, etc. — a compact, rounded and formally perfect integrity and harmony. . . . On the contrary, the psychological school strove for integrity and harmony, cosmic completeness and perfection not so much through the selection, systematization, interlacing, conjugation and juxtaposition of themes, as through the meditation following each stage of the Game, which they considered most important. . . . The world of the Game, abstract and evidently withdrawn from time, was flexible enough to correspond, in a hundred of nuances, to the spiritual make-up, voice, temperament and other aspects of personality. . . . After the meditation is completed. . . . the Game . . . encircles the player as the surface of a sphere encloses its heart, and makes him feel that a certain faultlessly harmonious world has accepted him and withdrawn him from the world of the random and confused."

The language of the Game, as distinct from the everyday language was closed, or almost closed: new symbols and rules were introduced there only in rare and exceptional cases, which is quite natural for a language with a hard structure.

The book by Hesse has many facets: sometimes there can be noted a fine irony concerning the idea of universal language, and in other places there is a dream of creating such a language.

Characteristics of Symbolic Language Systems

From the above collection of statements about language, it is easily seen how difficult it is to give a pithy definition revealing the concept of language. Difficulties arise primarily as a result of the fact that traditionally disposed linguists and, after them, all the encyclopedias of the world confine themselves to studying the most complicated system, everyday language. But linguists–dissenters attached to semiotics have assumed a different, enormously broad stance: they began to consider all conceivable symbol systems, and natural language was of interest to them only because it was part of such symbol systems. Non-linguistic scientific thought has perceived everything in quite another way: new systems turned out to be related to the category of language. There has emerged a notion of the language of a biological code and the language of music; languages of programming have been created. Quite a curious situation developed: linguists–semioticians went from studying a particular language to studying symbolic systems in general, while scientific thought concentrated on studying language, having widened this concept by including other systems similar to it in some sense. I believe that such a widening of the concept of language allows us to understand its nature better. Considering systems simpler than our everyday language, which has undergone an extremely complicated and prolonged evolutionary history, we can better understand some of its peculiarities: they may find their extreme expression in certain languages and in other ones may be present in a degenerate form which does not hamper observation.

Let me try to formulate the structural characteristics and functional properties of the symbolic systems which we would intuitively regard as languages. To do so, I shall resort to a kind of argument related to inductive forms of thinking. It seems pertinent to remember here a remarkable formulation from the *Tractatus* by Wittgenstein:

> The process of induction is the process of assuming the simplest law
> that can be made to harmonize with our experience. This process,
> however, has no logical foundation but only a psychological one.
> (Wittgenstein, 1955, paradoxes 6.363 and 6.3631)

Functional characteristics.   Let us begin with an analysis of the functional characteristics of language. Following the commonly accepted tradition (see, for example, Mel'chuk and Frumkina, 1966), we shall assume language to function first of all as a means of communication, that is, a system serving to transfer information.[6] Information transfer in the process of human communication may be effectuated not only with words but also with other symbols. Dance, music, symbols of religious cults, and abstract paintings all are symbolic systems performing the function of communication. Exchange of information may take place not only among people but also between a human being and a computer; hence, it seems quite natural to speak of the languages of programming. The next step is the possibility of communication between inanimate mechanisms, e.g., between two computers. Having made this step, it is natural to go farther and to think that exchange of information is possible between any inanimate objects. But such an assertion confronts an opposition even on the intuitive level of our ideas. Many phenomena of the physical world can be regarded in terms of the receipt and transfer of information. However, we would hardly like to interpret a photoelectrical effect in physics as a response to the monologue of a light source addressed to the metal, and quanta of light as words of this monologue. If we adhere to this strategy, physics and chemistry will immediately turn into linguistic disciplines, and the term "linguistics" will become synonymous with the word "science." Fulfillment of the communication function cannot be considered as a necessary and sufficient requirement for elevating a symbol system to the rank of language. This is rather only a necessary demand. Sufficient conditions will fulfill some limitations imposed on the symbol systems by specific structural language characteristics which I shall describe a bit later. These sufficient conditions cannot simultaneously be necessary since they may sometimes acquire a degenerate character: we cannot demand that all traits characterizing a language be fulfilled with an equal degree of precision.

Now we shall examine another functional characteristic of language: information reduction, storage, and retrieval. This aspect of language has not received much attention in traditional linguistics papers. Indeed, in everyday practice, information is stored without reduction: books have been written in a slightly changed conversational language, and, therefore, no special problems connected with information storage have arisen. This problem was clearly formulated for the first time in mathematical statistics when it became necessary to present the results of observations in a compact form fit for publication. Indeed, there is no point in publishing all the results of observations if, say, they are a sample from the normally distributed universe. In this case, it would suffice to publish sample parameter estimates, namely, mathematical expectation and

---

[6] We cannot define what "information" is, and we shall consider it to be a complicated concept whose meaning is revealed by its context. Such an approach should not surprise anybody. Even in attempts to strictly formalize mathematics, concepts have to be introduced whose meaning becomes clear from axioms formulated by use of the same concepts.

variance, and to give the number of observations underlying the computation of parameters. However, here we immediately face a set of complicated problems: parameter estimates should be unbiased, i.e., devoid of systematic errors, and efficient; i.e., they should be received with the maximal accuracy. There arises a problem of constructing such algorithms of reduction which would elicit all information contained in the observed results. After the work of Ronald Fisher, many statisticians hold the opinion that information reduction is one of the central problems of mathematical statistics. This problem has become especially acute since the appearance of computers. Imagine, for example, the problem of specifying various constants. This work is being done almost continuously. Novel data are introduced into the computer from year to year; they are obtained sometimes under rather different conditions, and they should be presented well reduced so as to enable the computer to produce reasonably specific results. Later, quite a grandiose task appeared: using computers for the storage and retrieval of all information contained in scientific papers. A more modest task is that of searching some publications on the basis of certain groups of data. All these tasks are indubitably linguistic; computers gradually become the means of our communication, and language acquires new functions.

The reduction function is of exceptionally great importance in the language of a biological code. The whole somatic and, probably to a great extent, psychic structure of an organism is coded in the genes of sex cells in an amazingly compact way. It is hard to tell how many times information is reduced here, but it seems perfectly fabulous. Another peculiarity here attracts our attention: the mechanism of restoring reduced information. It seems surprisingly accurate: one-egg twins, at least in early age while the influence of environment is restrained and code errors have not accumulated in the process of cell restoration, are absolutely identical.

According to the Kolmogorov definition, the complexity of a message is determined by the information necessary to restore it (for details, see the review by Zvonkin and Levin, 1970). If, say, we deal with a sequence of digits consisting of zeros and unities, the complexity will be characterized, roughly speaking, by the minimal number of binary symbols necessary to substitute for the sequence in transferring it along the communication channels. Such a definition of complexity is well perceived intuitively. Imagine that we must transfer such numbers as π and e. It is clear that there is no need to transfer the whole computed set of figure symbols giving the approximate value of the numbers; it will suffice to transfer the algorithm of computation. If, however, these figure symbols are presented as a sequence of numbers, then, applying all known statistical methods of analysis, we shall not be able to distinguish them from a random sequence of numbers put down by, for example, a counter measuring radioactive decay. In some algorithms, figures were used to generate pseudorandom numbers, forming the numbers e and π, and random numbers thus obtained were successfully used in the problems of simulating by the Monte Carlo method. However, only the sequence of numbers received in registering radioactive decay is truly complicated: it cannot be expressed with a shorter symbol sequence. In this sense it is a random sequence (if we, after Kolmogorov, call random the elements of a large finite universe of symbols with the maximal complexity). Another example: imagine that we are generating a pseudorandom number by successively putting down the last symbol in five-digit logarithms of natural numbers. At first sight we seem to be dealing with a good generator of randomness, but if we bear in mind the above-mentioned criterion, the generator no longer seems good enough since the sequence is easily put down by an accurate description of the generating procedure.

Now let us turn to analyzing texts of everyday language. Imagine that we deal with a literary work. It cannot be transferred along communication channels with the help of a briefer text of a résumé character. Thus, we must acknowledge this work to be complicated, the complexity being so great that we cannot relegate it to the category of random texts. This is also true of any somewhat serious scientific publication: its content cannot be restored from the abstract. Carry out the following mental experiment: an abstract of a new paper yet unpublished is handed over to a group of scientists working in the same field with a request to restore the original text. It is not too difficult to imagine the way the new texts will differ from one another. Here a question arises unintentionally: Is it possible to state that abstract journals can replace original ones? Even a purely mathematical article cannot be unambiguously given by its abstract. From Gödel's proof (which is to be discussed later in greater detail) it follows that, in the language of commonly used formal systems, it is impossible to give a strictly formalized definition to the notion of proof inside the same system in mathematics. Still, every author has to convince the reader of the correctness of the method of proof that he has found, and this, as a rule, cannot be done in a text of a résumé (abstract) character. Now let us return to the biological code. We have already mentioned the striking identity of one-egg twins. Despite the complexity of biological organisms, information concerning them is reduced with almost faultless precision. Therefore, organisms should be viewed as simple non-random texts: the language of the biological code is truly amazing.

Thus, we see that the notion of *randomness*, one of the principal philosophical categories, may be viewed from a purely linguistic standpoint, if information storage and retrieval is recognized as a language function. Assigning any phenomena to the category of *randomness is determined only by our linguistic potentialities*. It may turn out that the phenomenon described today as a random one will in time, when new linguistic means for its description and analysis are found, be regarded as non-random. Special attention should always be paid to the relativity of statements associated with the peculiarities of using language means. It is quite possible that the first messages from other worlds—if received at all—will be perceived merely as random and, therefore, senseless signals (this has also been emphasized by Kolmogorov). So far, we have been speaking about intralinguistic reduction; now let us try to look upon the problem of reduction from a broader standpoint. If we oppose language to thinking, then is it not possible to consider language itself as, perhaps, a not too compact, but still coded, system? Albert Schweitzer (1960), the well-known philosopher, brilliantly explained this idea:

> Thinking being necessarily connected with language absorbs abstractions and symbols fixed within the latter. This coin is in use only so far as it allows us to present things in a short way instead of introducing them substantially as they are given themselves. But then it appears that thinking operates with these abstractions and symbols as if they denote something actually given. Such is the general temptation.

Linguistic structure: alphabet and grammar. Now let us pass to describing structural traits of language. First of all, it seems pertinent to speak of subelementary linguistic symbols, morphemes, for the written language of the alphabet whereby the elementary signs, "words," forming the language vocabulary, are built, and of "grammar," i.e., the rules whereby texts are built from words.

One might ask here: Is the presence of alphabet and grammar sufficient and necessary for a symbol system to be regarded as a language? Answering this question is not so easy as it might seem. We may point, for example, to a symbol system intuitively perceived as a language but at the same time void of explicitly expressed alphabet or grammar: i.e., the language of bibliographic references in scientific publications. This is a specific language in which every reference is associated with ideas contained in previously published papers corresponding to the reference. There is no need for a scientist to repeat the content of the papers he is referring to; it is enough to refer to them. Looking through a journal, we first of all pay attention to the article bibliographies, and it is on this basis that we make a decision whether the paper is worth reading. By means of references, information is coded very compactly and restored very accurately: we just find the publication from the reference. Let us try to analyze the structure of this language. The reference as a whole seems to be an elementary symbol here. Its constituents — authors' names, their initials, the title and the number of a journal, the title of an article (if any) — have no independent meanings and may be regarded as subelements of a symbol, resembling lines and other letter elements of our everyday alphabet. Every new publication is coded with a specific new symbol. The primary symbol system is open and, strictly speaking, cannot be regarded as an alphabet since an alphabet is usually defined as a closed or almost closed subsymbol system, i.e., a system where the set of possible subsymbols is given beforehand and remains unchanged for a long time. It is even more interesting that in this language one can hardly observe any grammar, i.e., the rules whereby certain operations are made with the symbols. True, we know how to use the symbols of this language, but these quite vague procedures can hardly be called grammar. In any case, they lack the rules for constructing complex logical structures.

Black (1962), criticizing the concept of universal grammar, draws our attention to the fact that familiar grammatical categories are not always observed in our everyday speech. Here is one of his examples: a full verbal report of a chess move, such as might be found in nineteenth century manuals, has the form: "The king moved from this square to another square." Here the word "king" is clearly the subject. But in the modern recording of the game, "e2-e3," it is very difficult to discern a subject and a predicate. Further, referring to Entwistle (1953), Black points out that Chinese, which is fully equipped for every sort of civilized communication, makes no use of the formal categories devised for the Indo-European languages. Even more interesting is his allusion to Whorf (1956): in polysynthetic languages of American Indians, an isolated word is something like a sentence, and a sequence of such words–sentences makes a kind of compound sentence. Let us try to imitate such a compound sentence in English.

> "There is one who is a man who is yonder who does running which traverses it which is a street which elongates." The exotic sentence consists simply of the predicate lexemes "one," "man," "yonder," "run," "traverse," "street," and "long," and the proper translation is, "A man yonder is running down the long street."

Of such a polysynthetic tongue it is sometimes said that all the words are verbs, or again that all the words are nouns with verb-forming elements added. Actually, the terms "verb" and "noun" in such a language are meaningless. Such construction in a way resembles the language of references: it is void of common grammatical categories.

The final conclusion from our system of judgments is as follows: alphabet and grammar are, of course, the structural elements of the language; they are clearly seen in the majority of symbol systems perceived as languages, but in certain cases they may become degenerate. Later, we shall have to face more than once the fact that certain probably quite essential language traits become degenerate in some linguistic systems; therefore, this will no longer be a sufficient criterion for regarding such degenerate systems as not being languages. The very attempt to formulate precisely the requirements necessary and sufficient for recognizing a symbol system as a language category seems doomed to failure. Language refers to some notions which we can speak about but cannot define.

Symbol and meaning.   I shall try now to examine the way a symbol is used to transfer the meaning of a message. First of all, we are not able to give any precise definition of what a "symbol" is. Again, we have to confine ourselves to stating that this is a complex conception whose meaning is revealed in its usage. What is obviously worth discussing is the problem of the connection between a symbol and a meaning. Recall again the statement by Ryle cited above that twentieth century philosophy has been largely the story of the idea of sense or meaning. It is not too difficult to understand the source of such extreme judgments: human culture is expressed in symbols, and the study of symbol systems is an analysis of the spiritual content of culture and delusions connected with it.

From the standpoint of those holding to the model of a hard language structure, a symbol should be in one-to-one correspondence with the referent. This demand has probably been most precisely formulated in the *Tractatus* by Wittgenstein. According to him, in order to avoid fundamental errors abundant in philosophy

> . . . we must employ symbolism which excludes them, by not applying the same sign in different symbols and by not applying signs in the same way, which signify in different ways. A symbolism, that is to say, which obeys the rules of *logical* grammar — of logical syntax. (Wittgenstein, 1955, paradox 3.325)

And further:

> In the proposition there must be exactly as many things distinguishable as there are in the state of affairs, which it represents (Wittgenstein, 1955, paradox 4.04)

Everyday language indubitably lacks such correspondence between the symbol and the referent: under some circumstances we may use one symbol to signify something usually signified by two essentially different, antisynonymous symbols. To illustrate this thought, I borrow an example from the book by Black (1962). Imagine that a person learning to drive is steering a car. Instead of telling him "stop" and "go," you may whistle and he would by all means understand you since he will start the car and stop it at necessary moments. The whistle substitutes for two seemingly different words. The fact is that the symbol system is organized so that the whistle means the necessity to "change the state"; in another symbol system this action would have been signified by two different words depending on the state of the car at a given moment. This is an example attractive for its paradoxical nature, but there are many other less paradoxical examples which often occur in our everyday communication. This gives rise to many questions: What is the cause of this symbolic polysemy? Whether it is good or bad, should we, following the early ideas of Wittgenstein, seek to overcome it, at least in the language of science? These are crucial problems in teaching about language, and I shall devote the next chapter to their discussion.

The matter stands no better in terms of understanding the semantic role of grammar. When it is stated that grammar is rules for operating with symbols, it is not quite clear what is meant here: pure grammar, i.e., syntax operating with symbols independently of their content, or the classification of symbols according to their meaningful usage as well? Wittgenstein (1955) in his *Tractatus* wrote:

> In logical syntax, the meaning of a sign ought never to play a role; it
> must admit of being established without mention being thereby made
> of the meaning of a sign; it ought to presuppose only the description
> of the expressions. (paradox 3.33)

> What does not get expressed in the sign is shown by its application.
> What the signs conceal, their application declares. (paradox 3.62)

But if the symbol meaning is revealed in its usage, grammar, then, cannot be separated from the meaning of the symbols. Indeed, the grammar of everyday language is indubitably based upon the latter. At the same time, the grammar of abstract languages entering mathematical logic and the theory of automata has to deal only with operations performed with symbols lacking meaning in the common sense of the word. Later, I shall use the word "grammar" in various senses, assuming that the reader will have no difficulty in catching what particular meaning I intend to convey.

Hierarchical structure of language.   Language structure can be analyzed from another standpoint, namely, considering its hierarchy. One of language's peculiarities is that one and the same language can be presented with several symbol systems forming a hierarchical system of several levels. For example, for an everyday language (say, written Russian) we have a system of levels consisting of letters, morphemes (a morpheme is a meaningful part of a word: the root and the affix—prefixes, suffixes, etc.), words (a word is a fragment of a text between spaces), segments (a segment is a fragment of a text between two punctuation marks), and phrases (a phrase is fragment of a text between full stops), etc. Shreider (1966) even thinks that this language property may serve as its definition. In his terms it sounds as follows: "A category of equimorphous symbol systems will be called a language."

Certainly we could go even farther and try to build a hierarchical classification of the language's logical structure. An attempt can be made to look for certain units of sense which would be analogous to words, units of speech. Wittgenstein in his *Tractatus* tried to analyze the hierarchical structure of the logic of statements introducing the terms name, proposition, structure, saying, showing. Such an approach seems very tempting but, as a rule, in practice it proves unrealistic. Just as was the case with the sense hierachy of words, suggested by the neopositivists, where words were divided into theoretical and non-theoretical, and the latter, in their turn, were divided into primitive (for these necessary and sufficient conditions were not formulated) and precisely defined (for them these conditions were formulated). I have already mentioned that it is practically impossible to observe such a structure of terms without falling into logical traps.

It should be acknowledged that the logical hierarchy of statements exists in the language, but it is so concealed that in practice it cannot be directly observed. One has to limit oneself to analyzing a symbol hierarchy. The presence of the latter, indeed, may be viewed as a condition necessary for regarding a symbol system as a language. This is a bridge linking language and thinking. Phenomenologically, thinking is a process of constructing complicated symbol systems from simpler ones, which is outwardly reflected in the hierarchical structure of language. It should be noted that we understand thinking in a broad sense, assuming that this process takes place during the functioning of a computer and during the development of an organism from an impregnated cell, with the symbol system acquiring more and more complicated hierarchical structure.

If we raise the hierarchical structure of symbols to the rank of the language's principal trait, we shall immediately be able to exclude from the linguistic categories simple informational processes occurring in inanimate nature, such as the above-mentioned photoelectric effect in physics; we shall have enough formal reason not to include physics and chemistry in linguistics.

True, when using this criterion, one must take precautions. In separate cases the hierarchical structure of the language, like all its other properties, may prove quite degenerate. Let us return once more to the language of bibliographic references mentioned above.

At first sight it lacks a hierarchy. But, as a matter of fact, this is not so. Selecting articles with common subject matter by proceeding from the

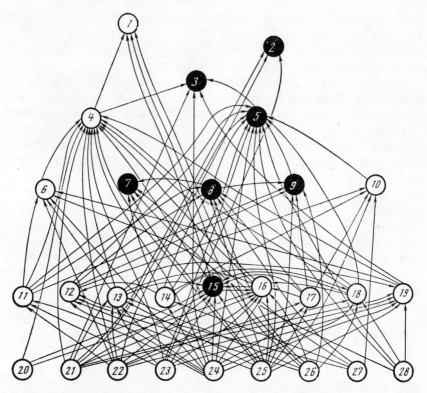

Fig. 1. *Paradigm, formed by the net of bibliographic citations (Garfield, 1970). To construct this paradigm only those publications have been used which are cited in a wide range of papers on DNA not less than five times. Blackened circles indicate publications most frequently cited. Numbers in circles allow identifications of the particulars as to place and date of publication. Paradigms of this kind can be used for practical purposes: beginning studies in the new field of knowledge, the researcher worker can fix his attention on the nucleus formed by associatively connected publications.*

community of their references, we are performing the procedure of hierarchical arrangement. Figure 1 shows a paradigm[7] of references in the review of literature on DNA (Garfield, 1970). The first level in the hierarchical structure of the reference language is a single reference, the second level will be paradigms analogous to those in Fig. 1, and the third

---

[7] Paradigm is a very polysemantic scientific term. The literal translation of the word from Greek is "example," "model." When considering an example, we usually expect that some associations are generated. For this reason, in its most general sense the term "paradigm" means an explanation of elements on the basis of association, and it is in this meaning that I shall use the term. It is also common to speak of a proof from paradigm, which is based only on comparison with a well-known example. Paradigm as a grammatical term is a pattern of speech formation.

level will consist of SCI (Science Citation Index) by Garfield, which is nowadays well known. In this publication all references to a given article are arranged, which allows one to observe quite clearly a high degree of hierarchical arrangement of the elementary symbol — references.

Having acknowledged hierarchical structure to be a criterion for raising a symbol system into the rank of a language, we also exclude from the linguistic category almost all information created by the art of images. In particular, abstract painting may be regarded as a language, since there the observer can easily find an alphabet, grammar, and hierarchical structure (for details, see below), but representational painting can hardly be called a language, at least on this level. For representational painting it is difficult to build a sufficiently compact alphabet and grammar and trace the hierarchical structure. If we try to present a picture of this type, say, one by Rubens, as a sequence of certain elementary signs, an alphabet of painting handled according to some grammar, we shall get something oddly cumbersome. In ordinary representational painting, the image itself is simultaneously the primary and the finite sign.[8] An image may turn into a sign only in specific instances, e.g., in surrealistic painting: if female breasts are placed other than where they ought to be, they turn from an image into a sign. An image may acquire a partial likeness to a symbol because of the style of painting. This is especially clearly manifested in icon painting. Experts can immediately tell the Pskov school of icon painting from the Moscow school. As far as I know, the linguistic analysis of style has not so far received much attention. True, Florenskii (1967) understood that contemporary rules of painting perspective which had been formed during the Renaissance were but a peculiar set of expressive means not excluding other systems of painting. He analyzed one of them, the so-called reverse perspective in ancient Russian icon painting. This question was later elucidated by Zhegin (1970).

Excluding image-generated information from the language category may arouse certain objections. Word constructions structurally resembling images are used in some branches of knowledge, not only in the humanities but also in certain sciences, e.g., in biology. Reading a serious paper on the theory of evolution, one may come across an interruption of logical exposition with a spacious insertion describing, say, a gray hamster. Authors try to supplement the logic of their judgments with certain images created in the reader's consciousness. Can

---

[8] It is probably pertinent to make the following statements: an image is not a sign but a symbol, an integral representation of something, which cannot be subjected to logical operations. Voluminous literature is devoted to the theory of symbolism. The papers by Langer seem especially interesting; e.g., see her book (Langer, 1951). One may get an idea of her conception from the article by Ye. M. Nemirovskaya (1972).

this method be considered extralinguistic? The image is here created by means of signs, but the need to supplement the logic of judgments with an image still seems rudimentary. Another example is the pictographic and, probably, the hieroglyphic art of writing, which is an experience of constructing a language with an explicit hierarchical structure where, at the same time, an image plays the role of the elementary sign. Perhaps the hieroglyphic art of writing is a transfer of a certain symbol system from image thinking to logical thinking, the latter demanding symbols of abstract structure to be used, in accordance with its nature, while the hieroglyphic symbol system reflects the pre-symbolic, image thinking.

Hierarchy of languages; metalanguages. Languages with highly developed logic have another peculiarity: emergence of a hierarchy of languages. This happens when a language becomes the object of another hierarchically higher one or, as it is customary to say nowadays, of a metalanguage whereby we may judge the correctness of statements made in the object–language. The idea of metalanguage entered science in connection with the papers of Hilbert, the well-known German mathematician (1862–1943). In his papers he discussed the problem of creating metamathematics, a metatheory[9] dealing with the proper method of constructing judgments in mathematics.[10]

Mathematics and its logical foundations are discussed in the meta-mathematical language. The goal of mathematics is certain structures—a collection of inwardly consistent áxioms and logical inferences from them made in the language of formulae. The object of metamathematics is statements about such formal systems; e.g., the statement "arithmetic is consistent" belongs to metamathematics.

Our everyday language is a metalanguage in relation to the "language" of things surrounding us. In terms of everyday language, we operate not with things but with their names. Making judgments about the things of the outer world, we try to arrange them in some consistent structures, which is equivalent to searching for logical foundations of the world of things.

It is possible to go farther and to demonstrate that our everyday language is constantly fulfilling two different functions: sometimes it is used to formulate statements; other times, to judge the precision of these

---

[9] The term "metatheory" was created after the term "metaphysics," and the latter had first been used by Andronicus of Rhodes, an Alexandrian librarian. When classifying the works by Aristotle, he introduced the term "metaphysics" to put philosophical papers by Aristotle on the prime causes on the library shelf behind his papers on physics. The Greek word μετα means "after," "behind."

[10] Historically, the notion of metalanguage emerged for the first time in ancient India. In a paper by ancient Indian scholars, a special grammatical language was used to describe Sanskrit (see the article "Language" in *Filosofskaya Entsiklopediya*, 1970). Indian logicians were aware of the necessity to discriminate between statements made in the object–language and in the metalanguage.

statements. This gives rise to contradictions unsolvable by the means of the same language. The contradiction will immediately disappear as soon as we understand that the statements concerning the correctness of judgments belong to another language, metalanguage, while the judgments analyzed are made in the object–language. The simple non-hierarchical union of two of these statements into a phrase may formally generate contradictions intuitively perceived as not existing in reality. When common laws of formal logic are applied to the semantically closed language, this gives rise to semantic paradoxes (this was well explained by Tarski,[11] though Russell had touched upon the problem earlier).

Russell introduced the idea concerning the types of words and types of statements relating to different hierarchical levels. Vulgarizing a little, we can say that the words "a table," "a chair," and "a sofa" are words of a lower level than the word "furniture"; at least, it is impossible to say, "I see two things: a chair and furniture" (see Hutten, 1956). Russell's concepts had a powerful influence on the development of modern logic. It became clear that not every grammatically correct phrase was a meaningful statement. It became necessary to introduce limitations to expressive elements of a theory (and not only to deductive ones as it had been earlier). This helped to overcome some paradoxes of the naïve theory of sets in mathematics.

Let us examine several examples of semantic paradoxes. In the novel *Rudin* by Turgenev an argument is described during which Pigasov declares that there are no convictions. His opponent is Rudin:

"Very well," Rudin murmured. "You assert, then, that there are no convictions?"
"No—they do not exist."
"Is that your conviction?"
"Yes."
"Then how can you say they do not exist? Here you have one for a start."
Everyone in the room smiled and exchanged glances.

This kind of argumentation is often resorted to in scientific discussion as well. Black (1949), controverting Lewis, the author of the book *Mind and the World Order* (New York, 1929), declares that if Lewis is right then it is only he himself who is in a position to understand his own statements, claiming that all statements are collections of indefinite symbols. Lektorskii (1971) draws our attention to the fact that, in its fight with

[11] A. Tarski (b. 1901), a Polish scholar, one of the principal representatives of the Warsaw school of logic. In 1933, he emigrated to the United States, where he became a professor of mathematics at the University of California. For details about Tarski's statement on logical semantics, see Smirnova and Tavanets (1967).

metaphysics, analytical philosophy has gone so far as to regard the principal declaration of "anti-metaphysical nature" as metaphysics. Then he adds, "Thus analytical philosophy in linguistic analysis comes to the boundary when it denies itself, as a matter of fact, and surpasses its own limits." I consider this quite a natural way of reasoning—the boundary in question is a demarcation line between statements made in the object-language and in a metalanguage. The British school of philosophy has crossed the boundary. Strictly speaking, this is no longer philosophy but only metaphilosophy. From the standpoint of traditional philosophy, this direction seems empty since it does not consider philosophical problems proper.

We come across paradoxical statements like those above both in everyday conversations and in scientific discussions, and, as a rule, we do not pay special attention to them. We respond to them as if we realize that in our speech the object–language and metalanguage are mixed illegally. I should like here to quote Wittgenstein (1955):

> That which mirrors itself in language, language cannot represent.
> That which expresses itself in language, we cannot express by language. (from paradox 4.121)

A number of difficulties in constructing our system of judgments are connected with the necessity of formulating in everyday language statements related to the class of judgments possible only in metalanguage. Everyone who is familiar with the problem of optimization knows how difficult it is to formulate the concept of goal. Once the goal has been formulated, it is quite easy to construct the procedure for optimal actions; but the more complex the system to be studied or controlled, the more difficult it is to formulate the goal. Formulating the goal is part of the problem whose solution is to be searched for only in metalanguage. These are the words of Wittgenstein (1955) concerning the matter:

> The sense of the world must lie outside the world. In the world everything is as it is and happens as it does happen. In it there is no value—and if there were, it would be of no value. (paradox 6.41)

We often prove not to have sufficient grounds to formulate a meta-statement, and the search for goal turns into an unsolvable problem. We want to do something well, but we do not know what "well" is. We always have to face such a task in organizing experimental research. It is not so easy to define what a good experiment is. Usually it becomes quite clear after the experiment has come to an end. Then we have at our disposal its description made in the object–language, and discussing what is formulated in this language, we may go up a hierarchical step and understand what a good experiment is.

Analytical philosophy gave up the construction of Weltanschauung doctrines. Its task is action, *or therapy*: critical analysis of our philosophical language by means of special, technically ingenious rules. This activity is of a purely metalinguistic nature. The task of analytical philosophy might be reformulated as follows: to build metaphilosophy and to create a suitable metalanguage. Any efforts aimed at comprehending the way judgments are built in science should be a metascience: a special metalanguage should be created for them.

Dialectical materialism, since it explains the development of science, its logic and structure, should also be considered as a metatheory though, as opposed to the analytical school, it remains a substantive philosophy as well.

Here are several formulations by Wittgenstein (1955) in which he attempts to reduce philosophy to a metatheory:

> The object of philosophy is the logical clarification of thoughts.
> Philosophy is not a theory but an activity.
> A philosophical work consists essentially of elucidations.
> The result of philosophy is not a number of "philosophical propositions," but to make propositions clear.
> Philosophy should make clear and delimit sharply the thoughts which otherwise are, as it were, opaque and blurred. (paradox 4.112)

It is noteworthy that the role of metamathematics and its relation to mathematics can be described with the same words. But it is also important that Wittgenstein remains fairly consistent. Here is what he says of his own statements in his next to last paradox:

> My propositions are elucidatory in this way: he who understands me finally recognizes them as senseless, when he has climbed out through them, on them, over them. (He must so to speak throw away the ladder, after he has climbed up on it.) (paradox 6.54)

Wittgenstein realized quite clearly the insufficiency of linguistic means for explanation of something which is situated one step higher in the hierarchical level of thinking. *Tractatus* finishes with the following phrase:

> Whereof one cannot speak, thereof one must be silent. (paradox 7)

There have been attempts to establish rules for the formulation of metalanguages.

Attention should first of all be paid to the opposition of the language of mathematics to the language of metamathematics. Mathematics is a strictly formalized system: logical operations within it are performed without giving any kind of interpretation in terms of the phenomena of the external world. A mathematician deals with a specially invented system of signs; he watches only those signs and not what can be found behind them. In contrast to mathematics, metamathematics proves to be intuitively consistent (though it can also be formalized), and its statements are formulated in the everyday language. Kleene (1952) writes to this effect in his well-known book *Introduction to Metamathematics*:

> The assertions of the metatheory must be understood. The deduction must carry conviction. They must proceed by intuitive inferences and not, as the deductions in the formal theory, by applications of stated rules. Rules have been stated to formalize the object theory, but now we must understand without rules how these rules work. An intuitive mathematics is necessary even to define a formal mathematics.

Below I shall demonstrate that the properties of metamathematical language stated above are not those which are obligatory for any meta-language. Mathematics (as will be shown in the discussion of mathematics as the language of physics in Chapter 4) may be a metalanguage itself as related to other fields of knowledge, and in this case the metalanguage proves to be formalized to a greater extent than the object-language.

Tarski puts in other claims for a metalanguage. I have already mentioned above that he sees the cause of semantic paradoxes in the semantically closed nature of language. Therefore, the notion of semantically unclosed language is introduced. Then the statements about semantic properties of the given object-language are worded not within this language, but in the metalanguage. Semantic notions may be introduced into a metalanguage in two ways: as primary notions, the properties of which are given by means of a system of axioms, or as notions for which the definitions are formulated. The second way is more interesting for us: it is closer to the real phenomena of our everyday language. A metalanguage should be richer than the object one — only then can we define in it such notions of logical semantics as the truth, the denotation of definability, etc. It means that it must contain a logical vocabulary no less rich than that of the object-language, and it must also have supplementary variables belonging to a higher logical type. (Logical variables are signs which may serve to denote various concrete ideas; logical constants serve to denote a single idea.) A metalanguage should be so rich that everything stated in terms of the object-language could be said in the metalanguage; particularly, it should have the means for constructing names of the object-language.

Certainly, this is an idealized scheme aimed at the rigid solution of semantical paradox problems formulated in the frames of logical semantics. I shall demonstrate below that in reality there exist many languages which do not satisfy Tarski's requirements, though indubitably they are all placed hierarchically higher than the object–language and to some extent they always contain stronger statements. Remaining at the formal level, we must assume that we are dealing with a metastatement each time this or that theory is discussed or when several theories are compared. Some metastatements may seem to us absolutely dull, but formally they are stronger than the object ones, for object theories are a subject to be discussed here. To estimate metastatements, we must build a system of metareasoning. We often come across complaints that our culture is more and more littered with statements about statements, which replace the original statements.

As was already mentioned above, in our everyday language in some hardly distinguishable way, the statements in the object–language are constantly mixed with statements in a metalanguage. The metalanguage of everyday speech uses the same sign system and the same logical means as the everyday language, which is here the object of statements. On the basis of psychological criteria, we often ascribe more weight to meta-statements than to object ones, and, as a rule, we never compare these two types of statements from the viewpoint of their logical compatibility. The paradox, if you like, lies in the fact that semantic paradoxes disturb nobody but logicians. The latter did not notice the difference between the statements of different levels for a long time. Here again, we can see two approaches to language—the hard one and the soft one. Only by considering language as a hard structure can we reveal semantic paradoxes, and in this case the hard system of overcoming them should be built in a manner similar to that used by Tarski.

The teaching about hierarchy of language—or, in the terms of Russell, about types of statements—must be, evidently, considered the most serious result of post-Aristotelian formal logic.

The interpretability of sense content expressed in a sign system. A sign system has a right to be called a language if it can be interpreted into another language (into terms of another language which can be either more rich in its expressiveness or, for one reason or another, more comprehensible for a certain group of people). It is with awareness that I speak here only about interpretability, but not about translation from one language into another. Strictly speaking, such a translation is impossible even for absolutely hard languages (I shall return to this question later). Our whole language behavior is permeated with interpretation procedures. Speaking to a foreigner, we interpret our mother tongue in the system of another language, and actually it is not a translation but a mere interpretation. Considering serious physical problems, scientists interpret abstract symbols of the mathematical language of physics. The performance of musical plays is the interpretation of texts written in notes. We face the problem of interpretation in our everyday language. This kind of interpretation can be illustrated by theatrical performances. Books, even of fiction, are often accompanied by interpretation expressed in graphic illustrations. A play—the text written in the everyday and, it would seem, absolutely understandable language—needs, in the author's opinion, interpretation in another, richer language, which uses supplementary expressive means: voice intonations, gestures, and, perhaps of primary importance, the images created by the actor's stage play. Here we return to pre-sign, image-bearing transmission of information. Any serious play—let it be "Hamlet"—can be interpreted absolutely differently by two directors without any distortion of the lexicographic text. (This example was suggested to me by Prof. Doerffel from the German Democratic Republic.) The image-bearing embodiment of a sign text can in its turn be interpreted in a sign system, that is, in critical reviews. But, like all the characteristics of a language, the possibility of interpretation can become degenerate; below I shall give an example of non-interpretability or, to be very cautious, of poor interpretability of a term in the language of physics.

Non-entropy of language.   Certainly, the analysis of a sign system may be approached from quite different positions. I consider the thermodynamic approach to the analysis of symbols in the book by Kobozev (1971) to be very interesting. The question is formulated there in the following way: "Which mechanism allows an entropic physico-chemical apparatus of the human brain to create idealized non-entropic constructions; to perform with their help logical thinking, precise coding and unmistakable recognition of symbolic recording of any thought production?" According to the author, "it is not a physico-chemical or morphological body of symbols itself that is non-entropic, but only its *recognition* by consciousness or by a mechanism which is assigned the function of this consciousness." Non-entropy of the perception of symbols releases human consciousness for activity on a higher level, and here, according to Kobozev, lies the basic distinction between human and animal psychics, since for the latter, the intensiveness of information of physico-chemical signals plays a great, often crucial role. The animal's consciousness is completely filled with "perception and analysis of sounds, colors, smells and with estimation of their intensiveness and direction." Non-entropy of language is not a peculiarity of human consciousness, but only of a sign system. Imagine that we deal with a computer. We can put some information in its memory. Naturally, some energy would be spent on it. The storage of information will be connected with preservation of a certain ordering. But all these energetic processes do not depend upon the kind of information put in, be it very serious or very frivolous; the observable relation between the morphological complexity of an object and its informativity is absent here. Only in this sense can we speak about non-entropy of sign systems.

Now we can formulate the following statement: a sign system turns into a language when signs are perceived without entropy or almost without it. This is one of the characteristics of language. And, like all its other characteristics, it can become degenerate; e.g., this happens in musical language, where loudness of reproduction of certain sounds is already a distinctive feature of a sign. The approach discussed here allows one to regard language as a sign system which enables the thinking apparatus of a human being, functioning without the external negative informational entropy, to reconstruct the order which would be broken spontaneously if thinking were organized in the same way as the physical world.

Language dimension and non-linearity.   Evidently, Bally (1932) was the first linguist to note one peculiarity of human everyday language — its *non-linearity*, resulting from its two-dimensional sign system. "Signs are linear, when they follow each other without penetrating each other during the speech," he wrote, and to exemplify a nonlinear[12] sign combination he gives the French expression "tout à coup," where the words "tout," "à," and "coup," taken separately, are deprived of any sense. The sense of this expression is given only by the *interaction* of elementary symbols; the text proves non-linear. Here, a *two-dimensional* sign appeared to be expanded into one line of written speech, a sign which we must have included in a phrase something like:

il a aperçu tout un . . .
à
coup

Only in this case the sign would enter our speech linearly; it would have the same status as all other signs of speech. If we want to consider our speech to be linear, then we must acknowledge that at least some figures of speech are of two-dimensional character.

It is notable that Bally in this discourse about non-linearity of speech had foreseen those important practical problems which we face when translating the language of chemical formulas into a code suitable for input of information into a computer. The language of chemical formulas is two-dimensional, and sometimes even three-dimensional, while the language of computers is linear. Many an algorithm was suggested which

---

[12] Here we use the analogy: if a polynomial $y = b_0 + b_1 x_2 + b_2 x_2$ contains a term characterizing interaction of variables, we shall already have a non-linear (along the variables) model $y = b_0 + b_1 x_1 + b_2 x_2 + b_{1,2} x_1 x_2$.

could transform two-dimensional recording of chemical formulas into a linear sequence of signs. The trouble is that, in the process of coding, the personnel make too many mistakes—up to 20%. In writing chemical formulas as linear sequences of signs, we lose the clarity of two-dimensional representations which allows one to avoid mistakes in the ordinary records. A two-dimensional language, from the viewpoint of a human receptor, possesses more possibilities than a one-dimensional language.

The language of note recording also proves to be two-dimensional.

It turns out that in our everyday life we deal with languages of even higher dimensions. The language of our color perception is an example of a three-dimensional language. Grossman's law of addition of colors has been proven experimentally (see Fedorov, 1939). It is formulated as follows: if some four intensively colored stimuli are given, a color equation between the multiples of those stimuli can always be composed. Marking the unities of the four stimuli as $W, X, Y,$ and Z, we can find coefficients whereby the equation

$$wW = xX + yY + zZ$$

will be satisfied. Coefficients $x, y,$ and z may be negative as well. Physically, it can be interpreted as follows: if some stimulus F is given which is subject to reproduction, it may turn out that in order to receive the same impression on a color photometer we must mix in a definite proportion two stimuli Y and Z on one field, and on the other field mix the analyzing stimulus and the third standard stimulus X, which can be symbolically written as follows:

$$F + xX = yY + zZ$$

In accordance with a certain convention, the monochromatic flows are chosen as isolated symbols $X, Y,$ and Z.

Thus, the language of color perception proves to be three-dimensional, though the language of the external world—the energetic spectrum—is two-dimensional. But here there is a peculiarity: in the language of spectrum presentations, we should have written any color stimulus as a part of a continuous straight line, marking frequencies on the abscissa and energies on the ordinates. In the language of color perception, the continuous two-dimensional recording is interpreted in a discrete three-dimensional recording. The dimension of the language of color perception does not coincide with the dimension of the world it describes (if the world is built in the way physicists present it).

We have no reason to think that the dimension of a language reflects the dimension of the world of things described in this language.

Classical physics was satisfied by the naïve notion of three-dimensional space existing independently from time. A relativistic physics could not be rendered in the language of these conceptions—hence, the language of four-dimensional space-time continuum. But space-time distance in Minkowski's world

$$ds^2 = dx^2 + dy^2 + dz^2 - c^2 dt^2$$

with the imaginary time axis could hardly be interpreted in terms of everyday language. Kant's notion of space and time as innate categories which are not given to us experimentally came in obvious conflict with modern physics, which filled these notions with entirely new, extraordinary content. This new content has come from experience or, to be more precise, from the necessity of finding a language for the description and interpretation of experience. And Kant's statements must have been no more than a guess about space-time categories having a linguistic nature.

The linguistic character of concepts of multidimensional space is very clearly seen in mathematics. Let us consider the problem of the classification of objects according to a variety of properties. Assume that we must classify the world powers according to a variety of different properties which are typical of them or classify some biological or social (human) population according to a set of properties characterizing, say, the physical state of their organisms. All such problems are of purely linguistic character. We want to divide the individuals subjected to classification into certain groups so that it will be convenient to speak about them from some definite positions. It is far from being an ontological problem: we are not at all disturbed by the fact that the discovered groups of homogeneous (in some respect) people or states do not actually form actually existing, independently acting systems. To solve such a language problem, we must develop a proper taxonomic vocabulary. The problem of classification, then, consists in uniting individuals into some groups in this property space. The metrics of this space can be arranged in different ways. The properties may be given in different scales: some of them may be linear, and for others—for highly dispersed properties—the logarithmic ones, we may proceed from the space of properties given by the matrix X, to the space of covariances, given by the matrix $(X^*X)^{-1}$. The results of classification will depend on the way we organize the metrics of the space of independent variables just as any other statement of ours made in everyday language depends upon our point of view. Arranging the space metrics differently, we can look at one and the same system in different ways.

So far, we have spoken about the symbolic, or semiotic, dimension of language. We may also speak about the semantic dimensions, set by language polymorphism. It is only the language of strictly definite words which could have been semantically unidimensional. The meaning of multidimensional polymorphic words reveals itself in their interaction during their use. Consequently, we may say that our everyday language is semantically non-linear. The language receiver, the human being, acts as a non-linear transformer.

Concluding the first chapter of this book, I plead with the reader not to be irritated by certain instabilities of the whole system of reasoning. Language is too complicated an organism, preserving and curiously combining everything gained during a long period of evolution. Its description cannot be put into the framework of simple logical schema. And, at the same time, we can describe nothing without turning to logical constructions. We cover a fine ornamentation with a rough net of our constructions. Certainly the net can be made more and more intrinsic, but we would risk blurring the coherence of the judgments.

In this chapter I had to place certain limitations upon the meaning of certain words. However, this should not be regarded too seriously, since the ideas emerging in these cases have no stable meaning. I shall readily give them up the moment we need this in some other place.

Chapter 2

Probabilistic Semantics

Introduction

This chapter might as well be entitled "probabilistic semasiology." It occupies the central place in my system of judgments. Our principal task is to build a model reflecting both the logical structure of language and its complexity expressed by the absence of one-to-one correspondence between a symbol and its referent.

Communication between people takes place on a logical level. Chains of syllogisms are often interspersed with our everyday speech. Nobody formulates postulates explicitly, but we easily catch them in the simplest statements. The logical structure of speech is learned in childhood. For example, a woman insistently asks a little boy, the son of a mathematician, "Why aren't you a girl?" After a moment of pondering, he answers, "Probably because I am a boy." In this syllogism an axiom is used stating that it is impossible to be a boy and a girl simultaneously. Hence, the boy comes to the conclusion that since he is a boy he, therefore, cannot be a girl. But this judgment does not seem too profound even to a child, and for this reason he adds the word "probably."

Even tipsy people try to reason logically.

Once in a dining car I asked a young man why he was so gloomy. The answer was brief, "Because my wife has left me." And to the question, "Why has she left?" he gave another brief answer, "Why? Because I have not left her first." A hidden postulate in this syllogism sounds as follows: the situation in the family demanded a divorce; hence the wife took this step only because the husband had not done so earlier.

Certainly, in everyday speech not only logical means are used but also plausible reasoning, such as judgments based on analogy, felicitous illustrations, etc. But they are still of lesser weight: remember the French proverb, "Comparaison n'est pas raison." The fact that in everyday speech initial postulates are not explicitly formulated allows one to ascribe different weights to them, which, of course, enriches the system of judgments and broadens its limits, though this makes it less strict.

Black (1949) paid attention to this circumstance when he criticized strictly axiomatic means of constructing theories with their unconditional democratism in evaluating both axioms and the consequences from them. If not all consequences are equally important, some of them which are inconsistent with other observations or in opposition to them may be omitted, and this will not destroy the whole system of judgments. True, statements with only implicitly formulated premises are difficult to analyze critically. It is interesting to note that the most remarkable critical structures of the eighteenth and nineteeth centuries, like the philosophy of Kant or of Hegel, are built so that initial premises are not made explicit.

The logical structure of speech has attracted the attention of logicians. Studying language, they could not but pay attention to its logical insufficiency. Hence, a desire arose to rigorize language, especially that of science and philosophy. Thus the program of the neopositivists appeared, which I have already mentioned. And when this trend proved inconsistent and began to degenerate, it was replaced by *logical semantics*, whose origin, it is true, goes back to the works of Peirce (1839–1914) and Frege (1898–1925).

Logical semantics is a branch of metalogic dealing with the interpretation of strictly formalized statements (logical calculus) studying such problems as names, sense, meaning, truth, and falsity. With the help of these notions, logical semantics studies the means of expression of artificial and scientific languages. My task here is more modest: the diagnosis of language and not its therapy. One can readily observe profound genetic links of two trends, logical positivism and logical semantics. The same authors may in some of their papers adhere to both trends simultaneously. Methods and problems of logical semantics have turned out to be deeply related to those of mathematical logic. Great contributions to the development of logical semantics were made by Russell, Carnap, Church, Tarski, and Kemeny. Somewhere at the crossing of mathematical logic and theory of automata another trend has emerged, *mathematical linguistics*,which constructs strictly formalized models of natural and artificial languages. It is concerned with building strictly formalized grammars for symbolic languages.

Another alternative to a formal logical approach to language proceeded from the belief in the power and richness of the natural language, of its inexpressibility in the system of formal–logical constructions. In opposition to the statements of the neopositivists, here it was stated that the natural languages should not be drastically altered (every correction would impoverish them) but rather should be studied and used correctly. This trend had already originated at the beginning of the twentieth century in the philosophical milieu of Great Britain.

It was then that the question of correct comprehension of texts and the rational interpretation of paradoxical statements, abundant in Western philosophy, became especially acute.

The first steps toward the foundation of the British school of linguistic philosophy were made, as I have mentioned, by the British philosopher Moore at Cambridge. His widely known book *Principia Ethica* (Moore, 1903) was published in 1903, and was followed by another book, *The Conception of Reality* (Moore, 1959), in 1917. In the first of these books, he says that in ethics, as in other philosophical studies, difficulties and troubles arise for a very simple reason: from a desire to answer a question without taking the trouble to understand its sense. Philosophers often face more than one question: they confront complex issues.

One such polysemantic question is the central problem of ethics, "What is good?" Moore wrote that if he is asked how good is to be defined, the answer is that it cannot be defined and that is all he has to say about it, disappointing though this answer may appear. In the second book, Moore subjected to a linguistic analysis a paradoxical statement of the British philosopher Bradley, "Time is unreal," and showed that these words mean something quite different from what ordinary people would think they mean. Later, the statement that all troubles in philosophy are due to using words of everyday language in an arbitrary and uncommon sense became the burden of reasoning of British analytical philosophers.[1]

Another example will illustrate more clearly the way Moore subjected philosophical statements to a critical analysis. In analyzing the statement that the universe is spiritual, he remarked that too many different meanings are ascribed to the word "spiritual." If the universe is declared to be spiritual, he said, then ". . . chairs and tables, and mountains which seem to be very different from us, will be more like us than we think."

However, Moore, as opposed to the neopositivists, did not deny the value of metaphysics and did not demand a reform of language; he remained an analyst purporting to have a more profound comprehension of ideas and objects of investigation. He was reproached with making a fetish of the natural language and declaring it holy. [A more detailed de-

---

[1] Much earlier, the wrong usage of words in philosophy was dwelled upon by Helvetius (1758) in his tractatus *On Mind*. One of its chapters is entitled "On Wrong Use of Words." His arguments strikingly resemble the arguments of Moore.

scription of Moore's ideas can be found in a brief but highly readable article (Paul, 1956); what is written above is borrowed from this article.]

I shall not dwell here upon the progress the British linguistic school has made; it had many supporters in the United States as well. I shall confine myself to several remarks on Ziff's book *Semantic Analysis* (1964) published in the United States rather recently. It deals with the semantic analysis of statements not found in philosophical texts. In the preface, the author notes that his writing the book was inspired by the idea that it would be helpful to say what the phrase "good painting" meant. The author faced this question while working on a manuscript on aesthetics. There the following questions arose: "Why should anyone believe what I said?" and "What made me think it was so?" In the last chapter of the book (Ziff, 1964), 160 phrases containing the word "good" are subjected to a comparative semantic analysis. Here are three phrases from the list:

(7) This is a good strawberry.
(8) This is a good lemon.
(9) This is a good carving knife.

It is readily seen that the word "good" has quite different meanings in these phrases. A good lemon should be sour; a good strawberry, on the contrary, should not be sour; and a good carving knife should be sharp, which has nothing to do either with the quality of a lemon or with that of a strawberry. Ziff finishes his book with a statement that the meaning of the word "good" varies but is always associated with answering questions reflecting some special interest or value of ours.

In the papers of representatives of the British linguistic philosophical school, one always, or almost always, comes across sharp opposition of their views to those of the neopositivists. However, the paper by Strawson (1956) contains the statement that it is not clear whether philosophers trying to construct an artificial language and those engaged in analyzing the natural language should be regarded as two hostile camps; he suggests that they supplement each other to a certain degree, and often these two trends are unified under the title of analytical philosophy since they have a common goal—the analysis of language. It seems that we should go farther and formulate the problem more broadly. There is a need in a language model to reflect both its many-sided and illogical character and its logical structure. These two tendencies which seem diametrically opposed are combined in some poorly understood interaction and create our everyday language in all its diversity. Studying these two tendencies separately and independently from each other will hardly be fruitful.

Language Polymorphism and Gödel's Proof

I consider the papers of the British linguistic philosophical school interesting not so much for the results, and even less for the methods of concrete linguistic analysis elaborated for this purpose, as for certain judgments of a general character concerning language, which we can name, following Gellner (1959),[2] the conception of language *polymorphism*. The term "polymorphism" should obviously be considered more apt than the term "polysemy," widely used in linguistic literature, since here not only words' polysemy is involved but also the general irregularity of language.

The diversity of everyday language is considered its most essential characteristic and is no longer regarded as an index of its deficiency. It is due to its polymorphism that natural language is richer than any artificially created one — in this way the answer of British analytical philosophers to the neopositivists may be formulated. To strengthen this almost self-evident statement, I shall now mention Gödel's famous proof of undecidability. I shall not give here its proof in the strict sense of the word, but only an analogy which seems sufficiently interesting and profound.

Gödel's proof is of an extreme epistemological significance. It completes a whole epoch of profound and unconditional belief in determinism, a belief whose last bright flash was the appearance of neopositivism.

The foundation of the scientific vision is confidence in the necessity of verifying hypotheses. This idea has been formulated especially clearly by the neopositivists, though, of course, it is as old as science itself. Thorough analysis of the logical content of the verification principle, made lately, has shown that, even if we confine ourselves to the natural sciences, we shall see that all is not as well as it should be (for details, see Popper, 1965).

As a matter of fact, according to the Popperian school, verifiability should be replaced by falsifiability: the only thing we can do is to show that a hypothesis formulated by us does not contradict the results of our observations. But if the hypothesis in question cannot be falsified, it does not yet follow that it will be impossible to formulate another, probably even stronger hypothesis which will not contradict observations either. However great the number of observations supporting our hypothesis, they are always insufficient for its unconditional acceptance. At the same time, a single negative result is enough to reject the hypothesis. In view of

---

[2] The book *Words and Things* by E. Gellner is devoted to a critical analysis of the principal ideas of the British linguistic philosophical school. It is highly readable; the author's criticism is not tiresome and irritating. A critical account of the ideas of the British philosophical school is also presented in the recently published book by Kozlova (1972).

such a troublesome logical asymmetry, we have to introduce a system of conventions formulated in the language of probability theory in order to be able to assess the degree of reliability of our hypotheses [for details, see Chapter II of my earlier book (Nalimov, 1971)]. The problem of verification in mathematics is even more complicated. The heart of mathematical constructions is *mathematical structures*, systems of axioms rich in their logical consequences (Bourbaki, 1948). The verification is here reduced to testing the inner consistency of the structures. The question of inner relations of axioms has troubled mathematicians since ancient times, immediately after the Euclidian axioms, the first mathematical structure well known to us, were formulated. Numerous efforts were wasted in the attempt to infer the fifth postulate from the basic ones. But after non-Euclidian geometries appeared, another problem arose: it was necessary to show their inner consistency. First, mathematicians were satisfied with a *relative* proof of consistency, using a method of mathematical simulation. In the system of old and recognized mathematical structures, models should have been built on which the axioms of new structures could be fulfilled. One system of mathematical constructions was interpreted with the help of another. Thus, it became possible to show that a plane in Riemannian geometry is simulated by the surface of a sphere in three-dimensional Euclidian space, and in this way the postulates of Riemann turned into theorems of Euclidian geometry. Further, it was shown that Euclidian postulates are fulfilled in a certain algebraic model and, consequently, are consistent if algebra is consistent.

The problem of inconsistency in mathematics became especially acute when contradictions were found in Cantor's theory of sets. At the beginning of our century (in 1904), Hilbert, the famous German mathematician, set out to prove the *absolute* consistency of arithmetic, recognizing the insufficiency of relative proofs when one system of mathematical construction is simulated by another. Later, in the 1920s and 1930s, Hilbert and his school published a number of papers in which certain precise results were obtained. These results seemed to prove the consistency not only of arithmetic but also of the theory of sets. But in 1931, Gödel published his remarkable theorem "On Formally Undecidable Propositions in *Principia Mathematica* and Related Systems," whence followed the failure of Hilbert and his school.

Gödel's proof concerns certain logical systems constructed in a certain way. Axioms are there regarded as lines of symbols, and rules of inference are regarded as ways of deriving new lines from lines. Two demands are imposed upon the rules of inference: they should be strictly deterministic and finite. That means that absolutely unambiguous rules are used, and that using them we should not resort to transfinite induction, a method where one would resort to transfinite numbers which appear through generalizing ordinal numbers on infinite sets.

Certainly, I shall not give here the proof of Gödel's theorem (strictly speaking, there are two theorems, but the second one is a mere consequence of the first), as it is too complex. It is preceded by forty-six definitions and several auxiliary theorems. Attempts to give quite simple proofs of Gödel's theorem may be found in Nagel and Newman (1960) and Arbib (1964). Here, I shall mention only briefly that in proving this theorem arithmetization of mathematics is of great importance. Every mathematical statement is encoded with an arithmetical formula. The study of mathematical statements is reduced to studying arithmetical relations.

From Gödel's proof it follows that the generally used consistent systems whereby arithmetic is expressed are incomplete. There exist true statements expressible in the language of this system that cannot be proved within such a system. Further, it follows from the same theorem that it is impossible to prove the consistency of an arithmetical system by use of methods expressible within this logic. From the theorem it also follows that no matter how much expanded the axioms of the logic (the expansion being finite), it will never become complete; there will always be new truths expressible by its means but not inferable from it.

On the basis of Gödel's theorem, certain statements can be made of a generally methodological or even epistemological character. First of all, from the theorem it follows that it is impossible to give a formal definition to the concept of "proof" in mathematics. In the process of the development of mathematics, new methods of proof appeared which were not foreseen earlier. Further, in the above-mentioned book by Nagel and Newman (1960), the impossibility of building thinking machines is asserted since the programs for computers are always composed on the basis of strict logic. General conclusions from Gödel's proof may be formulated as follows: *human thinking is richer than its deductive form.*

We do not know how a human being actually thinks, but we know fairly well that, on the level of communication, formal logic is widely used. In our everyday speech, to say nothing of scientific language, we can easily trace the logical structure (I have already spoken about this earlier). Here, the question arises immediately: What is the mystery of our language? Why does the logical form of communication not submerge any other modes of human thinking which we, perhaps, do not understand but which are obviously much richer? In what way is Gödel's difficulty overcome in our language?

The conception of polymorphism is one answer to these questions. Vague and ambiguous meanings of words, indistinct demarcation lines between words, and the diversity and heterogeneity of words—all of these create the possibility of breaking out of strictly deductive forms of thinking, the breach being polite and not irritating the interlocutor. Human judgments should, on the one hand, be sufficiently logical; i.e., they should be based on deductive logic. On the other hand, they should be built so as to allow breaches in the strict logic of a system of postulates and rules of inference; otherwise, the system will be tautological. Polymorphism of language is a means allowing such breaches to occur without breaking the illusion of strict logic: it allows us to introduce into our system of judgments the inconsistency without which it would be incomplete. This is also true of judgments in the language of mathematics. I shall remind the reader of the following statement from Gödel's proof: ". . . if arithmetic is consistent it is incomplete." Perhaps the same idea has been expressed by the British school of philosophy, which stated that precision and extreme strictness of the language lead to intellectual spasms (Gellner, 1959). Polymorphism of the language allows us to make our *system of communication non-Gödelian* (Nalimov and Mul'chenko, 1972). [After this manuscript had been finished, I became acquainted with the book by Popper (1962) in which he bases his criticism of the logical positivists' conception of an artificial scientific language on Gödel's proof.]

At the same time, we understand that the inner inconsistency of judgments created by language polymorphism should not go too far; otherwise, the situation of an asylum will result. The limit of unstrictness allowed is somehow set by itself. I shall show further that our everyday language occupies an intermediate position in the semantic scale, on one end of which is situated a hard language with precisely determined meanings of symbols, and on the other end, soft languages with an altogether arbitrary relation between a symbol and a referent. Our everyday language does not occupy a strictly fixed place on this scale; it embraces a broad indeterminate area there.

We should not close our eyes to the fact that people have to pay for the polysemy of the language. Odd disputes quite often arise as a result of different interpretations of the meaning of one and the same word, though probably this is an unavoidable component of human creative activity, one we cannot program in an attempt to create an artificial intelligence. The problem of mutual misunderstanding is perhaps most acute in philosophy, which is only natural since there the most complicated ideas are discussed. The British analytical school accused philosophers of using words of everyday language in an unusual sense. And in contrast to the neopositivists, they did not demand correction of language but confined themselves to a more modest program: interpretation and clarification of word meanings and judgments built of these words.

In fact, I believe that a philosopher can construct an interesting model merely by using common words in an uncommon sense. Obviously, this leads to the necessity of interpreting what has been said. Even the well-known *Tractatus* by Wittgenstein needs an interpretation, but all interpretations are poor in one respect or another. If a brilliant thinker tried to present his ideas in such an interpretative manner, they would look too dreary. Certainly, the *Tractatus Logico-Philosophicus* could not have appeared if such style had been required from the author, though the book deals with the rigor of language.

Games including a random component are a peculiar model of language behavior. One such game is cards. When people of different intellectual background meet somewhere—say, in a train compartment—they feel a desire to replace language behavior with its simplified model, a card game. Card games possess strict rules and well-developed strategies applied in random situations. These rules act like the rules of logic in our language; they cannot be broken or you will play not *this game, but another one* (Vendler, 1968). Shuffling cards is here a generator of randomness. Randomness combined with a complex system of rules makes the game intellectually rich, recalling verbal behavior where randomness is given by the language polymorphism. What is important here is that our verbal behavior, as well as a card game, should have several alternatives; otherwise, everything will turn into a farce, into solving a charade, and will be as dull and sad as a trial with a predetermined outcome (Gellner, 1959). Random constituents resting upon a logical structure enter our verbal behavior.

Bayesian Model of Language

Let us now try to build a model of language which will contain overtly the probabilistic structure of the meaningful content of a sign. First of all, I should say a few words about the theorem of the Englishman Bayes[3] and the neobayesian approach to the foundation of the rules of

[3] Thomas Bayes (1702–1761) was a member of the first secure generation of English religious Nonconformists. His father was a respected theologian of dissent; he was also one of the group of six ministers who were the first to be publicly ordained as Nonconformists. Privately educated, Bayes became his father's assistant at the presbytery at Holborn, London; his mature life was spent as minister at the chapel in Tunbridge Wells. Despite his provincial circumstances, he was a wealthy bachelor with many friends. The Royal Society of London elected him a fellow in 1742. He wrote little: "Divine Benevolence" (1731) and "Introduction to the Doctrine of Fluxions" (1736) are the only works to have been published during his lifetime. The latter is a response to Bishop Berkeley's "Analyst," a stinging attack on the logical foundations of Newton's calculus; Bayes's reply was perhaps the soundest retort to Berkeley then available. Bayes is remembered for his brief "Essay towards Solving a Problem in the Doctrines of Chance" (1763), the first attempt to establish firm foundations for statistical inference. (*Dictionary of Scientific Biography*, vol. 1, New York, 1970).

inference in modern mathematical statistics. The principal idea lies in the fact that, making certain decisions after this or that experiment, we always use both the newly received and the previously known information about the phenomena under study. Before an experiment, the experimenter always has some knowledge expressible in probabilistic language; we can call it prior probability or, alternatively, subjective or personal probability. [Ramsey was the first to introduce the concept of personal (subjective) probability in 1926.]

Bayes' theorem allows us to formalize the process of decision making by simulating a procedure where both prior information and that received as a result of an experiment are used; the answer is given in probabilistic terms as a posterior probability.

Let us explain this theorem in ordinary statistical terms. Let us assume that the measurement of a certain attribute μ of a certain object H is effectuated. There is a region Y of all possible results of measurements y. In this region probability $p(y|\mu)$ is given; in the simplest case the errors in the measurement of object H are normally distributed. Further, we shall assume that we know prior probability $p(\mu)$; that is, that a priori before the experiment we know the distribution of all possible values μ. Then Bayes' theorem may be put as follows

$$p(\mu|y) = kp(y|\mu)\,p(\mu)$$

where k is a constant to normalize the result. Prior probability being introduced into consideration gives the entrance into the system, and with the help of Bayes' theorem, we provide a logically faultless exit which is put down as a posterior probability, $p(\mu|y)$. The difficulty of this approach consists in comprehending what prior probability, $p(\mu)$, is. As a matter of fact, this question has been widely analyzed [see, for example, von Wright (1962) and Good (1962)]. In any case, it is clear that a person always estimates probabilities of various events in both his scientific and his everyday activities. These estimates are always subjective in the sense that they are determined by the intellectual disposition and experience of a given subject, and the degree of his being informed; they are at the same time objective to a certain extent, or, it is probably better to say, general since it is assumed that we deal with reasonable observers rather similarly disposed. Another thing is important here: subjective probability of an event estimated by any method may be handled the same as the probability introduced mathematically if it has the same properties and obeys the same axioms.

If a priori we know nothing about the distribution $p(\mu)$ our ignorance may be expressed thus: all values μ are equally distributed on a straight line. In this case it is easily seen that the posterior distribution will be brought down in statistical investigations to the initial distribution of errors in measuring $p(y|\mu)$, built in relation to value $\bar{y}$ found in the experiment. In the long run, we shall compute the estimated value $\bar{y}$ with the same two- or three-sigma limits of traditional statistics. The only difference lies in the logical foundation, but it proves to be very profound. It allows us to avoid the difficulties we have to face in traditional statistics where the confidence limits are given before the measurement is taken; in fact, it is not clear why they should always remain valid after the measurement is taken.

I shall illustrate some logical difficulties arising here with an example. Assume that we are measuring small quantities of a substance in a sample near the limits of detection (Slavnyi, 1969). At first sight it seems natural to regard the value $\bar{y} \geqslant 3\sigma$ (criterion of Kaiser) as a threshold signal (the limit of detection being a standard deviation characterizing the average of background fluctuation). Then we have a simple rule of decision making: the substance in the sample is not found if $\bar{y} \leqslant 3\sigma$. But then we are not using all the information present in the observations. In particular, we do not pay attention to the fact that the value $\bar{y} < 0$ was found for a certain sample though we know beforehand that the content of the substance in a sample cannot be less than zero. Negative values could also serve as a basis for a statement that the true content of the substance in the probe is lower than a certain value significantly less than the 3σ limit of detection. The trouble is that using traditional statistical methods we cannot build a distribution function around the value $\bar{y}$ when $\bar{y} < 3\sigma$ without getting into the region of negative values of a signal, which, of course, lacks a physical sense. In a Bayesian approach, everything becomes much simpler. A prior statement of the impossibility of negative concentration results should be introduced into the decision-making rule; further, all positive values of the signal should be acknowledged to be equally probable (of course, within certain limits). Then at the output of the decision-making system we shall naturally obtain posterior probabilities. In the case of a uniform posterior distribution, the problem will finally be reduced to renormalization: the part of the square under the portion of the curve of the differential distribution function which corresponds to the positive values of the signal will equal 1. This is presented graphically in Fig. 2.[4] Of course, in practical work, it is more rational to take not an equally probable distribution but a decreasing one; however, this is a detail which we shall not dwell upon.

---

[4] One might ask whether it is necessary to present the results of the substance analysis in such a complicated manner as it is done in Fig. 2. The answer depends here on the problem formulation. If this is the case of a mass quality control, it may not be necessary, but we may come across problems in which we must make a responsible decision on the basis of the results of an analysis carried out in the vicinity of the limits of detection. In this case, a Bayesian solution will seem attractive.

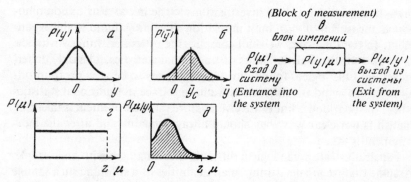

FIG. 2. *Graphic illustration of the application of the Bayesian theorem in the problem of finding small contents of substances.* **Classical solution of the problem:** *(a) the distribution function of the error of measurement known by an experimenter before the performance of the given measurement; (b) constructing of 95% confidence limits for the results of measurement by way of centering of the distribution function* **a** *in relation to a new result of measurement* **ye** *(it turns out that we must admit the existence of negative concentration of substance with great probability).* **Bayesian solution of the problem:** *(c) a block-scheme of the Bayesian solution; (d) à priori distribution function for the contents of substance in a probe (here the hypothethis of almost complete à priori ignorance is accepted: impossibility of the existence of negative concentrations is the only fact we know); (e) à posteriori distribution function p(μ|y), obtained by means of multiplying à priori distribution function* **d** *by the distribution function of the errors of measurement* **b** *obtained by measuring the given probe.*

This example shows how a Bayesian approach allows us to avoid a logically unfounded method of action: ascribing to the observation results the limits of confidence suggested by a statistician before taking measurements. It is especially important that we have managed to build a new procedure for estimating observation results only on the basis of using prior knowledge. A new algorithm of decision making seems quite natural: it is as if it simulates our everyday behavior since in this kind of behavior we make decisions using our prior knowledge and the additional inputs from most recent experience.

At this point, I should probably make a reservation: in the frame of classical statistics it is indubitably possible to overcome logical difficulties connected with defining confidence limits for very small concentrations. But it cannot be done so elegantly as in the Bayesian approach.

Let us now return to the semantic analysis of sign systems. Our principal statement may be formulated as follows: both in everyday language and in many other languages, every sign is connected in a probabilistic manner with a variety of meanings. We may speak of a prior function of distribution of sign meanings. This distribution may be constructed, for example, as follows. The receptor's consciousness contains a certain notion of possible sign meanings: one of them has a greater probability; another, a lesser one; etc. All this may be represented with a distribution function built so that on the abscissa the ranks of meanings are plotted according to their probability of occurrence and on the ordinate probabilities themselves are plotted. The scale of the abscissa may be imagined as continuous: sections of this scale with vague boundaries (such as vague demarcations between colors on the wave scale for the white light spectrum) may be meaningful units. Looking through dictionaries, bilingual or explanatory, we shall see that every entry word is explained by several or many words. These explanatory words are usually ordered according to the strength of their connection with the entry word. Thus, the notion of a distribution function of the word meanings is implicitly present in the structure of our dictionaries. The meaningful content of a sign is given there as a *semantic field* whose elements are ordered on a linear scale. We want to strengthen this arrangement by ascribing to the sections of the semantic scale those probabilities with which they are associated by use of signs. The probabilities appear in the consciousness of the receptor, a subject, and for this reason the corresponding distribution functions may be called prior or, as is sometimes said, subjective or personal.[5] Two examples of such an arranged semantic field are given in Fig. 3. In building distribution functions we have made use of the analysis of the words "game" and "to read" in Wittgenstein's *Philosophical Investigations*, as well as data from the dictionaries of Webster and Dal'.

It is quite obvious that a person with another intellectual background may have quite different distribution functions. This especially refers to the word "game," since it is not difficult to think of a person for whom

---

[5] There exists a voluminous literature devoted to the techniques of estimating subjective probabilities [see, for example, the paper by Winkler (1967), which has a bibliography of the most important papers]. In elaborating these techniques, the following requirements are taken into account: (i) an expert should obey the postulates of concordance, which means that he must express his judgments so that they corresponded to the existing notions of the probability theory; (ii) the expert's judgments must be numerical expressions of his personal opinion. The first of these requirements can easily be tested; the second one cannot, since it deals with purely subjective notions not corresponding to any objective reality, or, to be more correct, to a reality existing outside the expert. Estimating subjective probability is an interesting psychological challenge. If we have a right to state that human behavior is probabilistic, it does not yet follow from this that a person has an ability to express his judgments in the system of probabilistic notions used in mathematical statistics. Real experiments of estimating subjective probabilities are carried out as if a mental lottery is in operation and the expert places bets. Different formulations of the problems often lead to different results. Other difficulties arise as well. For example, it may prove that the expert's sum of probabilities is 1.2. What will he do in this case? He may norm it to a unity dividing it by 1.2, or he may subtract from certain probabilities so that their sum equals a unity. Then, it has become experimentally obvious that naïve experts tend to build truncated distribution functions. They regard the probability of rare events as exactly equal to zero and not as close to zero. In any case, it is clear that experts should be specially instructed. It should also be remembered that probability estimates obtained at various moments may differ significantly, and this must be regarded as experts' natural behavior.

FIG. 3. *Possible à priori (personal) distribution functions of the meaningful content of two words.* (a) *The word "game": 1–game as playing situation, a procedure with a variety of nondetermined alternatives; 2–game as a model to describe complex systems (a game model of language, a game model of the world in the Buddist philosophy, etc.); 3–game as a mathematical model of decision making, mathematical game theory; 4–game as passionate activity (gambling, gambler, etc.); 5–game as competition (in intellectual and political activity, etc.);*

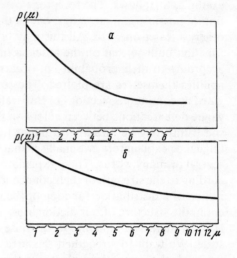

6–game as competition in sports; 7–game as joke, enjoyment, mockery; 8–game as theater. (b) *The word "to read": 1–to pass from symbols to speech sounds; 2–to read something learned by heart; 3–to read to oneself, 4–to read proofs, checking the written material by comparing it with another text; 5–to translate unambiguously one sign system into another; 6–to carry out measurements; 7–to interpret in ordinary language something written in other languages; 8–to guess something written in an altogether unfamiliar language; 9–to interpret images; 10–to guess something concealed behind the external manifestation, e.g., to read others' thoughts; 11–to predict, to read one's fate; 12–to deliver lectures (to read a course).*

this word will be primarily associated with gambling games and will in no way be connected with a branch of mathematics.

The prior probability permits the first step in the process of perceiving the text read. The process of reading is used here in a broad sense as a procedure of text perception because the texts are formed of various signs, and we can thus form the $p(y|\mu)$ distribution function. It is given by several factors: by means of combining the sign read with other signs of a phrase or by the general emotional–intellectual disposition of the receptor and by his attention at the moment of reading. The two last factors introduce the same element of uncertainty as an error in ordinary physical measurement. In any case, it seems reasonable to speak of the errors in semantic perception of a sign in the same way that we speak of the errors in any other measuring procedures, as well as to introduce the notion of a distribution function. The analogy can be continued as far as one wishes. Imagine, for example, that you are finding by means of a spectrochemical analysis some element in a sample with a complex structure. The errors of analysis will first of all depend on the general sample composition and on its physical state; further, they will depend on the attention of a laboratory assistant, and on the unavoidable irreproducibility of all elementary measuring procedures, including here the condition of measuring instruments.

At the *exit* from the system, we shall have a posterior distribution function $p(\mu|y)$: after reading, the sign read will still be associated not with one meaning but with a field of meanings whose elements will be arranged in some probabilistic manner. In a particular case of full prior ignorance (or prior indifference), the function $p(\mu)$ will be just a uniform distribution (on a straight line) and then $p(\mu|y)$ will be reduced to $p(y|\mu)$, but this can hardly happen when the receptor is a sane human being. If $p(\mu)$ is more or less similar for the receptor and the transmitter, the process of reading will introduce only casual distortions. But it may turn out that the receptor and transmitter ascribe to the sign system completely different senses. This is evidently what is happening to a certain degree in Western philosophy, and this is what has led to an appearance of a critically minded trend in analytical philosophy which I have already mentioned more than once. This is expressed even more obviously in abstract painting, which I shall dwell upon later. In everyday life, people of one social circle usually meet and they have certain agreement as to the prior distribution functions. But this is not always so. And the more interesting the idea stated, the more striking is the transmitter's prior distribution function connected with the signs used: speaking of something new, he uses old signs. I should like here to recollect one of Wittgenstein's statements, "The silent adjustments to understand colloquial language are enormously complicated" (Wittgenstein, 1955, paradox 4.003).

Different people may read signs differently as well. Divergence of the results of one and the same text being read by different people seems always to be larger than reproducibility during the repeated reading of the same text by the same person. The same happens during physical measurements. Errors of interlaboratory reproducibility are always larger than errors of intralaboratory reproducibility.

It is interesting to note that, using a neobayesian approach in physical investigations, different observers may assume different prior probabilities. This is especially obvious in the problems of discriminating hypotheses, when one has to choose a hypothesis from a number of rival ones.

Inappropriate choice of prior probabilities does not lead here to any grave troubles. Both general theoretical reasons and calculations made when problems are solved by simulating them show that the Bayesian system of decision making has a short memory in the system of sequential procedures: wrongly chosen probabilities are quickly forgotten after several experiments. The same is believed to take place in reading texts. Imagine that the receptor has a prior distribution function different from that of the transmitter. Reading attentively one and the same text, or, better, various texts by the same author or group of authors, the receptor will be able to switch over in the process of reading. This is a process of learning accompanied by forgetting old information. But does it always take place? To provide for this, the receptor should not be too conservative. In any case, prior information is understood here not in the Kantian sense but the way it is commonly understood nowadays in mathematical statistics: in relation to the $(n + 1)$th experiment, prior information will be that received in the nth experiment.

The model described above proceeds from a profound analogy existing between the process of measuring and its interpretation and the process of reading a sign system. It may be contrasted to the well-known concept of *logical atomism* of Frege, Russell, and Wittgenstein (in his early period) (see, for example, Pears, 1956). Logical atoms, elementary and indivisible particles of sense, may be opposed to a continuous distribution function of meanings, and this contrasting goes even farther; I believe that meaning cannot be ascribed to a sign before a text is read, though we have some prior idea of the meaningful field of a sign. This is analogous to the impossibility of ascribing to a value estimated in a physical experiment the confidence limits we believed it to have before the experiment. The analogy with a physical experiment may be continued. If we deal with a continuously changing random variable, the probability of hitting a strictly fixed point in measuring equals zero. A notion of certain unique and strictly fixed meaning of a sign will be a similar non-degenerate case.

Our model can also be contrasted to the statements of Wittgenstein (in his later period). In the *Investigations* (Wittgenstein, 1953) there is his famous phrase that the meaning of a word is given by its use. Some Western philosophers believe it to be the strongest statement of twentieth century philosophy. In our model, the process of word perception is given both by its use expressed as distribution function $p(y|\mu)$ and by the prior knowledge distribution function $p(\mu)$. If the receptor a priori has no meaningful associations with the sign read, then the distribution function is degenerate: the probability of all meaningful associations proves to equal zero, and in this case our model shows perfectly formally that the text cannot be read. This is probably what will happen to messages from other worlds if they are received some day. In his *Investigations* Wittgenstein puts a question: What does it mean that we have begun to understand a text? My answer to this question, contrary to the author of *Investigations*, is as follows: we have succeeded on the basis of our experience to build a prior distribution function of the meaningful content of a sign which previously aroused no associations in our mind.

What is said above may be illustrated with an example from the book

Star Diaries of Ijon Tichy by the Polish writer of science fiction Stanislaw Lem (1971). The reader can find there several words of non-terrestrial origin. Here is how the word "sepulka" is explained in the "Cosmic Encyclopaedia":

> Sepulka — an important element of the civilization of Adrides (v.) on the planet Enteropea. v. sepulkarium.
> Sepulkaria — objects for sepulking (v.).
> Sepulking — activity of Adrides (v.) on the planet Enteropea (v.) v. Sepulka.

Then a dialogue takes place.

> I came up to the counter and with a feigned calm asked for a sepulka.
> "For what sepulkarium?" asked the salesman descending from his peg.
> "Well, for a common one," I said.
> "For a common one?" He was surprised. "But we have only sepulkas with a whistle."
> "Well, I want one."
> "And where is your zhutka?"
> "Ehm, I have not it with me."
> "Where will you take it, then, without a wife?" asked the salesman scrutinizing me and growing dim.
> "I have no wife," I said imprudently.
> "You . . . have . . . no wife?" mumbled the salesman growing black and staring at me thunderstruck. "And you want a sepulka? . . . without a wife . . ." He was trembling all over.

Here we see that an extensive and logically correct text is insufficient to understand the meaning of a foreign word. We have not at our disposal the set of meanings μ upon which we could build the distribution function $p(y|\mu)$. We not only cannot understand, we cannot even feel vaguely, the word-meaning if it has no prior distribution function in our mind. Its logically correct use does not yet reveal its meaning.

If we hold to the Bayesian model of sign perception, we shall have to acknowledge that, although reading a text will cause our consciousness to absorb not a certain discrete meaning connected with a sign read but rather a whole field of meanings, the range will be narrower than the meaning connected with the sign before the text was read. A Bayesian model may be interpreted as a many-valued probabilistic logic; here, the answer is given by a distribution function of sense content.

In the frame of the model suggested here, many facts well known in linguistics are easy to interpret. First of all, we can speak of what lies behind the notion of the term *"precision"* so widely used in discussion of scientific terminology. From our point of view, this very exact notion is determined only by a degree of vagueness of the prior distribution function $p(\mu)$ related to a scientific term μ.

Another well-known problem is that of synonymy, one of the characteristics of language polymorphism. However, it remains unclear what we understand under this term. A statement by Nida (1965) is very interesting in this respect. He denies altogether the existence of synonyms, saying that no morphemes or their combinations are ever identical with respect to the meaning they contain. It is always possible to give an example in which generally acknowledged synonyms proved unequivalent. This is especially readily seen if we turn to set expressions. For example, in the expression "as right as nails" the word "right" cannot be replaced with the word "correct," though these two words are considered synonymous according to a dictionary of synonyms (Aleksandrova, 1971). In our system of ideas, synonymy is given simply by a coefficient of rank correlation between meanings of two different words. We can also estimate a degree of meaningful coordination between several words by means of the coefficient of concordance, well known in non-parametric statistics. It becomes immediately clear whence come the difficulties in defining what synonyms are. In fact, it is doubtful that the rank ordering of the meanings of two different words can be completely identical, and for this reason the phrase by Nida should be understood in the sense that there are no synonyms whose coefficient of rank-order correlation would equal unity. Evidently, we regard as synonyms the words whose rank-order coefficient of meanings is not too small; i.e., speaking the language of mathematical statistics, it should be significant for a certain previously chosen level of significance. Besides, we should not forget that prior distribution functions are subjective, and we should always think of some average sense ranking which characterizes semantic behavior of whole groups of people. Nevertheless, it is reasonable to believe that in reality everything happens the way our model presupposes, and a certain level of significance for the correlation coefficient which is not fixed anywhere is somehow set spontaneously. This allows us to recognize some words as synonyms.

I have attempted to investigate quantitatively the frequency of occurrence of synonymous groups of different sizes in the English and Russian dictionaries of synonyms. The frequency of groups containing two, three, or more synonyms in dictionaries (Webster, 1942; Aleksandrova, 1971) was determined, and the results obtained are graphically presented in Fig. 4. Distribution functions proved to be strikingly different, though, of course, we are not sure that the writers of these dictionaries meant the same level of significance for the correlation coefficient.

The first thing that surprised me was the large difference in the number

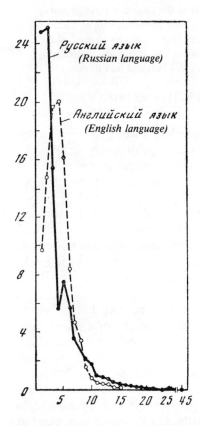

FIG. 4. *Frequencies of occurrence of synonymous groups of different size in Russian and in English. On the abscissas the number of words is marked which enter the synonymous groups; on the ordinates, the frequency of appearance of such groups in the dictionaries of synonyms (Aleksandrova, 1971; Webster, 1942).*

of entries. The Russian dictionary is compiled for 8,322 entries, whereas the English one contains only 1,954. For the latter dictionary an obvious concentration of frequencies is observed for words with a small number of synonyms (from one to five), and then the curve begins to decay rather rapidly; the maximal number of synonyms is 15. The distribution function for the Russian dictionary is extended: there are words with more than 20 synonyms, and the maximal number is 59. Is it a real difference in the semiotic structure of the two languages or just a result of different approaches to the definition of synonyms? In this case, the definition of synonyms in the two dictionaries is formulated so that it is impossible to answer this question, but I believe that statistical study of the synonymy of various languages, if properly organized, could prove very interesting.

A Bayesian model allows us to understand the nature of a joke. Here is an example.

> Recently I made a report in a biochemical laboratory on the way the teaching of mathematical statistics to these specialists should be organized. I began my speech by telling the audience how the for-

mulation of the problem emerged during the talk at dinner in our canteen. After a thorough discussion of the problem, one of those present at the table said, "Now we may come to the conclusion: the service at our canteen should be improved." This remark animated the audience, but a mathematician who was late and had missed the beginning of my report got up and asked with a perplexed air what it meant—probably he misheard my words. However, when it was explained, he began to laugh too.

What has happened here? After my speech, the word "canteen" in the minds of the audience began to be associated (with a very small probability) with the problem of teaching mathematical statistics to biochemists. After the concluding remark, in accordance with the Bayesian theorem, the posterior distribution function connected with the word "canteen" was reduced to a meaning of the word which was associated with it only weakly in the prior distribution function. This shocked and pleasantly animated everybody. The mathematician who had missed the beginning of the report did not have this additional weak association in the prior distribution function; therefore, he did not understand the joke.

A human being is put together so that he does not like dull verbal behavior; it wearies him. A joke breaking the monotony of a speech consists in suddenly transferring associations with small probability into dominant ones. Jokes are based on using the tail part of the prior distribution function. To understand them, one must possess a "stretched tail" part of the prior distribution function. In order to be able to make jokes, one must be able to use this tail part. People who do not understand jokes have a truncated prior distribution function; they can use only those meanings of the word's semantic field which are associated with the word with a large probability.

Many jokes are based on the fact that a phrase contains a word to which two quite different meanings can be ascribed with almost equal probability. As a matter of fact, a word having simultaneously two equally probable meanings is the basis for innumerable puns. The following anecdote based on the present-day Soviet reality is an illustration of this:

> One nationalistic Jew says to another during the six-day war, "I say, yesterday our soldiers shot down six of our aircraft."

The gist of this anecdote is based on the two meanings of the word "our"; in the first case it signifies Soviet soldiers and in the second one Israeli aircraft.[6]

---

[6] In Russian the anecdote sounds better since the Russian pronoun "our" (наши) in the first meaning is substantial; i.e., it does not require a noun.

Now let us see in what way we can interpret this joke in Bayesian terms. It seems that upon hearing this phrase I recall my own prior distribution function of the word "our." If I try to ascribe to the meanings of this Russian word the probabilities with which they occur in my mind and rank them, I'll get roughly the following sequence: kith and kin, my friends, my colleagues and members of our invisible college, my distant acquaintances, my compatriots, people whose native tongue is Russian. Somewhere at the end of the list, the word "наши" with a very small probability will acquire the meaning of the national minority from which my father comes.

In order to get the gist of the joke, it is very important to remember the remark that this is a conversation of two nationalistic Jews. Taking this into account, the distribution function $p(y|\mu)$ should be constructed proceeding from the peculiarities of nationalistic psychology. In this case the greatest probability among the meanings of the word "наши" is ascribed to belonging to one's nation. The probability of all the other meanings decreases sharply. The product of the two functions — the prior distribution function $p(\mu)$ constructed above and the function $p(y|\mu)$ constructed while reading the phrase and its context — gives a bimodal distribution function $p(\mu|y)$. The word "наши" thus may have two essentially different meanings with almost equal probability, and the phrase may be understood in two different ways. Here lies its pungency.

A brilliant example of a pun based on the two meanings of the word "to shoot" — (i) to aim and fire and (ii) to photograph — may be found in Evelyn Waugh's novel *Vile Bodies*.

> As Adam walked up the drive two lorries thundered past him. Then a man appeared with a red flag.
>
> "Hi! You can't go that way. They're shooting in front . . ."
>
> Wondering vaguely what kind of sport this could be, Adam followed the side path indicated. He listened for sounds of firing but heard nothing. . . . He had not gone very far in his detour before he was again stopped . . .
>
> "Here, what in hell do *you* want?" said the Bishop.
>
> "I came to see Colonel Blount."
>
> "Well, you can't, son. They are just shooting him now."
>
> "Good heavens, what for?"
>
> "Oh, nothing important. He's just one of the Wesleyans, you know — we're trying to polish off the whole crowd this afternoon, while the weather is good."
>
> Adam found himself speechless before this cold-blooded bigotry.
>
> "I dare say you'd like to come round to the front and see the fun," continued the Bishop. "I should think they'd be just singing their last hymn now. It's been uphill work," he confided, "and there's been some damned bad management. Why, yesterday, they kept Miss La

> Touche waiting the whole afternoon, and then the light was so bad
> when they did shoot her that they made a complete mess of her—we
> had the machine out and ran over all the bits carefully last night after
> dinner—you never saw such rotten little scraps—quite unrecogniz-
> able half of them. We didn't dare show them to her husband—he'd
> be sick to death about it—so we just cut out a few shots to keep and
> threw away the rest. I say, you are not feeling queer, are you? You
> look all green suddenly."
>
> "Was—was she a Wesleyan too?"
>
> "My dear boy, she's playing lead. . . . She's Selina, Countess of
> Huntingdon. . . . There, now you can see them at work."

The pun of the dialogue proceeds from the fact that Adam's partner
speaks so that his interlocutor chooses the meaning of the word "to
shoot" which is irrelevant for the situation.

Here is an example illustrating how misunderstanding of the second
meaning of a word can be turned into a joke.

> Once in a shop I was a witness to the following conversation.
>
> "Have you any cinnamon?"
>
> "We don't sell it."
>
> "And where can I get it?"
>
> "Here."
>
> "But you say you don't sell it."
>
> " 'Don't sell it' means 'sell it only very rarely.' "

Here, the salesgirl explained to the customer a Bayesian model of understanding the two meanings of the phrase "we don't sell it."

A Bayesian model may help to explain the mechanism of comprehending "contracted" phrases. And the meaning of such phrases becomes
clear not because of their grammatical structure, but through the Bayesian procedure of passing from a broad meaningful subset of word
meanings to one of its subsets. This latter becomes the field of elementary events on which the probability of comprehending the word meaning in a given context begins to be redistributed. It is noteworthy that the
mature English language with its highly expanded polymorphism contains such contracted phrases much more often than the comparatively
young Russian language in which the tendency to build expanded phrases
prevailed up to recent times. By the way, here lies the origin of the well-
known fact that after translating an English text into Russian it always
becomes slightly longer (in the number of printing symbols). However,
this problem is to be studied separately.

As an illustration of the differences in the two languages, I shall use
the word combination "New English Bible." Its meaning is quite clear for
English-speaking people. Their prior distribution function for the word
"Bible" is such that its being combined with the word "new" may mean

only a new version of translating the Bible. But the Russian reader, even with some knowledge of English, is puzzled by the title. According to the tradition of Russian lexicographers, the meaning of this phrase should be interpreted, "This is a new Bible, the English one," but such an interpretation contradicts the prior meaning of the word "Bible." Thus, the title of the book should have been translated into Russian as "New English Translation of the Bible."

The English language, despite its strict grammar, allows formally directed phrases. For example, phrases like "It's the last tram but one; the last one will go by in an hour" have become linguistic clichés. If the word "last" is ascribed a discrete meaning, the phrase will have to be acknowledged as logically illicit, since then the existence of idioms would be impossible. But if we believe the word to have a fuzzy meaning including not only the latest event in a time sequence but also an event close to the end of the sequence, then it becomes clear that the word combination "but one" allows us to select from the fuzzy semantic field of the word "last" its subset of meanings pertinent here.

The probabilistic model of language can explain certain peculiarities of the verbal behavior of insane people (my attention was drawn to this fact by psychophysiologist I. M. Feigenberg). It may be suggested that schizophrenics have much flatter slopes of the prior distribution functions of meaningful word contents than normal people, and sometimes the slopes may go almost parallel to the horizontal axis. In any case, the values of word content which with normal people are situated in the tail part of the distribution function arise in the insane consciousness with a probability equal to that of the principal meaningful components of the word. It is not logic but rather semantics of speech which is broken here. Say a patient is asked, "Are there any common features between a plum and a river?" He answers, "There are stones both in a plum and in a river." When asked, "Are there any common features between gasoline and a symphony?" he answers, "If you make a hole in the gasoline can, the gasoline will run out and produce a melody." These answers are not in the least humorous. Patients with such verbal behavior cannot perceive humor, which, as we have already pointed out, is connected with unexpected use of a word's meaningful content. With such patients, the prior distribution function of word content is arranged so that there can be no unexpectedness.

According to I. M. Feigenberg, such psychic disturbances are the breach of probabilistic ordering in the memory "card index." In psychiatry a very curious, though rare, phenomenon is known—that of a "second life" of a patient. Having recovered, the patient returns to normal life but he chooses a new, intellectually simpler profession. He turns out to have maintained his previous knowledge; it is not forgotten but is probabilistically disordered. Here, it must be pointed out that the formal construction of the speech of this kind of patients remains logically strict. Speech disturbances are not of a logical but a semantic nature.

In his book Feigenberg (1972) develops a very interesting conception of probabilistic expectation of human behavior. Imagine, for example, that you are at the railway station, where the broadcasting center gives out quite incomprehensible messages. Still, you will immediately recognize the number of your train. This is Bayesian recognition. This is also true of listening to broadcasts in one's native and in foreign languages: in the former case we get the meaning even if the message is accompanied by noise, while the understanding of foreign texts requires a very high quality of program listenability. Our recognition in this case is hampered since in our consciousness there does not flash a set of alternative words (they must appear very quickly so as to match the tempo of the program), one of which we must recognize. When tuning the radio, you come across some foreign program, and you first of all wish to guess what it is about. As soon as you succeed, the Bayesian mechanism of recognition starts working.

Probabilistic expectation is well illustrated by the well-known Charpentier experiment. Imagine two objects of equal weight but essentially different volume which seem to be made of the same material. A normal person, having picked up the object, will immediately state that the smaller one is heavier. This is a shock response since, judging by their appearance, he expected the smaller object to be lighter. If the same procedure is carried out with closed eyes and the objects are picked up by the string fastened to them, the weights will be perceived as equal; in this case, probabilistic expectation is absent. Schizophrenics do not possess it either: they will not state that the smaller object is heavier even if they see the objects before taking them into their hands.

Now let us pass to discussing the most interesting problem — that of constructing a system of logical judgments by using a set of signs of a polymorphous language. Is it at all possible to build any logical structure if words have a variety of meanings?

A statistician, when formulating judgments on random variables, gives a distribution function by their parameters: mathematical expectation, dispersion, asymmetry, excess. Not all of these parameters are necessary; often it is enough to deal with one of them, mathematical expectation implying the mean of a random value. In our verbal behavior in the process of constructing logical structures, we replace distribution functions with average meanings which are signified by this or that word. An average word meaning is its semantic invariant with a poor sense content. Logical structures may be constructed on various levels of abstraction. On the low levels, the average meaning is very important. On the highest levels, we operate with words simply as with signs, forgetting about their average meanings. In such an abstract phrase, words play the role of logical variables. Thinking over the statement given by this phrase, we try to interpret its meaning by means of words, turning to the mechanism given by a prior distribution function and Bayes' theorem. Strictly speaking, logic can deal only with signs and not with sense. Here, I should like to recall the well-known statement by Wittgenstein (1955) in his *Tractatus*:

> In logical syntax, the meaning of a sign ought never to play a role; it must admit of being established without use being thereby made of the *meaning* of a sign . . . (from paradox 3.33)

Cherry (1957) illustrates this thought by the following syllogism:

> All hoodles are snurds.
> This gabooge is a hoodle.
> Therefore it is a snurd.

This is an example of a deductive inference that is clear for us though built from meaningless words (we have no prior distribution function of sense content for them). We perceive the words of the syllogism as abstract symbols, being quite aware that the moment we get the key to their understanding the syllogism will immediately be interpreted.

The progress of logical thinking is related to passing to still more and more profound symbolization which we generally call abstraction. The language of complex statements becomes two-staged. On one stage, logical statements about abstract symbols are constructed. On the other stage, these symbols are interpreted. The two-staged language structure is especially vividly seen in describing physical phenomena in the language of mathematics. We have already spoken about the profound links between logic and mathematics. In principle, any logical statement may be expressed in mathematical language, and any mathematical statement may be interpreted as logical, but, of course, it is very difficult to do this in practice. Symbols used to fulfill this task have a definite physical sense but not so precise a one as the neopositivists used to demand. At an early stage of development, the physical meaning of symbols played a great role in the process of building a mathematical theory of physical phenomena. But gradually, as the progress of physical knowledge continued, the abstraction of conceptions became more profound. After certain mathematically expressed logical operations, sometimes quite complicated, are defined in terms of relations constructed from abstract symbols, we obtain new relations to be interpreted in the language of experiment.

A very interesting question may be formulated which, for some reason or other, has not been discussed by philosophers: What is the difference between the modern tendency toward mathematization of knowledge and the program of the neopositivists? Both seem to concern the same problem: transforming sciences into formal calculi. Two very different approaches are suggested for the solution of this problem. The neopositivists wanted to construct a calculus on the terms of a new language with strictly unambiguous word meanings. The modern tendencies toward mathematization of knowledge are directed at constructing a calculus over symbols whose meaning does not seem very pertinent. Certain formalization of knowledge is allowed, the set structure of scientific language being preserved. Strictly speaking, two languages are introduced in this case. One of them is a language of mathematics by means of which the system of inference over abstract symbols is built. Another one is an everyday polymorphous language of science by means of which statements received in a symbolic form are informally interpreted.

Now let us consider the problem of translation. Assume that we have to translate a text from μ-language into η-language. From experience it is known that each meaningful word of μ-language may be represented by several seemingly equivalent words in η-language. This means that the word μ_i in question has a field of meanings that completely, or at least in its major part, intersects with the fields of a certain x-subset of $\eta_1, \eta_2, \ldots$ η_x words of η-language. Hence, the following recommendation for translation would seem rational: choose the word from the x-subset which has the greatest rank correlation coefficient with the word μ_i. However, this recommendation is not correct. It might turn out that the phrase in μ-language may be built so that the word makes use of the tail part of the content distribution function which is absent in the words of the x-subset of η-language. To make sure of that, we have to use the procedure of Bayesian reading. Thus, two possibilities emerge. The first is to select a word in η-language into which the meaningful content (understood for μ-language in the Bayesian way) would enter with the maximal probability (this word may prove outside the x-subset). Such a translation will be but a clumsy paraphrase of the text. The second way is to construct in η-language a phrase so that in order to convey the sense expressed in μ-language one will also use only the tail part of the content of a certain η-word. This will be a translation reflecting not only the meaning of the phrase but its mode of expression as well. Now imagine the problem of a dialogue between a human being and a computer. The logic of the conversation must be so arranged that the computer would understand the subtlety of human speech and then start translating the text into some clumsy language, "thinking" in that language, and answering in it. This is a model of our conversation with foreigners: speaking with us, they use the whole richness of their language, but answering them in their language, we use only primitive phrases. Hence comes the paradox: it is easier to speak the foreign language than to understand it; comprehension requires the mastery of all of the most complicated aspects of language. Technically, it seems easier to create programs for a dialogue between a human being and a computer than for a good translation.

From the above-developed standpoint, it seems very interesting to consider the structure of jargon languages. One of them is the "filthy" or obscene language. In some microcollectives in the USSR, it is used every day in place of our usual language. This is an extremely interesting phenomenon of Russian culture, and, of course, it is worth a serious study. Since similar social phenomena occur in other countries (though they have different linguistic features), I shall confine myself to separate statements to the point.

The words of the "filthy" language are devoid of the selective prior distribution function. Strictly speaking, they mean nothing or everything. Their direct meaning has nothing to do with the statements built from them: it only adds a saucy flavor to speech. But if this saucy flavor is viewed as negligible (which is really so from the point of view of semantics), then the filthy words can be replaced by any other words-symbols with equal probability signifying anything one wishes.

Naturally, a conversation in such a language has very poor semantics. People speaking in the filthy language do not use all their rich information about the world encoded in the prior distribution functions of the semantics of the words of everyday language. Language games, in their usual sense, prove impossible in the filthy language.

But where lies its attractiveness? In no way is it in the saucy flavor of the statements. It turns out that the filthy language is fit for fairly special and very attractive language games. At least two constituents of such games can be indicated. The first one is guessing the sense the interlocutor wants to express, in the given situation, in the words of the filthy language. The second one—and this seems especially interesting— is an amazing possibility of creating words: formation of new, quite unexpected words from one root, the initial obscenity.

This question is worth a more detailed discussion. Word formation by means of broad use of suffixes and prefixes is one of the features of the Russian language that makes it very rich. In Russian we can derive from one word, by means of affixes, at least five or six other words of the same grammatical class, which is utterly impossible in English. In French such derivation is possible only to a small degree. (For some reason or other, in his comparison of Russian and English Nabokov did not pay attention to this peculiarity; this comparison is mentioned in the discussion of mathematics as the language of physics in Chapter 4.) This amazing peculiarity of the Russian language was especially vividly revealed by the outstanding Russian poet Velemir Khlebnikov. One of his most famous poems illustrating the versatile ramifications of the derivatives of the word "laughter" is as follows:

О, рассмейтесь, смехачи!
О, засмейтесь, смехачи!
Что смеются смехами, что смеянствуют смеяльно,
О, засмейтесь усмеяльно!
О, рассмешищ надсмеяльных - смех усмейных смехачей!
О, иссмейся рассмеяльно, смех надсмейных смеячей!
Смейево, смейево,
Усмей, осмей, смешики, смешики,
Смеюнчики, смеюнчики,
О, рассмейтесь, смехачи!
О, засмейтесь, смехачи!

What is this? This is a dance of words, in which they are bending, serpentining, wrapping themselves in a cover spun from suffixes and prefixes; they change their clothes before our eyes and turn naked again. The rhythm of this dance-masquerade carries away with it semantic fields of such simple words as "laughter," "to laugh," "burst out laughing," etc. But the principal thing is not the meaning; it does not become clearer due to this masquerade. The principal thing is rhythm and it is utterly untranslatable into any other language, including even Polish despite its genetic relation to Russian.

This poem is based on the single Russian root "смех," which means laughter. Almost all of the derivatives used here do not exist in Russian and are not registered in any dictionary. The thing is that these words were created by Khlebnikov. They are neologisms formed according to the laws of the Russian language. Since they are made by using affixes with whose meaning we are acquainted from our verbal experience, we can get the meaning of each word, though we have not come across them before and will never meet them again. However, their meaning is understood only vaguely, and when we try to render it in English, a language with different means of word derivation, the result is a monster of a poem:

O, burst out laughing, laughing creatures!
O, start laughing, laughing creatures!
They who laugh with laughters, who are engaged in laughter laughingly,
O, start laughing, rocking with laughter
O, of mocking roar of laughter - laughter of risible laughing creatures
O, die with laughter laughingly, laughter of mocking creatures
Laugh 'em to death, laugh over, little laughters, little laughters,

Teeny laughters, teeny laughters,
O, burst out laughing, laughing creatures!
O, start laughing, laughing creatures!

In order to render the poem in English we have had to use about three dozens of extra words with roots other than "laughter." The words **"смехачи"** and **"смеячи,"** which translate into English in the same way, as well as **"надсмеяльные"** and **"надсмейные,"** which are translated as "mocking," are morphologically quite different words in Russian.

Now it seems pertinent to ask: Where does the Russian language realize its rich possibilities? The answer is sad. If this potential is realized anywhere, it is, first of all, in the filthy language with its unusually versatile and almost arbitrary word formations. Not wishing to join the ranks of authors writing obscenities, I won't give an example. I am sure that any Russian can easily reproduce them, guided by his imagination or resorting to folklore or even works of the well-known Russian writers; however, it is unlikely that anybody remembers now such once widely known poems by Yesenin as "Большой матерный загиб" and "Малый матерный загиб" (these are the poems which are mostly written in obscenities and their derivatives). One thing I wish to emphasize here is that there cannot be an analogue to the Russian profanities in English, since the latter lacks this specific faculty for creating short-lived words (ephemerides).

It is a pity that Wittgenstein's proposition that a word's meaning is given by usage can be referred to the utmost degree only to such jargon languages as the one described above.

In any case, I consider the questions touched upon worth a most serious analysis. Their study allows us to understand peculiarities of our language. Should we avoid them as a result of false shamefacedness? We know that only that which we have agreed to consider as such becomes obscene.

Concluding this section, I should like to note that our model of language [first briefly formulated during our study of the language of abstract painting (Andrukovich et al., 1971)] is a completion and development of a widely accepted English-American linguistic literature model of a "dipper" (Laird, 1961). According to this model, we may speak first of all of the concept of reference. A word is referred to a definite object or several objects. This property of words is defined more or less precisely. Reference creates but a poor language; people go farther and ascribe a particular meaning to a word. It is stated that the meaning of words is "dipped" from the human consciousness. A word is a "dipper" common to everybody, but the content drawn by the dipper is far from being the same for different people. Laird (1961) gives the following example: Imagine that a man is going to the theater, and his woman companion tells him, "Wait a minute." In this phrase the word "minute" is very far from the astronomical concept of a minute. Depending on the circumstances and character of the companion, this word may at one time mean that it is no use hurrying now — you will have to wait for a long time; next time it may mean that in fact everybody is ready to leave home in a minute.

I would say that referring a word to a certain meaning is equivalent to our notion of its average meaning, and for this reason it unavoidably proves poor. Dipping profound content is equivalent to our notion of a mechanism of Bayesian reading. It is no use looking for some unconditional and unambiguous meaning in phrases. According to Hutten (1956) ". . . it is better to speak of sentences *being meaningful* rather than having meaning . . ." This elegant formulation is supported by our model.

I would like also to oppose our approach to that of the Swedish school of lexicostatistics formed in the 1950s and to its new ramification presented quite recently by Sankoff (1969). The school seems to proceed from the above-mentioned neopositivistic concept of logical atomism. In any case, the conception developed by them is based upon the postulate of the existence of a certain set of meanings. In the general case, this is just an analytical construct. In the particular case, in studying natural languages, this set may be built empirically, proceeding from the analysis of word frequency curves. The original formulation of the Swedish school even stated that it is possible to select 200 principal universal meanings independent of the peculiarities of a given culture, although Sankoff does not make use of this postulate. Further, a stochastic process is considered giving fluctuations and probabilities of using words to express this or that meaning. This is a diffuse process with a zero shift; in the simplest case this is a Brownian process.

Thus, we see that two approaches, apparently rather similar, are possible in constructing a probabilistic model of language, though they lead to essentially different constructions. According to our approach, a distribution function for the word meaning is built, which allows us to use the Bayesian theorem, introduce the notion of subjective probabilities, and obtain all the results described above relating to understanding the way the reader perceives the text. According to the Swedish school, the word fluctuation around logical atoms is studied, which allows one to comprehend certain lexico-statistical phenomena, e.g., the Zipf law well known to linguists which characterizes word distribution on the basis of frequency of occurrence in texts.

Our concept perhaps comes closer to a non-probabilistic approach to building quantitative semantics of the "fuzzy" meaning of words which is being developed by Zadeh (1971) on the basis of his concept of fuzzy sets of the logic of slipshod predicates. But in this system, as far as I can gather, all the attempts to build a communication model which would reflect the peculiarities of semantic disposition of the recipient ended in failure.

The Role of Contradictory Statements

Strange as it may seem, very little can be said about contradictory statements. As far as I know, nobody has made a systematic study of the problem from a generally linguistic stance, though it seems obvious that there is an object of study here: human thinking, contradictory by its nature, should reflect this characteristic in language.

Wittgenstein, at least in his early period, indubitably believed in the logical structure of language and thought that logically contradictory statements simply cannot exist. Here is one of his formulations from the *Tractatus*.

> To present in language anything which "contradicts logic" is as impossible as in geometry to present by its co-ordinates a figure which contradicts the laws of space; or to give the co-ordinates of a point which does not exist (paradox 3.032)

And further: "Most propositions and questions, that have been written about philosophical matters, are not false but senseless." He gives the following example of such a senseless phrase:

> . . . whether the Good is more or less identical than the Beautiful (from paradox 4.003)

Later, in his *Investigations* (Wittgenstein, 1953), he wrote:

> 500. When a sentence is called senseless, is not as it were its sense, that is senseless. But a combination of words is being excluded from the language, withdrawn from circulation.

At the same time logicians (and Wittgenstein also was a logician) from the times of ancient Greece did their best to formulate logical and semantic paradoxes. Many of the latter were perceived tragically like serious contradictions in theories nowadays. For example, it is known that Frege during the last twenty years of his life did not publish a single important paper on logic. This was due to Russell's finding an unsolvable contradiction in one of his publications.

However, this is true of gross irritating contradictions. Many of them, probably all of them, are removed under close scrutiny if we are bold enough to reject a too narrow comprehension of formal logic. I have already remarked that many contradictions arise only because of the heterogeneity of our language: in everyday language we are mixing judgments made in the object–language with those made in metalanguage. Other contradictions result from ascribing to words too precise meanings. These gross contradictions will disappear as soon as we make use of the probabilistic model of language. Let us consider the classical paradox of a liar.[7] It goes as follows: "A liar can confess he is a liar. In this case he will tell the truth. But a person speaking the truth is not a liar; thus it is possible that a liar is not a liar." From the probabilistic viewpoint there is no paradox here at all. The thing is that a person who makes truthful statements with a small probability will be called a liar. The paradox will also stop being such if we analyze it in the following manner: the liar's confession that he is lying should be regarded as a metastatement. Sometimes the paradox is formulated as follows: "The Cretan Epimenides said, 'All Cretans are liars.' However, Epimenides himself is a Cretan and then he has told a lie. What, then, will be the true meaning of his statement?"

Here it is quite easily seen how the statements made in object–language and metalanguage are mixed. If the demand of homogeneity was laid upon the language, Epimenides, being a Cretan, would not have any right to make any judgments of the truth or falsity of their statements.

Now imagine the following situation: a person says, "I am lying." What does that mean? If he has just been speaking about something else, e.g., proving a theorem or making calculations, we understand that in this phrase he informs us that he himself has hit a mistake in his logical reasoning or calculations. In this case the polymorphous word "to lie" realizes one of its meanings. But if it was only the above-mentioned phrase which had been spoken and nothing more, then it just cannot be interpreted. From a formally logical standpoint this grammatically correct phrase conceals an inner contradiction: it is unclear whether the person speaking tells the truth or a lie. This is a stumbling block for logicians. But from our viewpoint there is no contradiction here: this is just a good example of behavior of the probability model of language. We proceed from the fact that the verb "to lie" is a highly polymorphous word. If a phrase contains but two words and has no verbal surrounding, we cannot cope with the polymorphism of the word and have to ascribe to it one strictly fixed and unconditional meaning; one might note something analogous in the process of ascribing a zero probability to the point value of the results of a continuous random variable. This unavoidably leads to absurdity. It is also possible to interpret the above-mentioned phrase in a

---

[7] Curious legends are associated with the paradox, showing how tragically it was perceived. Diodorus Cronos, a Greek philosopher, died of distress seeing that he could not solve it; a certain philosopher Philip Kossky committed suicide; Chrysippus, a stoic philosopher, devoted three books to the paradox (Kondakov, 1971).

Probabilistic Semantics 77

broad sense assuming that the person speaking is telling the truth; namely, that usually, or more often than not, he lies. In such an interpretation the phrase immediately acquires the meaning coordinated with a probabilistic notion of the meaning of the word "to lie." But this interpretation is hardly correct.

The problem of the truth so much investigated in modern logic (see, for example, "Logical Truth" in volume 3 of *Soviet Philosophical Encyclopaedia*) loses its original sense if we ascribe a field of meaning to the words from which statements are formulated.

The probabilistic model of language allows us to understand the way fine contradictions are introduced into speech; they enrich speech and turn it into a non-Gödelian system. This primarily occurs on the level of interpretation when, in reading the words of a phrase, the reader puts into them prior information resulting in a situation of logical conflict and in a collision of ideas. From a formal standpoint this might annoy and even be perceived as nonsense. We shall refer here to an interesting paper by Danoyan (1970), who analyzed contradictions and tautologies in the scientific language of psycho-physiological problems. Danoyan regards as contradictions a binary combination of notions opposite in meaning and being in the formal relation of inclusion. These opposite notions are not mere antonyms but complementary components of a classical dilemma. He states that from the dilemma "physical–psychical" it follows that the phrase "the physical of the psychical" is contradictory; from the dilemma "mechanism–objective" it follows that "mechanism of the objective" is contradictory, etc. Then the following statements are all contradictory:

1. We do not know the physical basis of thinking.
2. What is the physical basis of memory?
3. The physical basis of recognition has not yet been studied.

The contradictory phrase "the physical of the psychical" is the invariant of all these statements. The following statements so frequent in our modern language are, according to Danoyan, of the same type.

1. We do not know the mechanism of thinking.
2. What is the mechanism of recognition?
3. The mechanism of recall has not yet been studied.

The word "mechanism" is here interpreted as "an instrument," i.e., a means of achieving an objective, where the objective is thinking, recognition, and recall. Thus, the contradictory statements "the mechanism of an objective" or "the means of an objective" are an invariant of the above phrases.

I believe that, were this analysis continued, contradictions of this kind might be found in any scientific paper or any discussion. But how we should impoverish our language if we regarded such statements as inadmissible!

It is interesting to note that our language possesses a special mechanism for introducing fine contradictions into it. This mechanism is the use of metaphors. This term cannot be given a good definition. The word "metaphor" comes from the Greek word μεταφορα — a transfer, in a figurative meaning. The *Oxford English Dictionary* gives the following definition of metaphor: "The figure of speech in which a name or descriptive term is transferred to some object different from, but analogous to, that to which it is properly applicable." According to an apt remark by Barfield, when we use a metaphor, we are "saying one thing and meaning another" (cited from Black, 1962). In our interpretation, speech containing a metaphor is constructed in the following manner: a word with a broad prior distribution function of the meaningful content is introduced into a phrase, a part of the word's meaningful content being in accordance with the other words of a phrase, and the rest of it contradicting them. In this way a fine contradiction is introduced into the speech, making it elegant and even, sometimes, refined.

In speech rich with metaphors, the transfer of meaning takes place on the basis not only of similarity but also of contrast. Words are used in a new and sometimes shocking sense; for example, the Russian word combination "сапоги всмятку" has the meaning "soft-boiled boots." Metaphorical speech is primarily associated with poetry, as in the phrases "murmur of the waves," "stacks of the sun," or the following lines from Yesenin's poems (my word-for-word translation):

Что ж ты смотришь так синими брызгами? . . .
Why are you looking with your blue sprays? . . .

Все равно любимая отцветет черемухой . . .
My beloved one will shed her bird-cherry blossoms . . .

We cannot formulate criteria that would enable us to tell a metaphor from a poetic image. For example, are the following lines from a poem by Yesenin metaphorical?

Словно я весенней гулкой ранью
Проскакал на розовом коне . . .
As if I rode a rose-colored steed
In the spring hollow early hours . . .

Не жалею, не зову, не плачу,
Все пройдет, как с белых яблонь дым . . .
I am not sorry, not calling, not crying,
All will pass as white apple-tree haze . . .

Another thing is important to note: our everyday, business and scientific speech are all filled with metaphors. Here are several examples from business speech:

> A fashionable branch of knowledge
> Intellectual field
> Statements orthogonal to
> To debug = to eliminate errors

The last is a word of American business slang that has the literal meaning "to squash a bug." The word "bug" has other metaphorical meanings: a technical blemish, a mad idea, insanity, clandestine listening device.

In the chapter devoted to the language of science, we shall return to the analysis of metaphors. To conclude this brief discussion of metaphors, let us note only that the metaphors listed above contain the same contradictions as the examples from the paper by Danoyan. In the first, knowledge is something serious and quite opposite to what is called "fashion." Intellect is something compact, purposeful, and logical — quite the opposite of what we think of as a field, i.e., something wide, fuzzy, and most surely lacking intellect. Our notion of statements is not in any way coordinated with that of vectors, though we know that if vectors are orthogonal that means they are linearly independent, and we understand that the statement in question does not coordinate with some others made earlier. Debugging is a process slightly similar to correcting a mistake but simultaneously quite different from it. Can we not infer, then, that metaphors are not a special category of our everyday language but rather a most vivid manifestation of the mechanism more or less inherent to any speech. Precisely for this reason it is difficult to formulate accurate criteria for defining and selecting metaphors — there is no clearcut line between common and metaphorical word usage. Metaphor is probably most vividly manifested in oral speech where it is accompanied with additional expressive means: articulation, pitch, and sometimes gestures. Black (1962) gives the following example: When Churchill in his famous phrase called Mussolini "that utensil," it was the tone of voice, the verbal setting, the historical background which helped the English people understand the meaning of the metaphor. From a formally logical standpoint, using metaphors is a rejection of one of the basic laws of logic, the law which may be put down as follows: A either is B or is not B.

Now let us see in what way science reacts to fine contradictions. I have already mentioned that Carnap suggested rejecting *Tractatus* by Wittgenstein as a work full of nonsense. However, nobody has done it and there is hardly anybody who would deny the remarkable intellectual power of this book, though many of its statements can give rise to strong objections. The power of the work is in fact due to its paradoxical nature; separate statements in a certain sense contradict one another though they possess a certain inner consistency, too. It is only through this game of consistency and contradiction that Wittgenstein managed to express elegantly a very complicated outlook which could hardly have been expressed in strictly deductive and inwardly consistent statements.

Here, it seems pertinent to draw the reader's attention to a very interesting though not well-known publication by the physicists Podgoretskii and Smorodinskii (1969) on axiomatic construction of physical theories. According to their veiwpoint, the creation of physical theories goes through two stages: (i) local theories with hidden contradictions, and (ii) revealing contradictions when local hypotheses meet. Overcoming these contradictions proves to be a starting point for the further development of physics. We would like to find out what language means are used in the first stage, in creating local theories. The contradictions should be well concealed at the beginning; otherwise, the paper could not have been published at all.

Even at the stage of completion, in constructing concepts generalizing a macroworld, we have to allow contradictions to arise. Classical logic proves insufficient for the description of the outer world. Trying to comprehend this philosophically, Bohr formulated his famous *principle of complementarity*, according to which in order to reproduce an integral phenomenon in a sign system, mutually exclusive *complementary* notions must necessarily be used. This requirement is equivalent to expanding the logical structure of the language of physics. Bohr uses a seemingly simple means: mutually exclusive use of two languages, each of which, being based upon common logic, is recognized as permissible. Such languages may describe physical phenomena that exclude one another, e.g., continuity and atomism of light phenomena, etc. Sometimes the principle of complementarity is regarded as a generalized principle by Heisenberg. Bohr himself was well aware of the general philosophical character of his principle (Bohr, 1958a):

> . . . Living organisms and the characteristics of people having consciousness as well as human cultures themselves possess the traits and qualities whose depiction demands using a typically complementary way of description.

In our philosophical literature, the principle was at first met with a great caution, but, according to the papers of a conference in Obninsk (*Printsip Dopolnitel'nosti i Materialisticheskaya Dialektika,* 1972), it has lately attracted attention and has begun to be interpreted broadly not only in conformity with physics but with other branches of knowledge as well. The principle of complementarity is, as a matter of fact, an acknowledgment of the fact that theories built in accordance with precise logic work as a metaphor: they become the basis of models, acting as if they were the outer world but not quite so. One logical structure is not enough to describe the whole complexity of a microworld. The peculiar philosophical significance of quantum mechanics consists in the fact that a demand to violate conventional logic in constructing the image of the world first made itself explicit here. It is interesting to cite here a statement by Heisenberg (1958): "Absolute fulfillment of the requirement of strict logical precision does not, probably, take place in any science."

Last but not least are contradictions in mathematics. We all have reasons to think that the mystical fear of contradictions has been pushed to the background. The problem has lost its acuteness and probably its precision as well. The statements by Hao Wang (1961), a well-known expert in the axiomatic theory of sets, seem very interesting to me:

> 23. So far as the present state of mathematics is concerned, speculations on inconsistent systems are rather idle. No formal system which is widely used today is under very serious suspicion of inconsistency. The importance of set-theoretical contradictions has been greatly exaggerated. . . . But the more modern search for consistency proofs is differently motivated and has a more serious purpose than avoiding contradictions: it seeks for a better understanding of the concepts and methods.

A very interesting article by Hao Wang can hardly be rendered here, but it is noteworthy that it proves very lenient toward the problem of consistency. He remarks that contradictions are often very interesting, though they are never an object and nobody will recommend a method on the grounds that it is powerful enough to produce contradictions. At the same time, Hao Wang assumes the existence of a mathematical structure containing contradictions. If the latter are revealed in a system, that does not mean that the inferences logically obtained from the system are useless, since the corollaries may not make use of everything inherent in the initial structure. And if we are going to discuss practical problems, he goes on, e.g., building bridges, it is not at all necessary to formalize mathematics and prove its consistency, since there one can find many other more important and quite real problems. I believe that these statements affect essentially the views of those who are now dealing with the foundations of mathematics.

Now let us return to our everyday language. We have already said that it contains the elements of formal logic, and these are learned from childhood, while the language is being learned. At the same time, our everyday speech behavior is never completely logical. Try to concentrate upon the phrases of cursory dialogues, upon numerous advertisements and instructions; everywhere you will find illogicality. Moreover, if anybody tries to be absolutely logical in everyday speech behavior, he is immediately referred to the category of schizophrenics. Thus, the charm of Carroll's *Alice in Wonderland*, at least for adults, lies in the fact that the reader is introduced into the world of absurdly strict logic. Indeed, the word "smile" is a noun, and not an adjective, and, consequently, it is not illogical that a smile of the Cheshire cat can appear without the cat.

Another thing is interesting to note here. Psychiatrists are well aware of the fact that patients with a lowered intellectual activity cease to understand metaphors: they only perceive their literal meaning. A simple metaphor such as "to be in somebody's skin" receives a literal interpretation that is quite absurd from the standpoint of a normal person. One of the diagnostic symptoms in psychiatry is the failure of a patient to understand proverbs. On the other hand, another sign of lowered intellectual ability is a gross breach of logic; e.g., a patient is asked to interpret a series of deliberately nonsense pictures and he is unable to discover gross absurdity there. Or he is asked to arrange a series of connected pictures in a logical order, and he cannot do this; even if schizophrenics do fulfill this assignment, it is done in an oddly whimsical form. At the same time, patients begin to use words at will. They produce metaphors clear only to themselves (for details see Kasanin, 1944).

We may conclude that the intelligence of a normal person lies in a very narrow interval, limited on the one hand by failure to understand metaphors, fine alogical statements, and on the other hand by gross breaches of logic.

Semantic Scale of Languages

Classification of phenomena is one of the ways to describe a complex system. Many ways of classifying language systems can be suggested. I shall dwell here on only one of them: on constructing a semantic scale of languages. This system of classification will place languages in accordance with the role of the probabilistic structure of meaning.

Imagine a scale with one end occupied by *hard languages*, e.g., those of programming: there every sign possesses perfectly unambiguous, precise, and definite meaning — a mathematical or logical operation. This part of the scale will also be occupied by various dialects of the language of pure mathematics and mathematical logic, where symbols are used independently of the phenomena of the external world. The meaning of symbols is defined when they are introduced or it becomes clear after some statement, e.g., axioms, is formulated from them. In some cases, e.g., in mathematical logic and in the theory of the so-called context-free languages, no special sense related to the external world is ascribed to symbols.

On the other end of the scale, perfectly *soft languages* will be situated, in which the probabilistic structure of the meaningful content is manifested most explicitly. An example of such languages may be the language of abstract painting. In a separate study of abstract painting (Andrukovich et al., 1971), we have shown that its sign system may in fact be regarded as a language. Here, I shall say only that the sign system of this language has prior distribution functions which are deeply subjective. In this case, it is difficult to trace coordination which is usually observed for the prior distribution function of the meaningful content of everyday language. In this sense the language of abstract painting proves degenerate: the tendency observed in everyday language here becomes extreme.

Our everyday language and the languages of science are placed somewhere in the middle of the scale and occupy there a broad interval. In both these languages, prior functions of distribution of the word are to a certain extent coordinated, especially for people with similar intellectual orientation. But the degree of coordination varies over a wide range depending on the field of knowledge. This coordination is expressed to a minimal extent in the language of Western philosophy: hence emerged the conception of analytical philosophy with its statement that traditional philosophy is a pathology of language. Certain dialects of chemical language, above all, the language of chemical formulas, are perfectly unambiguous. If in a chemical text we come across the symbol "Na" it means only the metal sodium and nothing more, though in the formula NaCl the symbol Na takes on the meaning an ion of sodium. At the same time, in the language of science we face polymorphism which is sometimes expressed more strongly than in everyday language. This problem is discussed later (in Chapter 3), and here I shall only remark, getting slightly ahead, that the language of mathematics, when used to describe the phenomena of the external world, becomes polymorphous.

Quite a peculiar position on the semantic scale is occupied by the language of ancient Indian philosophy. There the right of words to be half-empty molds is acknowledged; everybody can fill them to his own taste, and contradictions are openly introduced into texts.

All this makes us place the language of ancient Indian philosophy on the semantic scale somewhere behind our everyday language, close to the language of abstract painting. Later, I shall return to analyzing this language. Here I should like to draw attention to the point that from my position the classification of languages, in the case of a broad formulation of the problem, should be made not according to the people speaking them but according to epochs of culture: languages of two peoples (e.g., English and French) belonging at present to one, general European culture will not occupy different places on the semantic scale.

The semantic scale may also be presented as an open straight line, assuming that soft languages are tending to its one side and hard ones to the other. Then, according to topological considerations, it will follow that an addition of a distant point will allow us to turn a line into a circle. Such a distant point is the language of the religious–philosophical system Zen, a Japanese branch of Buddhism which has very little in common with the original teaching. The language of Zen is a strange language of absurd statements. The latter are built as illogical phrases, "koan," containing only hints. These are riddles without rational solutions. An adept of a Zen monastery would have to be immersed in meditation in order to reveal the "sense" strangely coded in unusual sentences. Months or even years may be spent on this. Here are several examples of such statements borrowed from the thesis of Pomerants (1968).

> Does a dog have the Buddha nature? Nothing!
>
> Two hands make a clap; and what is the sound of one hand?
>
> When much is reduced to one, to what can one be reduced?
>
> Call it a stick, and you state it; don't call it a stick, and you deny it.
> So, not stating and not denying now will you call it? Speak! Speak!

These statements cannot be called logically contradictory. If we use Wittgenstein's terminology, they can probably be called senseless, or, even better, prohibited from the standpoint of our everyday language. But, as a matter of fact, this is a language conveying certain strange profound sense. When a koan is solved, it becomes clear for an adept that it is a simple, clear and almost self-evident statement made by the teacher in the state of ecstasy. The teacher wants his pupil to achieve a similar lucid state, and for this reason he resorts to constructing statements.

Of course, Zen is not only a set of koan; it is something more — an outlook which has made a strong impresson upon the whole of Japanese culture (for details see Grigorieva, 1971). The influence of Zen on Western culture is easily traced in the works of such painters as Van Gogh and Henry Matisse, the writer J. D. Salinger, and, in its vulgar form, American beatniks, e.g., in the characters of Jack D. Kerouac. All this is well presented in the book by Zavadskaya (1970). But here we are interested in something else, namely, typological community of phenomena in Western and Eastern cultures which have emerged independently and without contact, according to the terminology of Konrad (1966). I believe that in the language of Western culture we can observe the tendencies which are manifested most vividly in the language of Zen. First of all, there are the metaphors of our language: they introduce into our speech the same shocking flavor of incompatibility which in its refined form is manifested in koan. In addition, I draw the reader's attention to some proverbs, sayings, captions to cartoons, and anecdotes, especially abstract ones.[8] In a grotesque form it is manifested in surrealistic painting. I am looking now at a reproduction of the picture "Invention of Monsters" by Salvador Dali from the Chicago museum. To the right there is a giraffe on fire; in the center, a table on which there is a sculpture of a horse head with female breasts; at the table, an almost human figure with little wings; in the right upper corner, nude figures in ridiculous postures; in the left lower corner, an odd group of people with an air of conspiracy; and in the right lower corner, a puppy. Each of the compositional constituents is painted quite realistically: both the giraffe and the fire look very realistic. The whole composition, however, is a riddle like a koan. It is its incompatibility that shocks the spectator.

Thus, our semantic scale is closed at the point where the language of Zen, the most unusual human language of all, is situated. And what seems especially interesting, in this language, is that the tendencies which are most explicit manifest themselves to a certain degree, sometimes very vividly, in the expressive means of other cultures.

Koan, in their logical structure, resemble very much the antiplays by E. Ionesco and S. Beckett (the reader can acquire a certain notion of them from Kulikova, 1970). Here, as well as in abstract painting, "the reverse side of logic" is used.

General Philosophical Prerequisites of the Probabilistic Model of Language

Our probabilistic model of language does not need strict philosophical prerequisites. When one is considering the question of language, it is not necessary to proceed from a very strong statement of world cognizability.[9] Without considering this statement in depth and without denying it, I shall only point to the fact that we shall be satisfied with the statement that our language should be capable of describing our idea of the world, which constantly develops and grows.

There is no need either to state with certainty that the mechanism of thinking is arranged in some particular way. Traditionally, it seems plausible to assume the existence of a hierarchy of thinking: (i) pre-logical, imaginative thinking [largely restricted to primitive civilizations (Lévi-

---

[8] Here is an abstract anecdote:
   "I say, there are bananas in your ears."
   "Sorry, I can't hear you: I have bananas in my ears."
It is not clear where these anecdotes have come from: whether they have come from the West or appeared independently.
   [9] I consider this question more thoroughly in my book *Faces of Science,* published in Russian in 1976.

Strauss, 1964)]; (ii) logical thinking; (iii) superlogical thinking whose mechanism remains unknown. Obviously, people may belong to various levels of the thinking hierarchies. However, communication, especially scientific communication, is preferably carried out on the logical level. Deductive logic is to a great extent a means of communication rather than a means of thinking. The task of logic is a development of ideas which are contained in a condensed, and for this reason not quite clear, form in the original premises. This is especially well seen in the language of mathematics where the deductive structure of constructing judgments is traced most easily. Here, I should like to quote the words of de Broglie (1960), the well-known French physicist:

> "The language of mathematics, due to its rigidly deductive char-
> acter, allows us to give a detailed description of intellectual values
> already obtained, but it does not allow us to obtain novel values, So,
> it is not pure deductions but bold inductions and original concepts
> which are the source of the great progress in Science."

While logic is a means of communication, language polymorphism is the way to overcome difficulties in a logically built system of communications rather than in the system of thinking. (We must divide thinking proper and the means of expressing it.) The probabilistic model of language is merely one possible explanation of the way the difficulty may be overcome.

At the same time, the fuzzy nature of our language makes us ponder the structure of our consciousness. But this is quite a separate subject which I shall briefly examine in Chapter 8.

I should like to draw the reader's attention to a certain parallel in the development of physics and linguistics. The concept of atomic word meanings, which seems to go back as far as Leibniz (or probably even the Cabala), was given substantial support by Frege, Russell, and the early work of Wittgenstein simultaneously with the seemingly finite conclusion of the atomic nature of matter clearly localized in space and time. At present, as a result of the progress of quantum mechanics, we are dealing with a fuzzy nature of subatomic particles. Here is how the physicist Capra (1976) in his paper devoted to comparing the ideas of modern physics with the ancient Oriental outlook attempts to sum it up:

> One of the main insights of quantum theory has been the recognition
> that probability is a fundamental feature of the atomic reality which
> governs all processes, and even the existence of matter. Subatomic
> particles do not exist with certainty at definite places, but rather
> show—as Heisenberg (1963) has put it—"tendencies to exist."
> Atomic events do not occur with certainty at definite times and in
> definite ways, but rather show "tendencies to occur." Henry Stapp

(1971) has emphasized that these tendencies, or probabilities, are not probabilities of "things," but rather probabilities of interconnections.

Any observed atomic "object" constitutes an intermediate system connecting the preparation of the experiment and the subsequent measurement. The properties of the object cannot be defined independently of these processes. If the preparation or the measurement is modified, the properties of the object will also change. (p. 22)

In the probabilistic model of language, the fundamental thing is a probabilistical setting of the text meaning. The prior distribution function of the word meaning $p(\mu)$ is but a "tendency for the word meaning to be realized," is a preparation to an experiment carried out in verbal behavior by constructing a concrete phrase. The likelihood function $p(y|\mu)$ arising while reading the phrase is a direct analogue of a physical measurement, as I have already mentioned in my discussion of the Bayesian model of language. The meaning of the text arises as a probabilistic description of the interacting "readiness to comprehend"—a "verbal experiment" aimed at comprehension.

The analogy proves to be a profound one. It is probably pertinent to say that the probabilistic model of language has resulted from a paradigm of modern physics. It turns out that both the concept of discrete subatomic particles in physics and that of discrete words of our language are but a conventional denotation of what is developed within the context which is at one time given by a physical experiment and at another time by a common phrase of an everyday dialogue.

We might continue the analogy by comparing words with hadrons — strongly interacting particles generating almost all of the subatomic particles known at present. Here is another quotation from Capra (1976):

The important new concept in S-matrix theory is the shift of emphasis from objects to events. Its basic concern is not with the particles, but with their reactions. Such a shift from objects to events is required both by quantum theory and by relativity theory. On the one hand, quantum theory has made it clear that a subatomic particle can only be understood as a manifestation of the interaction between various processes of measurement. It is not an isolated object, but rather an occurrence, or event, which interconnects with other events in a particular way. Relativity theory, on the other hand, has forced us to conceive of particles in terms of space-time, as four-dimensional patterns, processes rather than objects.

The S-matrix approach combines both of these viewpoints. Using the four-dimensional mathematical formalism of relativity theory, it describes all properties of hadrons in terms of reaction probabilities, and thus establishes an intimate link between particles and processes.

Each reaction involves particles which link it to other reactions and thus build up a whole network of processes. (p. 28)

The picture of hadrons which emerges from these bootstrap models is often summed up in the provocative phrase: "Every particle consists of all other particles." It must not be imagined, however, that each hadron contains all the others in a classical, static sense. Rather than "containing" one another, hadrons "involve" one another in the dynamic and probabilistic sense of S-matrix theory, each hadron being a potential bound state of all sets of particles which may interact with one another to form the hadron under consideration. In that sense, all hadrons are composite structures whose components are again hadrons, and none of them is any more elementary than the others. The binding forces holding the structures together manifest themselves through the exchange of particles, and these exchanged particles are again hadrons. Each hadron, therefore, plays three roles: it is a composite structure, it may be a constituent of another hadron, and it may be exchanged between constitutents and thus constitute part of the forces holding a structure together. (p. 36)

For language the analogy is striking. Words in dictionaries are explained by other words, but this is not to say that the meaning of a word consists of the meanings of the words by which it is explained. Phrases are composed with words, probabilistically interacting with one another. This is a phrase structure generating a new sense which is missing from the constituent words though, somehow, they "contain" it.

Concluding Remarks

In concluding this chapter, I should like to say the following. Humanity seems to have always realized the *insufficiency of its means of communication*. Human thinking, and more broadly human inner life, is evidently richer than language is. This idea has been expressed in various ways by many people. For example, a line from the poem "Silentium" by Tyutchev says, "A thought once uttered is untrue." In the poem "Благославляю все, что было" ("I Bless All That Happened") by A. Blok, we find the lines:

> Все, чего не скажешь словом,
> Узнал я в облике твоем
> (All that can't be said in words
> I saw in your image)

In Schopenhauer (1862) we read:

A thought lives while it is verbalized: then it is petrified and henceforth remains dead but unperishing like petrified primeval animals and plants. Its momentary life may also be compared to a crystal at the instant of its creation.

And as soon as our thought has clothed itself into words, it loses its heartiness and profound significance. Starting to exist for others, it stops living within ourselves, – as a child who, separating himself from his mother, enters his own existence. (p. 74–75)

In the words of John Ruskin:

To explain is to waste time. A clear-sighted man catches your hint; but an ill-sighted man will not comprehend after a long speech. (cited from Tolstoy, 1905, p. 191)

Heidegger stated:

A "true" man speaks "truly" only when he keeps silent. (cited from Stassen, 1973, p. 43)

Jung (1930) expressed the same idea:

One of the greatest mistakes of our culture . . . is an intense belief in words and exposition and infinite over-estimation of teaching by words and methods. (p. 88, my translation)

Zavadskaya (1970) cited the words of Matisse's teacher: "Regard painting as passionate silence." Remember the "noble silence of Buddha" with which he answered difficult questions. Well-known is the concept of word insufficiency in the "theory of silence" of Chuang-Tzu, one of the founders of Taoism. He said: "The sound of an unspoken word is louder than the thunder of a drum" (*Drevnekitaiskaya Filosofiya*, 1972, my translation). An important role is ascribed to silence in the religious philosophy of Yoga (Swami Sivananda, 1967): "Listen to soft, hardly audible voices of silence. . . . The power of silence infinitely exceeds the power of lectures, talks, speeches and discussions. . . . The language of silence is the language of God . . ." (my translation).

Hillel, a character in the novel *Golem* by Meyrink, says, "Do you think our Jewish books are written only in consonants just accidentally? Everyone has the opportunity to insert those vowels which will help him to reveal the mysterious sense intended only for him alone—otherwise the live word would have turned into a dead dogma" (my translation).

Doubts about word meanings have manifested themselves most vividly in the teaching of Zen. In modern times, this idea has been clearly formulated by the Indian thinker Krishnamurti.

Understanding does not come with knowledge. In the interval between words, between thoughts, comes Understanding, – this interval is silence unbroken by knowledge, it is the open, the unponderable, the implicit. (Pomerants, 1965)

In Wittgenstein's paper we read: "Whereof one cannot speak, thereof one must be silent"; this is the concluding paradox of the *Tractatus*.

However, people are always searching for a new language. New languages mean new cultures. And I believe that the statement that the history of human culture is the history of sign systems is perfectly correct.

Scientific development is also reflected in the development of a scientific language. According to Hutten (1956), "Science is a linguistic or symbolic representation of experience."

Almost the same formulation can be found in the book by Kopnin (1971): "Language is a form of knowledge of existence as a system of signs."

In Langer's (1951) book we read: ". . . the edifice of human knowledge stands before us, not as a vast collection of sense reports, but as a structure of *facts that are symbols and laws that are their meanings.*"

In the book *Marxism and the Philosophy of Language* by Voloshinov (1929), an even stronger statement is made: "Everything ideological possesses meaning: it presents, describes, replaces something outside it, i.e. is a sign. Where there is no sign there is no ideology."

Physicists also have asserted the insufficiency of modern linguistic means. For example, Heisenberg (1958), describing the impetuous reaction to modern physics development, says:

> . . . it probably means that one has not yet found the correct language with which to speak about the new situation and that the incorrect statements published here and there in the enthusiasm about the new discoveries have caused all kinds of misunderstanding. This is indeed a fundamental problem. The improved experimental technique of our time brings into the scope of science new aspects of nature which cannot be described in terms of the common concepts. But in what language, then, should they be described? . . . However, if one wishes to speak about the atomic particles themselves one must either use the mathematical scheme as the only supplement to natural language or one must combine it with a language that makes use of a modified logic or of no well-defined logic at all.

Peculiar features of a culture are most expressively reflected in the "language" of its architecture. Buildings are phrases of this language built from separate constructive elements–signs forming an alphabet of the language. Ensembles of building are texts of this language. The hierarchical structure of the language of architecture is quite obvious.

People are permanently searching for new forms of expression and sometimes find such sudden means as Zen. Language, having received an impetus to its existence, begins to develop as a self-organized system influencing human thinking. It seems rash to decide what is here of primary or secondary importance: it is only language that we can observe and analyze phenomenonologically. For this reason, it is more convenient to speak of one system: of the language of culture, and of its sign system. Here I should like again to cite Wittgenstein (1955): "The *limits of my language* mean the limits of my world" (paradox 5.6).

However, the same thought has been formulated much earlier by Humboldt (1843), who stated that the difference between languages is the difference between outlooks. The statement of Whorf (1956) that we perceive nature the way it is expressed in our native language sounds very similar. If language is viewed as an instrument, then, speaking of its impact upon the formation of our concepts, we may make an analogy with the impact of an instrument of measurement on the results of measurements in the microworld. (This comparison was suggested by S. K. Shaumyan.)

Even if we adhere to the point of Leibniz and believe in the existence of necessary logical truths that remain true in all possible Worlds, still they are not charged with any information about our World and the way we perceive it. The question remains open whether, and to what degree, we can understand languages of other cultures, say, the language of ancient Indian philosophy or the language of Zen. Many people now feel the necessity to enrich European culture with new ideas, to respiritualize it — hence the interest in other cultures and the languages by means of which they are expressed.

Chapter 3

The Language of Science

Terms in Science

In this section I make an attempt to consider some metalinguistic problems of the language of science. First of all, I should like to answer the question: How do scientific terms appear and evolve; why and in what way do we comprehend them? Strange as it may seem, it is not very easy to speak about this. Since our school days we are taught the concepts of some indubitable rigor and precision of judgments in science. Hence, it seems that in science we should have realized that the terms (at least, partly) do not come into being in the same way as new words do in our everyday language. So far, widespread opinion has been that the terms should be defined in the rigorous logico-linguistic sense of the word. That would mean that, when a new theoretical term is introduced, it is once and for all time ascribed a strict sense content expressed in a defining phrase; but this is hardly the case. Carnap's elegant concept of the semantics of scientific language was built not inductively, as a theory trying to comprehend and systematize actually observed facts, but deductively, as some idealized, logically perfect system—a program for the future. If somebody still feels like tracing in what way it is possible to approach the analysis of scientific terminology from the formally logical standpoint, I shall send him to the book by Hutten (1956), *The Language of Modern Physics*, which is highly readable and has already been mentioned above.

Another purely empirical approach seems to be much more interesting. This is a many-sided, theoretically unbiased analysis of the whole semantic diversity of scientific terminology. The recent book by Achinstein (1968) is written from this standpoint. If one takes this road, many interesting observations may be made, but even here it can hardly be hoped that some sufficiently general theory can be built which would explain the whole diversity of the phenomena observed.

I shall illustrate the complexity of the mechanism of forming scientific concepts by several examples. First of all, Achinstein draws our attention to the fact that some terms such as "copper," "metal," "metalloid," "brass," "semiconductor," "bronze," "fusion," etc., may be regarded as certain taxons—the elements obtained as a result of classification performed upon some multidimensional space of attributes. These attributes may not be necessary: the metal mercury is a fluid under normal temperature, though solidity is one of the indications of a metal. They may also be insufficient: one of the properties of copper, its melting temperature of 1,082°C, is not sufficient, because some other alloys have the same melting point. With scientific development, new attributes appear and the old classification schemes become insufficient. Thus, the traditional division of chemical elements into metals and metalloids also proved insufficient after the emergence of a clear-cut concept of semiconductors. True, the latter is already connected with the physical properties of the substance but not with its chemical ones. But in fact we do not know for sure which properties are chemical and which are physical. The demarcation between physics and chemistry has become blurred, though clear-cut distinction of these terms is of great pragmatic significance. In the editorial boards of the "abstracts" journals there are continuous and unsolvable arguments as to the headline under which this or that article should be published, either under "chemistry" or "physics," and when a new leading scientist, a chemist or a physicist, enters the editorial board, the headings of the respective issues are inevitably changed.

In the process of constructing the system of scientific terminology, we face the same difficulties as in ordinary statistical problems of multidimensional classification since scientific terms can be regarded as taxons, i.e., units of classification given over fuzzy fields of meanings. In statistical classification methods, there are a variety of techniques leading to essentially different results. For each technique not only is a classifying procedure given, but there is no stopping rule; in any case, there are no criteria which would permit one to insist that further division does not lead to obtaining actually new taxons. Every result of classification may be essentially changed, if the metrics of the space of variables is changed. In our case, it will mean the equivalent of ascribing various weights to certain properties. We should also keep in mind that taxonomy is a purely semantic problem and not in the least ontological. There is no use raising the question about whether there are some realities in the world of things corresponding to taxons. In any case, the criteria for this cannot be established.

No doubt, in scientific language there are some terms which may be clearly defined, say, "Bohr's atom," "the black body," "double-atomic molecule"; these are the examples taken from Achinstein's book. But it often happens that the definitions which look quite respectable from a logical standpoint prove insufficient; they cover too wide a range of things. This happened to the term "document." It could be defined as follows: "a document is any material carrier on which certain information expressed in a language is fixed." If such a definition is accepted, then the fence with the joke written on it by children immediately turns into a document, though it does not correspond to our intuitive notion of a document. We may attempt to save the situation by introducing the supplementary series of *operational* characteristics, and declaring that not any information carrier is to be called a document, but only the one which bears certain numerable functions. In many cases the introduction of operational characteristics helps considerably. But in our example with the word "document," it makes everything look more anecdotal: after the well-known apt expression, it turns out that the elephant in the zoo is a document, and all the other elephants are not. But at the same time, we know for sure what a document is. Moreover, there exists a special scientific branch called "documentation science"; certain journals are published whose title contains the word "document"; and in modern soceties dozens of thousands of people are engaged in "documentalistics" as a scientific discipline.

Evidently there is no sense in a further consideration of all possible ways in which terms emerge in science. The above examples seem sufficient to illustrate the difficulties encountered by scientists when they try to outline the boundaries of a term.

Now we shall go into more detail with another question, that of the analysis of certain phenomena which are specific for the language of science as a whole. Here we shall speak of the profound connection of terms with theoretical notions in science, of their code-wise character, of the role metaphors play in the generation of scientific words and of the possibility of using rather abstract notions with their ambiguous interpretation in the language of concrete representations.

The connection of terms with theory. Terms in science are closely connected with its theoretical concepts (Feyerabend, 1962). On the surface, many terms seem to be no more than names of some objects or phenomena. For example, the Raman effect would seem to be a name of some physically observed phenomenon. In fact, it is neither through the indication of what it denotes nor through some semantic definition that the meaning of this term becomes clear, but through the understanding of the theory of this phenomenon. The same is true of such terms as "atom," "electron," etc. A pupil in a secondary school attaches a different meaning to these words than a physicist does. The meaning of the words changes with time together with the development of our scientific concepts. In any case, the meaning we ascribe to the word "atom" differs considerably both from that ascribed to it by the ancient Greeks and from that used at the beginning of our century. But there is one especially interesting thing: it is possible that in science several concurrent hypotheses exist simultaneously which use the same terms but in a different sense. There can also exist some theories, one being above the other or one including the other, e.g., the relativity theory and classical mechanics, and they may both use the same terms in essentially different senses. Both classical mechanics and relativity theory make use of such terms as "mass" and "length," but they are interpreted differently. When we speak about space in physics, we may mean the space of both Euclidian and non-Euclidian geometry. And what is exceedingly surprising is that, as a rule, in science all this causes no trouble of the kind it does in philosophy. Being the adherents of different theories, scientists may use in an argument the same words in different meanings. From the standpoint of logical semantics, this does not seem possible (Achinstein, 1969). Actually, it becomes feasible when the word is associated with a distribution function of the meaningful content, given in scientific terminology by a scientific concept. Different scientific concepts will lead to different, though correlated, distribution functions of the meaningful content. From the semantic standpoint, a scientific discussion may often be regarded as a procedure aimed at the improvement of the correlation of the prior distribution functions of the meaningful content of the term.

The metaphorical structure of the language of science.   If, reading a scientific text, we stop for a moment and ponder the character of terms in our field of vision, we shall find that they are metaphorical. We have become so used to metaphors in our scientific language that we do not even notice it. We keep coming across such word combinations as "course of time," "the field of force," "temperature field," "the logic of experiment," "the memory of a computer," which allow us to express new notions with the help of rather unusual combinations of old, well-known, and familiar expressions. Recognizing the right of metaphors to existence in scientific language, scientists have permitted rather different senses for old terms with the emergence of these new theoretical conceptions. In science, theories are continuously changing, but the change does not cause a waterfall of new words. The new phenomena are interpreted through the old, familiar ones, through the old words for which the prior distribution function of meaning is slightly, but continuously, changed. Something remains unchanged but becomes of less importance; something new appears, entirely different from, and to a certain extent contradictory to, the former meaning of the word. Now the role of metaphors in the language of science is evident; it is alluded to in a most elegant way in MacCormac's work (1971). It is his example with reference to Feyerabend (1965) that is especially interesting. There he speaks of the term "force," one of the fundamental terms in physics. Emerging on the basis of the notion of human force, it has undergone a long history starting from the neo-Platonic philosophy via Kepler and Newton up to modern physics without being strictly defined; always it has remained at the metaphorical level. And the especially intriguing fact is that, obeying some unconscious inner pressure, entirely new terms are introduced into science as metaphors. In mathematics there recently appeared such metaphorical terms as "group," "bodies," "rings," "regression," and "regression analysis" (literally, regression means "backward movement," "reversion"), and "mathematical expectation"; eventually, all the terms received strict definitions. I shall dwell at more length on the meaning of the last term.

In ordinary speech the word "expectation" is modal and is used when something is expected; i.e., it may happen, but it may not happen as well. We can expect the weather to be nice tomorrow or our friend to arrive, but if today is Friday we shall never say that tomorrow is expected to be Saturday. And when we speak of the mathematical expectation of a random value, we mean its average which will necessarily take place, if we carry out averaging on the indefinitely large number of observations forming the so-called general population. The modality of the word "expectation" has undergone changes here, and this change is not logically conditioned by adding one more word. It is just to a certain, fixed combination of two logically incompatible words that we assign a particular sense.

"A new confrontation of words must create either strain or absurdity. If a metaphor does not provoke thought, then it appears as a symbol rather than a metaphor" (MacCormac, 1971). The metaphorical structure of the language makes it not only polymorphic, but also strained. Above, I have already spoken of the observation by Podgoretskii and Smorodinskii (1969) to the effect that a new axiomatic basis in physics emerged after the revelation of hidden contradictions in previously published papers. For a while these contradictions remained unnoticed, evidently, precisely by force of the metaphorical structure of the language, though, of course, this question needs further investigation. But it is noteworthy that, when introducing new words, scientists often yield rather to psychological influences than to logical ones. This can be easily explained. The transmission of thought is carried out on a logical level, but its perception is greatly influenced by some psychological factors which are not entirely understood. An idea is perceived more readily if it is shocking and requires an intellectual effort. A good scientific paper ought to be a bit incomprehensible; there is nothing like some reticence to express peculiarities of ideas. The papers which are too comprehensible seem childish. Incomprehensibility is most often created by some deliberate linguistic structure, which often becomes lost when the work is translated into another language: we sometimes cannot recognize our papers after translating — so dull do they become. Use of the metaphorical structure of language is only one of the techniques used to create intellectual strain. The creators of Zen culture apparently understood this psychological peculiarity of the mechanism of perception of complicated concepts especially well, and they widened its use to the extremes, introducing koans as special illogical forms of thought transmission.

Polymorphism of scientific terms.   Scientific terms have a more polymorphic character than the words of ordinary language. This is only natural: they contain more meaningful content than the words of our ordinary language. We may give innumerable examples to illustrate polysemy of scientific terms. In this book the term "prior information" is often used. To statisticians this term means the information contained in n initial experiments as related to the $(n + 1)$th one. In a particular case $n = 0$, and then the term "prior information" will mean the knowledge gained by the experimenter before this series of experiments, from some quite different experience, related in some way or another to the problem under consideration. But imagine that in the audience where the lecture is being delivered by a statistician a philosopher is present. He will be irritated and decide that here the restoration of neo-Kantianism is being propagated. Indeed, the term "à priori statements" was introduced by Kant, who opposed it to the term "à posteriori statements." Kant needed this confrontation in order to develop the notion of inborn ideas. By now, the epistemological sense of these terms has been pushed somewhere to the background for all non-philosophers, but in reading certain texts it is restored to life immediately. If in our texts we deliberately underline the non-Kantian meaning of the term "à priori information," still this will not make it indubitably precise. In the literature on mathematical statistics there are many shades in the interpretation of this term. Sometimes attempts are made in the direction of their classification, but in vain. It is useless to introduce many narrow notions instead of one broad notion; it will only make our speech clumsy and complicated. The latter assertion is not only a phenomenon observed, but also a normative statement. It is impossible to imagine the existence of a multitude of narrow notions on a fuzzy field of meanings: they will be unavoidably hard to distinguish.

Two other terms widely used in modern logic are also connected with the name of Kant: they are "analytical statements" and "synthetic statements."[1] Now they are used not in an epistemological but only in a logical sense. One and the same phrase may be regarded at one time as an analytical statement and at another time as a synthetic one. And still some vague connection with Kantian notions remains associated with these terms. This connection is the inner succession of thought. And it is one of the functions of scientific terminology to preserve such succession in some concealed, unobtrusive form. Developing new concepts, we always confront them with the old, well-known structures and thus add certain inconsistency to the new statements.

The polymorphism of some new terms has been subjected to special study. The term "model" — quite a fashionable one nowadays — was honored by such a study in the paper by Chao Yuan-Ren (1962). He gives a list of 30 synonyms, i.e., of characteristics of "model," and of 9 nonsynonyms, i.e., of notions contrasted to "model." We see that the synonyms of one and the same word are not always synonymous to one another, and sometimes a word is not even a synonym to itself. It is interesting to trace the historical development of the meaning of the word "model" (see, for example, Hornbey's dictionary). In English it means something ideal or perfect. In mathematics the word "model" was apparently introduced by F. Klein in the 1870s and later by Russell. One of the applications of this term in mathematics is connected with the concept of relative consistency. Above, it was already mentioned how a new system of axioms such as the axioms of Riemannian geometry is simulated on the spherical surface in the three-dimensional Euclidian space. Thus, Riemannian axioms turn into the theorems of Euclidian geometry, and hence it follows that the Riemannian postulates are consistent if the Euclidian geometry is also consistent. Further, the Euclidian postulates, according to Hilbert, are fulfilled on a certain algebraic model and, consequently, are consistent, if the same is true about the algebra. To this extent a model turns out to be a set of things, for which properties and relations are given by a certain theory — the theory which is being simulated. One and the same theory can be simulated on different ob-

---

[1] In the transcendental logic of Kant, such statements are called the synthetic prior statements, which remain prior, i.e., given outside experience, despite the fact that in such statements the predicate is not included in the subject; they are inborn statements. In modern logic, Carnap considers synthetic those statements which contain certain information about the external world: they are juxtaposed to analytical statements — tautologies — the truth or falsity of which does not depend on the connection with the external world. The division of statements into analytical and synthetic, despite its conditionality, proves very useful in the logical analysis of scientific texts.

jects. At present, we often ascribe a quite different meaning to the term "mathematical model building," meaning a certain simplified and rather approximate mathematical presentation of a complex system (Nalimov, 1971). The word "model" in this case is opposite to a law of nature describing phenomena in some rigorous way. One and the same system may be described by different models, each of them reflecting only one side of the system under study. If you like, this is the view of a complex system from a certain predetermined and apparently narrow angle. In this case, evidently, the problem of discrimination does not arise; different models may exist concurrently. To a certain extent, model, in this sense, behaves in the same way as the system it describes; yet the model is not identical to the system described. In linguistic terminology it must be said that a *mathematical model* is no more than a *metaphor*. This interesting idea was suggested by Hutten (1956). Now the question can be asked: Why was it only recently that building mathematical models of complex systems (such as those we come across in industry or in biology and sociology) became possible? No essential, hitherto unknown mathematical ideas appeared. The answer is simple: the psychology of research workers had changed. The standards for mathematical descriptions of the external phenomena have become lower. From the status of law they changed to the status of a metaphor. And psychologically we are quite ready for the possibility of using metaphors in science. All the arguments as to the possibility of applying mathematical methods in sociology are brought into focus by use of the word "model." If it is understood as something similar to the laws of nature, then nothing can be accomplished; if it is understood as a metaphor, than all the objections are eliminated at once.

Let us return to the confrontation of the two basic approaches to the notion of model in mathematics. In mathematical logic, the word "model" means the interpretation on a certain set of objects. One and the same theory may, as mentioned above, be simulated on different objects. Here we observe a multitude of interpretations, but this multiplicity is not of a metaphorical character. In applied mathematics, the word "model" means some theory of a complex system expressed in mathematical language. In this case one system is simulated by different models — by theories, and these models behave like metaphors. As we see, the difference in the understanding of terms proves very profound.

Sometimes in one and the same field of knowledge, and even in the same texts, we have to use the term "model" despite meaning by it quite different things.

Such contradictory reading of the term "model" in mathematical linguistics also has proved interesting. Trying to introduce strict and faultless clarity in his reasoning, Shreider (1971) supplied this term with three indices *m, l,* and *c.* In his interpretations, the term "model$_m$" corresponds to the strictly defined notion of model in mathematics; roughly speaking, this is an interpretation of the theory. The term "model$_l$" is the notion of model in linguistics, that is, the theory itself, or some hypothetical scientific construction. It turned out that the relation "to be model$_l$" is inverse to the relation "to be model$_m$." And lastly, the term "model$_c$" is a cybernetic understanding of this word. It had been proven that

$$\text{model}_c = \text{model}_m \text{ for model}_l$$

i.e., "the model$_c$ of a real object is a mathematical model ("model$_m$") of a theory ("model$_l$") of this object." The trouble is that if we ascribe individual indices to all other possible meanings of the sense of the word "model," then no doubt nobody will be able to use the word. In speech (especially in reports and lectures), we always use the word "model" in various meanings and interlocutors understand this. But they will hardly understand anything if we speak as follows: "Having built a model in the fifteenth sense of the word, we have achieved the understanding of the word "model" in its twenty-seventh meaning." And still, an analysis of word meaning similar to that carried out by Shreider often proves very useful, since it allows us to penetrate more deeply into the polymorphous meaning of the word though it does not allow us to cope with it.

In the appendix to this book, a list of definitions of the term "statistics" is given. First of all, it is interesting as an illustration of the enrichment and broadening of word meanings. This word first appeared in fiction (Yule and Kendall, 1950): in *Hamlet* (1602, act 5, scene 2), in *Cymbeline* (1610, 1611, act 2, scene 4), and in *Paradise Regained* (1710, book 4), but the meaning of the word is not quite clear. It seems to be derived from the Latin "status" which means "political state." Later, the term "statistics" appears in science as well. Roughly speaking, three basic stages may be traced in the evolution of its meaning. First, it was the collation of data about the economic condition of a country based upon the analysis of those economic factors which can be expressed quantitatively. Perhaps in this meaning the term became connected with the German word *Staat* or the French word *état,* both of which mean "state." In the second stage of development, the term "statistics" was used for denoting the processing of any quantitatively expressible data, no matter the source: in science or in any other field of human activity. At this stage, statisticians were not worried about the reason and the way the data had been obtained. Nowadays, the term "statistics" is sometimes defined very broadly—as a metascience. The object of this science is logic and methodology of the other sciences, the logic of decision making in other sciences, and the logic of experiment. But such a broad interpretation is by no means widespread. At present we can still hear that the methods of statistics should be used cautiously, keeping in mind the priority of the quantitative over the qualitative. If some statisticians consider it senseless to divide statistics into mathematical statistics and statistics as a social science, others think such a division obviously necessary. Sometimes the aim of statistics is stated to be decision making under conditions of uncertainty. In a way, this definition is narrower than the definition of statistics as a metascience: it does not take into consideration all the questions connected with the logic of the sciences which are the concern of a metatheory. But at the same time it is broader, for it embraces both the problems of game theory and the problems of decision making in business. In this connection I should like to emphasize that the argument about the meaning of the term "mathematical statistics" is not a mere discussion about the limits of this or that scientific discipline. It is something much wider: it is the consideration of one of the problems of the philosophy of science. The discussion about the role of a probabilistic approach in grounding the methodology of scientific research has turned out to be an argument about the meaning of the term "statistics." In this respect it is especially interesting to observe the sharp divergence in estimating the role of the large-numbers law in social phenomena made clear in the articles by O. Yakhont and F. Lifshitz. This is not only the difference of opinions of the two authors but something much more significant since these opinions are given in the two leading Soviet encyclopedias: *Philosophical Encyclopaedia* and *Large Soviet Encyclopaedia*. It is noteworthy that the corresponding volumes of the two were published in the same year.

A collection of the definitions of the term "information," one of the main notions of cybernetics, would be of the same interest. A sampling of such definitions follows.

> Information is a name for the content of what is exchanged with the outer world as we adjust to it, and make our adjustment felt upon it. (Wiener, 1954)

> Information is . . . an attribute of objects, phenomena, processes of objective reality, man-made control computers, which consists in the ability of perceiving the internal state and the influence of the environment and preserving its results within a certain period of time; the ability of transferring the knowledge of the internal state and the obtained data to other things, phenomena and processes. (Kondakov, 1971)

> Information is the objective content of the connection between interrelated material objects, which manifests itself in the change of the state of these objects. (Mikhailov et al., 1968)

> Information is a philosophical category, considered side by side with

such notions as space, time and matter. Most generally information may be represented as communication, i.e. the form of a condition between the transmitter sending the message and the recipient perceiving it. (Vorobiev, 1971)

Information. The knowledge (in Russian "svedeniya") contained in a given speech excerpt and regarded as the object of transmission, storage and processing. (Akhmanova, 1966)

Information means order; to communicate means to create order out of disorder or at least to increase the degree of order that existed previous to the message received. (Hutten, 1967)

Even this small collection of the definitions of the term "information" demonstrates how polymorphic this word is in its range of meanings. Here, the development of polymorphism is primarily connected with the fact that none of the definitions corresponds to our intuitive understanding of the meaning of the word. And any attempt at defining ascribes some new features to this word, features which do not clarify but, on the contrary, make narrow and thus obscure its sense, and indubitably increase the word's polymorphism. For example, Mikhailov's definition connects this term with material objects in the most rigid way and thus excludes from the term "information" our idea of theorems in mathematics, in proving which the material objects by no means interact. The notion of information as objective content of the connection between interacting material objects makes us exclude music from this category as well, for it is hardly of an objective character. The desire to regard information as a philosophical category, similar to space and time, throws us back to Kant's era. At any rate, now physicists are not prone to consider space and time as philosophical categories. In Akhmanova's definition the international word "information" is replaced by the Russian word "svedenija," the meaning of which is not further explained.[2] Strict limitations are imposed upon the word "svedenija": not all the "svedenija" appear to be information, but only those which are contained in a given speech excerpt. Non-speech excerpts, e.g., the results of observations presented as curves or in a discrete code on a magnetic tape, turn out to be excluded from the concept of information. Hutten's definition sounds the most pleasant. It does not encompass the depth of the notions connected with the term, but it does reflect the content ascribed to it by physicists and, I dare say, experts in cybernetics. It is noteworthy that this definition sounds similar to the oldest idea of the role of a word in the creation of the universe. In the Gospel according to St. John we read: "In the beginning was the Word. . . . All things became through Him; and

---

[2] It is not easy to translate the word "svedenija." I have translated it above as "knowledge," but this translation is not quite adequate. It is better to translate this word as "information," but in this case Akhmanova's definition becomes a tautology.

without it did not anything become: that which became . . ." In the modern canonical versions of the Gospel of St. John the very polymorphous Greek concept λογος is traditionally translated as "word," and then the word acquires the role of a constructive and arranging force. It is in this sense that the word "information" seems to be understood nowadays.

It is interesting to call the reader's attention to the interpretation of the term in the *Philosophical Encyclopaedia* (*Filosofskaya Entsiklopediya*, 1962). It runs as follows: "Information (Latin — informatia) — see: information theory." Further, under the heading "Information theory" the questions with which this theory deals are enumerated, and various presentations of the quantitative estimation of information as a measure of order are given: according to Hartley and Shannon; to R. Fisher and A. N. Kolmogorov; to N. Rashevsky; to R. Carnap and Y. Bar-Hillel; and, at last, to Yu. A. Shreider. The definition of the term "information" proper is not given at all. The picture becomes very curious: a non-philosopher (Vorobiev, 1971) puts the notion of "information" under the heading of philosophy, but philosophers refuse to consider it from the philosophical point of view.

The above examples seem sufficient to back up the correctness of my thesis about the deep polymorphism of the language of science.

In the language of science, polymorphism manifests itself more clearly than in ordinary language. The reason is that here the words encode whole concepts. Scientific concepts may be very fuzzy and versatile. Many scientists understand only certain aspects of the complex system of notions. The above definitions of the word "information" are just a collection of judgments on different facets of the complex system which has recently been crystallized out in a separate scientific trend called cybernetics. The same is true of the term "mathematical statistics," and to a lesser degree of the terms "model" and "prior probability." The latter two terms encode not just one large but several small interrelated concepts. Such seemingly simple physical notions as mass and force are also theory laden. Here, I shall refer to Einstein and Infeld (1954): "Physics really began with the invention of mass, force and an inertial system. These concepts are all free inventions" (p. 295).

Concepts cannot be defined; they should be explained. The conceptual character of terms creates intensified polymorphism of the language of science. The deeper and more complicated the concepts encoded by the term are, the greater its polymorphism.

Here, a rhethorical question may be asked: If the polymorphism of language both in science and in ordinary speech grows with time, then won't language degenerate in the future, i.e., each notion will become all-embracing, and all the notions will have the same meaning? Indeed, asymptotically it may seem so in our model. But we have already agreed to regard language as a living organism, and like any organism, with age it must give way to another one. By the way, aging is no more than a natural process of information storage, which prevents further progress. The increase in the polymorphism of words does not go on smoothly. If the meaning of a word is imagined as a continuously widening field, then at certain moments part of this field may be lost, i.e., forgotten. Words undergo a complicated process of development; interesting examples of the semantic history of words are given in Budagov's book (1971).

Speaking about scientific terms, we must pay attention to another peculiarity. In the process of the development of science, its words gain *prestige*. Furthermore, the same occurs in social life, but here we shall restrict ourselves to the analysis of scientific terminology. When a scientist proposes a new concept, he wants to express it in old words. If he manages to do that, the new theory immediately gains the prestige already associated with these terms. If, for example, an absolutely new meaning is ascribed to mathematical statistics, it is considered a meta-science, and this new meaning is put into the old word "statistics"—a word which has already gained very high prestige. Now imagine that, developing a new concept, a scientist expresses it in new words. It will be equivalent to the loss of the game. More conservative colleagues of his will declare: "He says something entirely different about the problems we are concerned with." In Russia the word "statistics" so far has been strictly connected with economics, and to avoid depressing arguments I have suggested calling this new understanding of statistics by a new term: "the mathematical theory of experiment." The arguments about words in science, which irritate many of us, are sometimes not at all small talk. (The ideas developed in this paragraph were suggested by S. K. Shaumyan during our discussion of the manuscript.)

Specific languages of science, their slang character. To some extent the languages of science are organized in a way similar to the thieves' cant. In both cases the words and grammar of everyday language are used; it is seldom that new specific terms are introduced. These new terms and the new meaning ascribed to old words borrowed from the everyday vocabulary give an esoteric character to slang language: they prove comprehensible only to the initiated. And still, the similarity between the language of science and slang is only superficial, so it is better to speak of *specific languages of science*.

My understanding of the specific character of the language of science can be illustrated by an example. After a report on mathematical statistics to an audience of engineers in metallurgy and the science of metals, one of the listeners said that all this was certainly very interesting but, unfortunately, incomprehensible. Rather irritatedly, he added: "And why not change such incomprehensible terms as regression, correlation, variance into simple Russian words?" The lecturer answered: "Then let us give up such well-known terms as martensite, troostite, crystobalite, and substitute for them such simple Russian words as ticks, crosses, dashes, or dots according to what is seen under a microscope when examining metallographic and petrographical sections." This suggestion irritated the audience, and the reason is clear: the point is not that "perlite" and "martensite" are foreign words. The difficulty is of quite another origin: these words encode complicated metallographic concepts, and if we give up this system of codes and turn to the arbitrary but apparently understandable words, then in conversation we shall have to explain all the concepts from the very beginning. In the same way in mathematical statistics, the terms "variance" and "regression" encode whole scientific concepts, and the lecturer's difficulty lies in explaining them popularly and using them for developing the ideas which he wishes to state in his lecture. If a reader meets an unknown term in a paper on mathematical statistics, an explanatory dictionary of specific terms would be of no use for him because it is not a strict definition of the term (if it does exist) that it is important to know but all the concepts connected with it. Thus, such a language barrier may be also called a conceptual barrier. In contrast to ordinary human language, the language of science is of a much more distinctly *coded* character. The depth of coding or, in other words, the informational capacity of terms grows in time with the development of scientific concepts. The difficulties are also redoubled by the fact that specific languages often use the words of ordinary language in a special sense. For instance, everybody knows the common meaning of the word "replica," which is a French borrowing. In mathematical statistics there are such terms as "replica," "fractional replica," and "regular replica" which have a specific meaning. "Fractional replica" means some specially selected part of the complete factor experiment — its fractional, i.e., partial, repetition. The meaning of this term becomes clear after substantial acquaintance with the concept of experimental design. Finally, in optics "replica" is a copy of a diffractional lattice prepared in a special way. All three of these terms with different meanings originated from the French "réplique."

The slang-like character of speech manifests itself not only in the sciences but in the humanities as well. The Russian edition of this book contains several extracts from the reports made at a conference on the Oriental problem. These examples deal with specialized expressions that cannot be translated into English. The paradox is that sometimes foreign words are inserted into Russian speech in an extraordinary manner which makes it sound elegant and artificial. These word combinations are actually words with Greek and Latin roots, and substituting for them words with Russian roots will eliminate the effect.

Recall once more that specific languages of science are continuously changing. New concepts emerge, and old notions are often assigned a new meaning. Because of its continuously changing nature, scientific language is accessible only to those working in the field and thus constantly interacting with the informational flows in science. The same phenomenon, but to a lesser degree, can be observed in ordinary language. Suppose you give a foreigner who has been living in the Soviet Union for a long time a magazine in his native language and ask him to translate several pages. He will translate ordinary text easily, but will immediately stumble over new slangish or idiomatic expressions, and cartoon captions will pose almost insuperable difficulty for him: as a rule they are based on certain peculiarities of current life, encoded in specific words. No matter how long I study English, I shall probably never learn it to such a degree as to be capable of translating a caption under a cartoon in such an intellectually respectable American magazine as *The New Yorker*.

Babelian Difficulties in Science

With the development of science, more and more separate specific languages of science have crystallized. This facilitates the exchange of information on the borders of narrow branches of science, but hampers mutual understanding between neighboring fields of knowledge. If I am permitted to be a bit frivolous, I shall say that the situation is the same as that at the building site of the Tower of Babel.

Heated discussions as to whether or not this or that field of knowledge can be considered an independent discipline are common occurrences. In discussing this question the opponents define various criteria. One of these is the statement to the effect that every independent scientific discipline should have a research method of its own. I think that, proceeding from the above, another quite simple criterion may be suggested: the emergence of a new independent scientific discipline must be accompanied by the emergence of a new specific language (or, rather, a dialect). The emergence of essentially new problems immediately leads to the emergence of the new language in which they are discussed. In contrast, the creation of a new science is not necessarily accompanied by the creation of new research methods, especially nowadays when many new branches of knowledge appear at the junction of previously existing ones and use their research methods. For example, the design of experiment — a subdivision of mathematical statistics — seems to me to be a new independent scientific discipline. In the process of its development, solving its own specific problems, this discipline has developed its own specific language. This language irritates specialists in mathematical statistics if they are not specialists in the problems of experimental design as well. At the same time, this new discipline has no unique methods. It uses methods commonly used in mathematics: linear algebra, combinatorial analysis, numerical methods of analysis, and, in its most unique manifestations, the methods of functional analysis, set theory, and abstract algebra. The above statements sound similar to those of Shreider (1969), who asserted that we should ascribe the greatest profundity to the truths which change the human thesaurus to the greatest degree.[3]

We often hear discourses on differentiation and integration of science. The process of differentiation can be easily traced by the emergence of new local, specific languages of science. As far as the integration of science is concerned, it is wishful thinking rather than an actually observed phenomenon. If this process had taken place, then we should have noticed at least some vague signs of the emergence of a language necessary for it. How can we speak about the existence of a specific manifestation of scientific thinking if there is no language in which it can be expressed briefly and clearly? The only phenomenon we can observe now is the appearance of new branches of knowledge at the intersection of some already existing disciplines which seem to have nothing in common. This is not integration but additional differentiation of knowledge. Every newly created discipline of such a kind is clothed in the attire of a newly created language. Here again, we refer to the example of the emergence of a new branch of knowledge called "experimental design." This branch has appeared at the junction of many subdivisions of mathematics, but it has not led to their integration. Metamathematics — a science dealing with the foundations of mathematics — cannot be regarded as a discipline resulting from the integration of mathematical knowledge. It is just a new subdivision of mathematics with its complicated concepts and its own specific language in which its concepts are encoded. This subject is remote from the representatives of other subdivisions of mathematics. Similarly, modern logic cannot be regarded as a result of the integration of differ-

---

[3] This is a one-way criterion: if in any field of knowledge there appears a new specific language, it undoubtedly means the appearance of a new scientific discipline, but scientifically formed languages may emerge with the construction of a system of notions in a region which is far from being scientific. Freud's theory is an example; it has a scientifically formed language of its own, but, strictly speaking, it is not scientific for it is formulated in such a way that it cannot be verified. This is not to say that I have a negative attitude to this theory; besides, I do not think that human intellectual activity should be completely reduced to scientific categories. A characteristic feature of science is the possibility of verification of its hypothesis (although, strictly speaking, it is difficult to give a clear-cut definition of what we understand by the term "the possibility of verification").

ent branches of knowledge. Its language is as specific as the languages of other branches of knowledge, and quite a large group of scientists fail to understand it.

Specific languages of science have another function. Delicate refinement of language turns out to be a form of scientific aristocratism, a sign of belonging to a certain scientific community similar to the situation in old Russia when speaking good French indicated that one belonged to the nobility. The representatives of some fields of knowledge, especially mathematicians, or at least some of them, have always considered themselves to be at the Olympus of science. A young mathematician thinks that by vulgarizing his language he betrays the refinement he has been taught and, consequently, loses the right to belong to the scientific community which it had been so difficult for him to enter (Nalimov and Mul'chenko, 1972). Strange as it seems, this aristocratism is also taught in our universities—God knows how. Unfortunately, it commonly happens that the superior verbal behavior of young mathematicians insults the representatives of other branches of knowledge who have come to them for consultation.

The Problem of Standardization of Scientific Terminology

I do not want the reader to get the impression that I reject the necessity of making scientific terminology stricter. From my concept that the polymorphism of language makes it a truly powerful means of communication, it does not follow that in scientific language we should permit that innumerable variety of terms which can often be observed.

Preobrazhenskaya et al. (1974) present interesting data which deal with the frequency of statistical terms in publications on spectrochemical analysis and analytical chemistry. One of the histograms from this paper is given in Fig. 5. Such graphs are interesting in two respects. Firstly, they permit us to judge the degree of penetration of statistical terms into this or that branch of knowledge. Here we see that serious concepts of mathematical statistics, connected with such terms as "regression analysis," "the least square method," and "distribution," are rarely used in the field under study. Furthermore, from this graph we see that to denote a single concept of "error" a variety of synonymous terms are used: ошибка (error), точность (precision), отклонение (deviation), погрешность (fault), воспроизводимость (reproducibility), расхождение (divergence). The picture will become still more confused if we consider the word combinations: точность анализа (precision of analysis), погрешность анализа (slip in the analysis), ошибка воспроизводимости

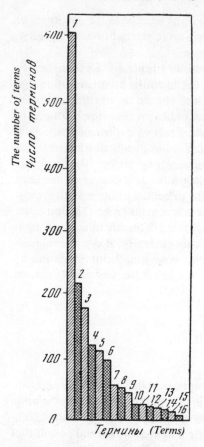

FIG. 5. *Distribution of terms of mathematical statistics according to the frequency of their occurrence in publications on spectrochemical analysis in the journal Industrial Laboratory (Slavnyi, 1969). (1) Error; (2) precision; (3) faultness; (4) deviation; (5) reproducibility; (6) variance; (7) confidence interval; (8) variance coefficient; (9) divergence; (10) criteria; (11) dispersion; (12) distribution; (13) correlation analysis; (14) least square method; (15) methods of mathematical statistics; (16) regression analysis.*

анализа (reproducibility error), отклонение результатов анализа (deviation of results), достоверность анализа (validity), оценка погрешности (error estimation), оценка достоверности (validity estimation), статистическая достоверность анализа (statistical validity), относительное расхождение анализа (relative deviation), средняя относительная ошибка (average relative error), относительная ошибка (relative error), случайная ошибка (random error), статистическая ошибка (statistical error), отклонение от истинного результата (deviation from the true value), относительное стандартное отклонение (relative standard deviation), относительная точность (relative precision), относительная величина дисперсии (relative value of variance — the expression is absolute nonsense), абсолютное расхождение (absolute deviation), средняя статистическая ошибка (average statistical error), относительная статистическая ошибка каждого измерения (relative statistical error of each measurement), вероятная случайная ошибка (probabilistic random error).

All these terms, formed by combining two or three words, are synonymous in the sense of "estimation of the degree of uncertainty, connected with the result of analysis." Naturally, the authors of all the publications investigated did their utmost to present their results in a form comparable to that used by other authors. But have they really reached this aim by using terms of such mixed and unintelligible character?

Recently, the State All-Union Standard No. 16263-70 was published in the Soviet Union with the title "State provisional system for the unity of measurements. Metrology. Terms and definitions." In this publication the term погрешность (mistakenness) is suggested as a standard.

Figure 5 suggests that it will hardly become established. This term, at least with specialists in substance analysis, is six times more rarely used than the unrecommended term ошибка измерения ("an error of measurement"). It seems useful to dwell upon the analysis of this Standard in more detail. In the Soviet Union it is one of the first attempts to *decree* the language of science in that branch which deals with an activity of all experimenters, and such a standard has the status of law. The preface to the Standard reads as follows: "The terms established by the present Standard, are recommended for use in documentation of all kinds of manuals, teaching aids, technical and reference literature." This Standard was developed by serious scientific institutions: Mendeleev All-Union Scientific Research Institute for Metrology and All-Union Scientific-Research Institute for Technical Information, Classification and Codification. Still, we find quite strange recommendations in it. One such oddity is the confrontation of the terms наблюдение (observation) and измерение (measurement). It runs as follows:

> Результат наблюдения (The result of observation). The value obtained by a single observation.
>
> Результат измерения (The result of measurement). The value obtained by means of measuring it.

Further, two more notions are introduced: среднее квадратичное отклонение результата наблюдения (the average square deviation of the result of observation) and среднее квадратичное отклонение результата измерения (the average square deviation of the result of measurements). One can hardly understand when and which of these terms should be applied.

It is also strange that in this Standard the terms точность измерения (precision of measurement) and правильность измерения (accuracy of measurement) are confronted. The following definitions are given there:

> Точность измерения (Precision of measurement). Quality of

measurements, reflecting closeness of their results to the true meaning of the value measured.

Notes:

1. High precision of measurements corresponds to small errors of all kinds, both systematic and random.

2. Quantitatively the precision may be expressed by the inverse value of the modulus of the relative error.

Правильность измерения (Accuracy of measurement). Quality of measurements reflecting closeness to zero of systematic errors in their results.

Here everything is puzzling. How can two separate terms coexist if one of them, правильность (accuracy), is given by reference to the other one, точность (precision). In Anglo-American literature, the terms "precise" and "accurate" are traditionally contrasted: random error is connected with the first one, and systematic error, with the second. The two terms "random error" and "systematic error" logically pertain to notions of different types (in the sense of Russell), and to build here a combined notion is as strange as to say, "I see two objects: a chair and furniture." What seems even more strange is the statement about measurements having qualities which are defined by quantitative characteristics. The concept of the true value of the quantity measured is defined in none of the above definitions; it remains a vague, philosophically shaped notion. It is very surprising that both the concepts of точность (precision) and правильность (accuracy) pertain only to measurements but by no means to observation, though it follows from the same Standard that the observations are also expressed quantitatively.

I have dwelt in such a detail on this example of the terminological Standard to demonstrate how great the difficulties are which are faced in the attempt to make scientific terminology stricter. The above-mentioned Standard will hardly be of any use for Soviet science. Nevertheless, this is a curious precedent: scientists are officially presented with terms which are beneath criticism from the standpoint of logical analysis and which do not correspond to the historical traditions of the scientific community. I wonder what will come of it.

We can formulate the following sufficiently general statement: the broader a scientific term is, the more difficult it is to define it. Here is an example. In the Soviet *Philosophical Encyclopaedia* (the article "Experiment" by B. Dynin) the term "experiment" is defined as follows:

Experiment — sensual-objective activity in science performed by theoretically cognized means.

Imagine that an experiment is performed which is aimed at the registration of infrared rays. The results of the experiment go into the computer, and the output order appears in mathematical language. What is to be considered "sensual–objective activity" here? Is it the obtaining of an infrared spectrum which we do not perceive through our senses? Is it correct to assume that the spectrograph, spectrum generator, and the aggregate for the registration of the spectrum are "theoretically cognized means"? The modern mathematical theory of experiment actually proceeds from the opposite assumption. It states that the experiment is being carried out in a situation which cannot be exhaustively described by theory. On this basis, it is suggested that the conditions of the experiment be randomized in order to avoid possible systematic errors. Randomization would be unnecessary if the experiment were performed in a situation absolutely under the experimenter's control. If the above definition is to be retained, then the largest part of scientific experimentation must be considered as non-scientific activity!

The difficulties in ordering scientific terminology seem enormous. Scientists want something to be done in the field, but such activity must be extremely cautious. To my mind, the terms should be explained rather than strictly defined. As a rule, every concept in science is closely linked with a field of meanings which has been formed in the course of a long history of development. Any attempt at rigorous definition may impose unwanted restrictions on the field. Following Spinoza, we may say that any definition is a negation — in our case, the negation of that part of the semantic field which has not entered the definition. Should such great restrictions really be imposed upon the semantic fields as has been done in the above example with the term "experiment" or still earlier with the term "information"?

Terms in science must serve not only for the expression of previously developed concepts, but also for the formulation of statements in the future. That is why scientific terms *must be open*. Even in mathematics, as was clearly demonstrated by one of the examples of Lakatos (1963–64), the criticism of the previously stated solutions leads to the broadening of the meaning of the conceptions.

In any case, it is clear that any terminologic recommendations must be preceded by substantial logico-linguistic analysis of the whole variety of actual scientific terms.

Chapter 4

Mathematics as a Language

Peculiarities of Mathematical Language in the Texts of Pure Mathematics

What is mathematics? Is mathematics, represented in all its modern variety, a single science? The answer to this clear-cut question was attempted by the French mathematicians who sign their papers with the name Nicolàs Bourbaki. In their article "Architecture of Mathematics" published in Russian as an appendix to *The History of Mathematics*[1] (Bourbaki, 1948), they stated that mathematics (and certainly it is only pure mathematics that is referred to) is a uniform science. Its uniformity is given by the system of its logical constructions. A chracteristic feature of mathematics is the explicit axiomatico-deductive method of constructing judgments. Any mathematical paper is first of all characterized by containing a long chain of logical conclusions. But the Bourbaki say that such chaining of syllogisms is no more than a transforming mechanism. It may be applied to any system of premises. It is just an outer sign of a system, its dressing; it does not yet display the essential system of logical constructions given by the postulates.

The system of postulates in mathematics is not in the least a colorful mosaic of separate initial statements. The peculiarity of mathematics lies in the ability of the system of postulates to form special concepts, *mathematical structures*, rich with logical consequences which may be derived from them deductively. Mathematics is principally an axioma-

---

[1] This is one of the volumes of the unique tractatus *The Elements of Mathematics*, which *was to give* the reader the fullest impression of modern mathematics, organized from the standpoint of one of the largest modern schools.

115

tized field of knowledge, and it is in this sense that mathematics is a unified science. Its uniformity is given by the peculiarity of its logical structure. This is the Bourbaki's central idea which mirrors their mathematical outlook.

Below, I try to give an idea of mathematical language. This language is a certain system of rules of operations on signs. To introduce a calculus, we must construct an alphabet of the initial elements, signs, to give the initial words of the calculus and to construct the rules for making new words out of the initial words. They are built upon a set of elements, the *physical nature of which remains unknown*. In order to give the structure, it is sufficient to define the relation between these elements in a certain system of axioms. The system of judgments in mathematics is built without turning to vaguely implicit assumptions, common sense, or free associations. The task lies in verification of the fact that the results obtained really follow from the initial assumptions. It is the question itself about verification of the correctness of the initial axioms in a certain physical sense that is pointless. Mathematicians care only about the logical consistency of axioms; they must contain no inner contradictions. But, again, the system of axioms must be constructed in such a way that it will be rich in its logical consequences.

The idea of a universal symbolism and logical calculation can be traced to Leibniz, though modern clear-cut definition of mathematics as strictly formalized calculus became possible only after the works by Frege, Russell, and Hilbert. In Kleene's work (1952) we find the following characteristic philosophical views of Hilbert.

> Those symbols, etc. are themselves the ultimate objects, and are not being used to refer to something other than themselves. The metamathematician looks *at* them not *through* or *beyond* them; thus they are objects without interpretation or meaning. (p. 64)

Chess playing is often regarded as a model of mathematics (Weyl, 1927) or, if you like, as a parody of mathematics. Chess figures and the squares on the playboard are the signs of the system, and the rules of the game are the rules of inference; the initial position of the game is the system of axioms, and the subsequent positions are formulae deduced from the axioms. The initial position and the rules of playing prove to be exceedingly rich: in skillful hands they create a variety of interesting games. While the aim of a chess game lies in check-mating the adversary, the aim of mathematical reasoning is the obtaining of certain theorems. In both cases it is important not only to achieve the goal, but also to do it beautifully and, of course, without contradictions: in mathematics some situations will be regarded as contradictory in the same way as, for example, the existence of ten queens of the same color would contradict the chess calculus. The most fruitful feature of such a comparison is that in chess, as in mathematics, logical operations are performed without any interpretation in terms of the phenomena of the external world: for example, it is not at all important for us to know to what element of reality pawns correspond or whether the limitations imposed upon the rules for moving the bishop are rational.

Still, it would not be correct to state that mathematics is a fully formalized branch of knowledge. Hilbert failed in his attempt to build a strictly formalized system of reasoning out of the absolute consistency of arithmetic. There are also some difficulties in defining formally the notion of proof in mathematics in general. In the process of the development of mathematics, new, previously unknown techniques of reasoning have appeared. (In particular, from this follows the irrationality of statements that the proof of mathematical theorems may be fully handed over to computers.) In the above-mentioned book Kleene (1952) states this idea as follows:

> We can imagine an omniscient member-theorist. We should expect that his ability to see infinitely many facts at once would enable him to recognize as correct some principle of deduction which we could not discover ourselves. But any correct formal system . . . which he could reveal to us, telling us how it works, without telling us why, would still be incomplete . . . (p. 303)

Sometimes it is said that all mathematical knowledge is implicit in those short statements which are traditionally called mathematical structures and that the proof of theorems is no more than an explication of the content of the structures. This statement would be quite correct if the process of reasoning were strictly formalized. But unless it is so, the proof of theorems themselves already contains some essentially novel information, which is not intrinsic to the structures they serve to elucidate.

There is one more reason that we cannot speak of a full formalization of mathematics: the reason is that in mathematics, together with deductive reasoning, plausible reasoning [in the sense of (Polya, 1954)] is also used; the conclusions built on analogy may serve as a good example. True, nobody can estimate the role they play in mathematical judgments. One final remark: mathematical papers still must use ordinary language as a kind of auxiliary means.

Mathematical Theory of Language in the Concept of Context-Free Languages

The American linguist Chomsky in the late 1950s tried to build a mathematical model of ordinary languages. Formal grammar of the context-free languages is built as a calculus for generating the variety of correct sentences of the natural language. As with any calculus, here we speak about the grammar, which must consist of some finite alphabet, that is, a variety of initial symbols, of some finite set of inference rules that generate chains, and of the initial chains, axioms. The chains generated by the inference rules are interpreted as sentences. The whole set of sentences is called language. Grammar, if it is properly formulated, must unambiguously define the whole set of correct sentences in language. Here, syntactic description is performed in terms of the so-called analysis of immediate constituents. Sentences are divided into fewer and fewer constituents down to the smallest ones (Chomsky, 1956).

The theory of context-free languages, as becomes obvious from the statement of the problem itself, is to be built as a purely mathematical discipline. This theory and the theory of finite automata are closely and deeply interrelated. In this book I cannot dwell in detail on the theory of context-free languages; to do so, I would have to write this paragraph in a language different from that of the rest of the book. A short and very popular rendering of this theory can be found in books by Shreider (1971) and Ginsburg (1966).

In one of the first papers dealing with the theory of context-free languages, Chomsky tried to establish the justification of his approach. He posed the following questions: Is it possible to formulate simple grammars for all the languages that we are interested in? Do such grammars possess any explanatory power? Are there any interesting languages which lie outside this theory? Is not, for example, English such a language?

Before long, it appeared that grammars of context-free languages provided very convenient means for the study of programming languages for computers. It would be interesting to pose a broader question: to try to find out to what degree this theory becomes useful for the description and understanding of natural languages which, unlike programming languages, are still non-Gödelian systems—at least from our standpoint.

This question can be answered in the affirmative if we introduce, after Chomsky (1956), a set of grammatical transformations which transfer sentences with one structure of immediate constituents into new sentences with another structure. The fundamental part of his conception is the notion of deep and surface structures of a sentence. A deep structure is something basic, directly connected with thinking and allowing one to give semantic interpretations of sentences independently of peculiarities of this or that language. Transformational rules transform sentences from the deep structure into surface ones which are different for different languages. But certainly, the broadened pattern—transformational grammar—may be regarded only as a model with the status of a metaphor, that is, if we assume that the simulated system—natural language—in a sense behaves like its mathematical model and in another sense, quite the other way around.

Chomsky's conception, i.e., the theory of generative grammar, has been discussed in many papers. Philosophical aspects of this approach can be found in his very interesting book (Chomsky, 1968) recently published in Russian. Another interesting book, *New Horizons in Linguistics* (Lyons, 1970), also dwells upon the impact of Chomsky's ideas upon the development of studies in the linguistics of ordinary languages (not free from the interaction between context and the sense of the phrase).

The most interesting results in the theory of context-free languages were obtained in solving the recognition problem when it is necessary to know whether this or that relation exists between various languages or between a language and a chain. The recognition is carried out by a determined mechanism according to a finite number of clear-cut orders, forming an algorithm. If such a solving algorithm does exist, the problem is said to be algorithmically solvable. Thus, the problem of an arbitrarily given chain belonging to some arbitrarily given context-free language has proved solvable. The solution of this problem is of great practical importance in computer engineering, where it is necessary to recognize programs automatically and to decide in which one of several possible languages this or that sequence of symbols is coded. The following problems proved algorithmically unsolvable: to judge by two arbitrary context-free grammars whether they generate one and the same language, whether the languages generated are intersecting, and whether there exists a finite transformer reflecting a language generated by a grammar into a language generated by another grammar. If such problems are faced by those who write such programs for computers, they have to introduce a number of restrictions, that is, to work with languages belonging to a certain specific subgroup of language, for which these problems are solvable, or to additionally formalized semantic aspects of languages, etc. (for details, see Ginsburg, 1966).

Now let us return to one of the central problems of natural languages, that is, to the question of whether it is possible, strictly speaking, to translate from one language into another. If somebody wishes to answer the question, he must begin with its clear-cut formulation. Only in the framework of a certain formalism is it possible to understand what we want to ask. In this case it is natural to turn to the model of context-free languages. Then this question can be formulated as the search for a finite transformer for representation of a language generated by one grammar into the language generated by another grammar, or as a problem of recognition of the fact that two grammars generate one and the same language. If this is actually the case, the formulation of the problem becomes so abstract that it is unsolvable; hence, it seems to follow that when dealing with natural languages it is better to speak about the *interpretation* in one language of something spoken in another one, rather than about translation from one language into another. I believe that an abstract mathematical model can be used for better understanding the fact that the difficulties we encounter in comparing natural languages have this principal character. They are intrinsic for the logical structure of the model of natural language which we assume to have some simple pattern. Hence, it is clear why not only professional linguists but also writers, scientists, and philosophers display such a great interest in the comparative evaluation of languages.

Here, I shall discuss the comparative evaluation of the expressive means of two seemingly related languages, English and Russian. These languages are related at least in the sense that in the latest stage of their development they adapted themselves to a common task: to express the ideas of modern culture. The following statement comes from a writer who has full mastery of both languages; in any case, he can hardly be accused of particular adherence to either of them (Nabokov, 1967).

> Movements of the body, grimaces, landscapes, languor of the trees, smells, rain, melting and iridescent nuances of nature, everything human and tender (strange as it is!), but also everything muzhik, rude, bawdy sounds in Russian no worse (or even better) than in English; but so typical of English delicate reticence, poetry of the thought, instant roll-call of the most abstract notions, swarming of monosyllabic epithet—all this and also everything dealing with technology, fashions, sports, sciences and perverted passions— becomes in Russian clumsy, loquacious and often disgusting as to style and rhythm. This discrepancy mirrors the principal historical difference between the green Russian literary language and the English language ripe like a matured fig: between a brilliant still insufficiently educated, sometimes even vulgar youth and a venerable genius combining the stock of motley knowledge with absolute spiritual freedom. Spiritual freedom! Breathing of the whole mankind is in these words!

This statement needs some comments. Certainly, it must not be regarded as a judgment arrived at by scientific analysis. It is just a piece of personal experience, an experience which is unique in itself, for Nabokov writes his fiction in two languages—Russian and English. Nabokov's words should be considered as a rather subjective, often debatable, but also picturesque description of the difficulty faced by an artist who is also a translator of his own works. At the same time, his judgment about Russian being a young language as compared with English seems to me quite accurate, if the historical conditionality of language development is accepted. Scientific life in England began several centuries earlier than in Russia. English people's intellectual life and, consequently, their language already began to be perfected by the logic of the great medieval scholars (though their language was Latin), but Russia had not experienced a scholastic Middle Ages. We consider Shakespeare to have been a perfectly educated philosopher, whereas in those days Russia had next to nothing except church literature. If we accept the historical conditionality of the semantic means of language, then we can propose a hypothesis that polymorphism in English is developed to a greater degree than in Russian. And possibly, it is just the greater polymorphism that gives English the flexibility noted by Nabokov; hence, the difficulties with translation resulting from different semantic structures of the two languages. My study of the distribution functions of words according to the number of synonyms connected with them (see above) has not allowed me to corroborate this hypothesis, but it does not disappoint me, for synonyms are not in the least the only and the strongest manifestation of polymorphism. Comparative and roughly qualitative estimation of bilingual dictionaries still gives us sufficient reason for supporting the hypothesis about the greater polymorphism in English. I hope to study this question quantitatively, using statistical methods for the analysis of dictionaries (though I am well aware of the difficulties, both technical ones and also those connected with choosing a methodology and interpreting the results expected).

I shall also cite here the statement of the well-known French physicist de Broglie (1960) on the different capacity of different national languages for expressing scientific ideas.

> Some languages have a complicated grammatical structure, but easily allow the formation of new compound words or new adjectives and readily express ideas by long phrases with a lot of parenthetical clauses. They are especially fit to express, in a not too precise but in a profound manner, great philosophical doctrines. They serve well for a detailed examination, sometimes a little ponderous, but often very instructive, of some branch of Science. Other languages, with contracted grammatical forms and especially simple syntax, represent the verbal instrument created by peoples with a pragmatic tendency towards action and activity, and are brilliantly adjusted to express scientific ideas in a clear and concise form and to formulate rigorous rules of predicting phenomena or affecting nature without taking much trouble to penetrate into all its mysteries.
>
> Among these expressive means, the French language occupies a peculiar and somewhat intermediate position. Its exigent grammar and sufficiently rigorous syntax to some extent restrain fantasy and excessive imagination. Being less supple than other languages, it assigns an almost necessary place to words inside the phrase and only

> reluctantly allows their inversions which, placing some words close together or isolating them, yield unexpected effects and in some languages, e.g. in Latin, give an opportunity to obtain contrasts of rare literary beauty. Furthermore, French dislikes lengthy periods overcharged with parenthetical clauses, which also deprives it of some possibilities. . . . But while this language is probably less fit than others to express, by diverse means of phrase construction, startling contrasts or to follow, along a phrase with many ramifications, the obscure mazes of a complex thought, its advantage becomes obvious when, following a solid thread of logical reasoning, one has to express a conclusion with precision.

We shall find the difference in languages still greater if we compare the languages of different cultures, such as European and ancient Indian languages (I shall return to this question later).

If we regard the problem of translation in terms of Chomsky's concept of the existence of a universal inborn grammar, underlying the whole diversity of languages, and of his notion of grammar being an algorithm generating all possible phrases of the language, then there seem to be no fundamental difficulties, even if a translation is done with the help of a computer. However, no interesting results in the field of machine translation have in fact been obtained.

We have had to acknowledge (see, for example, the paper by Bott in Lyons, 1970) that a person interpreting an ambiguous context makes use of all his knowledge about the external world, and it still remains vague in what way this encyclopedic information can be programmed. In my opinion, all this information is encoded in the language polymorphism which is decoded by the method I have tried to describe with the help of the Bayesian theorem. Imagine that a polymorphous language were replaced by a monomorphous language consisting of unambiguous words. It is possible to estimate, though quite roughly, the clumsiness of such a language. It will surely pass the limits of the possibilities of human memory. In addition, if we attempt to impose hard grammatical limitations upon monomorphous languages we shall immediately face the Gödelian difficulties.

A question may be asked as to whether the Bayesian approach allows one to overcome, at least partly, the difficulties connected with machine translation and other similar problems. At present this question cannot be answered, but serious work in this direction does seem tempting. In any case, the approach developed allows one to comprehend the difficulties which emerge.

Concluding this section, I should like to recall that we are living in a world of essentially different languages, which preserve their individuality even if they have to adjust to solving the same problems. The difference in national languages—and a scientist must speak several of them—is only one instance of the diversity of languages we have to cope with. Our intellectual activity manifests itself in diverse languages and is often reduced to interpretation—to the attempt to express in one language something which has previously been said, for one reason or another, in another language. The theory of context-free languages allows us to understand, from the purely formal standpoint, the statement that the existence of diverse languages enriches us. This statement seems strange on the surface, but actually, is it always so? Sometimes their existence turns into a barrier. Babelian difficulties in science are a good illustration of both sides of this process.

Mathematics as the Language of Physics

The language of physics is discussed in two interesting books by Hutten, an English physicist (1956, 1967). I shall begin this section by citing some of his statements.

In an attempt to carry out the logical reconstruction of any field of knowledge, one must, according to Hutten (1956), distinguish three stages of formalization.

The first is *mathematization*. Some propositions originating in a theory are expressed as equations. At this stage of formalization, mathematics is used just like a language. Statements made in the mathematical language do not yet form compact, inwardly consistent logical systems analogous to the structures of pure mathematics.

The second stage is *axiomatization*. At this stage of formalization, the fundamental premises of a theory should be formulated as axioms. The whole diversity of knowledge is reduced to very compact formulations. All the particular results of a theory, diverse as they are, are expressed as theorems derived from the principal premises given by a few fundamental phrases. All knowledge is implicit in compact structures; theorems merely serve for their explication. Such a construction of theory, were it possible, seems the ideal one. How easy it would be to write monographs and to teach students! But can this dream of "exhausted" scientists come true?

Finally, the third stage is constructing *rules of interpretation*. In addition to axioms and syntax (rules of inference), we should also have interpretation rules for the results predicted theoretically in terms of an experiment. This is the concluding stage of formalization.

If, Hutten goes on to say, we look at physics from this standpoint, we must admit that its formalization is restricted to the first stage, that is, to mathematization. There have been many attempts at axiomatizing physical theories, but it was only Caratheodory's axiomatization for the first and the second laws of thermodynamics that had been universally accepted. Even an attempt at axiomatization of Newtonian mechanics failed. [Some interesting statements about the difficulties connected with formalization of physical theories are to be found in Dishkant (1968).] As far as interpretation rules are concerned, strictly speaking, they do not exist at all, though in physics there are some bridges across the gap between formal description and the language of experimentation.

In his second book Hutten (1967) requires correct understanding of the statement (which has lately become trivial) to the effect that science is being mathematized in the process of its perfection. He says that mathematics is important in introducing a system of universal symbols rather than in being the means of quantitative judgments. Testing a hypothesis, Hutten continues, is not a mere problem of numerical correspondence. It is a manifestation of something greater, namely, the interpretation of mathematical formalism, which reflects rational human behavior. Mathematical equations themselves do not yet create a model. Mathematics used to describe reality needs interpretation, and this is carried out by means of a model. To support this idea, he gives the example of the non-linear relativistic wave equation. It has two equal solutions: one for positive energy and the other for negative energy. Dirac, an English physicist, interpreted the solution for negative energy as antiparticles (see Hutten, 1967, pp. 111, 133). This is an example of a physical theory proper being created not only by mathematically formalized inference procedures, but also and to the highest degree by their interpretation in the language of experiment. Another example: I do not think that it will seem simplistic to say that special relativity theory emerged after Einstein managed to physically interpret Lorentz's transformations. Thus, from a physicist's standpoint, mathematics is but a language. Here, it seems appropriate to cite Bohr (1958a), who spoke about mathematics while discussing problems of physics:

> . . . we shall not consider pure mathematics as a separate branch of knowledge, but rather as a refinement of general language, supplementing it with appropriate tools to represent relations for which ordinary verbal expression is imprecise or cumbersome.

At this point, we can ask the following question: What is the advantage of the language of mathematics in its application to physical problems? Answering this question, Hutten speaks about science being an abstract representation of reality. Growth of science, he goes on to say, causes the emergence of more and more abstract theories. I suppose that these statements by Hutten can be deepened by recourse to the probabilistic concept of language which is being developed in this book. The abstractness of the mathematical language of physics is manifested by the fact that, in mathematical phrases, abstract symbols are used as elementary signs, but not the words of the language of experiment. Logical operations embedded in mathematical language are performed on abstract symbols but not on words. True, there are words behind symbols, and behind the words there are distribution functions of their meaningful content. In the early stage of the development of physics, scientists, though using the language of mathematics, still kept in mind the meaningful content of signs. But gradually, with the complication of theoretical conceptions, the meaningful content of a sign becomes vague or even fully lost. A physicist begins thinking in the way a pure mathematician does, without any attempt to connect signs rigorously with the physical reality they denote. The physical sense of a theory is revealed only at its last stage—in interpreting the statements expressed in the language of abstract symbols by the language of experiment, i.e., ordinary language.

I call the reader's attention to the fact that, while interpreting an abstract theory in the language of experiment, polymorphism remains. In this connection, I should mention a very interesting report by Abel (1969), an American philosopher, at the XIVth International Philosophical Congress in Vienna. The very title of the report is curious: it is called "Language and Electron." Polymorphism in the description of phenomena connected with an electron proves so troublesome that Abel asks: Can we be said to know something which we have not been able to put into words? To illustrate his idea, he gives a very interesting collection of statements of well-known physicists and philosophers of physics about the probability waves—one of the fundamental concepts of quantum mechanics. I present this collection here in a somewhat shortened form.

> *Louis de Broglie.* . . . the wave is now simply a purely symbolic and analytical representation of certain probabilities, and is not a physical phenomenon in the old sense of the term.

> *Max Born.* Experiments show that the waves have objective reality just as much as the particles—the interference maxima of the waves can be photographed just as well as the cloud tracks of the particles. . . .

> *Heisenberg.* The probability waves . . . the intensity of which determines in every point the probability for the absorption (or induced emission) of a light quantum by an atom at this point . . . a strange kind of physical reality just in the middle between possibility and reality . . . not a three-dimensional wave like elastic or radio

waves, but a wave in the many-dimensional configuration space, and therefore a rather abstract mathematical quantity.

Schrödinger. We sorely need those spherical waves as realities . . . there are many experiments which we simply cannot account for without taking the wave to be a wave, acting simultaneously throughout the region over which it spreads . . . neither the particle concept nor the wave concept is hypothetical.

C. J. Davisson. The evidence that electrons are waves is similar to the evidence that light and X-rays are waves.

Walter Heitler. The wave function of an electron develops as a classical field does, i.e., its future course is predictable. . . . But its very nature and its physical interpretation (as a probability distribution) makes it clear that it is not itself the physical object we investigate (in contrast to the electromagnetic field of the classical theory, which is a physical object which we may consider, observe and measure), although it is inseparable from the object under consideration (an electron, for instance). Its predictable course of development . . . continues so long and until an observation is made.

P. W. Bridgeman. The unanalyzable probability which wave mechanics introduces as elementary can be a property only of the mathematical model, because the concept of probability is logically never applicable to a concrete physical system.

Albert Einstein. The probability waves are more abstract than the electromagnetic and gravitational fields. . . . The only physical significance of the probability wave is that it enables us to answer sensible statistical questions in the case of many particles as well as of one.

James Jeans. The waves cannot have any material or real existence apart from ourselves. They are not constituents of nature, but only of our efforts to understand nature, being only the ingredients of a mental picture that we draw for ourselves in the hopes of rendering intelligible the mathematical formulae of quantum mechanics.

Eddington. What precisely is the entity which we suppose to be oscillating when we speak of the waves in the sub-aether? It is denoted by psi. . . . The probability of the particle being within a given region is proportional to the amount of psi in the region.

C. F. von Weizsäcker. The concepts "particle" and "wave" or, more exactly, "spatially discontinuous event" and "spatially continuous event" appear therefore as interpretations demanded by the forms of our perception for processes that are no longer immediately perceptible.

Hans Reichenbach. The conditions through which the corpuscles pass are so arranged that their statistical regularity is described by waves.

Philipp Frank.   All the confusion is produced by speaking of an object instead of the way in which some words are used. . . . The mental or idealistic character of the new mechanics is occasionally demonstrated by calling the de Broglie waves "waves of probability." . . . This interpretation is certainly a misleading one. The new mechanics describes the percentage of electrons which strike on the average a certain region of the screen. There is nothing psychological involved . . .

We invite trouble if we ask the question what are the "real" physical objects in subatomic physics. Are the particles "real" or are the de Broglie waves . . . "real"? . . . If we say that these "waves of probability" are "real," we use the word "wave" in the same sense that it is used in expressions like "wave of suicides," "wave of disease," etc. . . . an unusual use of the word "real."

I think that the question put by Abel can be answered in the affirmative. No doubt, physicists know something about the world of an electron, though this knowledge cannot be given an unambiguous formulation in the language of experiment.

Apparently, our knowledge of the external world can be represented in the language of such abstract speculations that their interpretation in terms of experimental concepts proves difficult — there are no means in our everyday language to denote the reality of a phenomenon in some new quantum–mechanical sense. Actually, a theoretical physicist does not need this: he perceives and describes the world in the language of the abstract quantum–mechanical concepts. Uninterpretability of theoretical constructions in the language of ordinary notions is the indicator of the abstractness of the language. Physics appears to be a *bilingual* discipline. Some physicists understand mainly one language, and some, another language. This divergence apparently increases in the course of time; Babelian difficulties are revealed even in a single field of knowledge. But no matter how much physicists complain of this bilingual system and of the mutual misunderstanding that follows, it is still by virtue of this variety of language that the development of modern physics was possible. One of the languages of physics proved suitable for experimentation, and the other one, for constructing complex logical patterns. A physical theory proper is created somewhere at the intersection, where logical constructions are interpreted in the inconvenient language of experimental ideas. As a result, physical theories, when verbalized, turn *fuzzy*. This difficulty must be familiar to anyone who has tried to get acquainted with these theories using only the language of experimentation.

Now I shall make a small digression and then go back to our ordinary language. If we compare it with the language of physics, we shall see that there is no essential difference here. The language of physics, with its bilingual structure, embodies in the most picturesque way the features which are to some vague degree intrinsic in our ordinary language. Our ordinary language carries in itself the elements of abstractness – the words of a language represented in a text need interpretation which, according to my theory, is given by a Bayesian model. Accepting the Bayesian model, we assume that one word is interpreted in the many words which we use to explain its content after the text is read and its general sense understood. Actually, in our everyday speech, we deal with a bilingual construction. We can mentally imagine a language with a unilingual structure: it would be extremely clumsy, and the phrases would be immensely long. Uttering something, we would have to interpret the utterance on the spot or use an enormously rich vocabulary. The progress of verbal thinking lies in a transition from the image thought to the logical one. Outwardly, it found its expression in language which, adjusting itself to logical thinking, became more and more abstract. Logical constructions must be compact and not as fuzzy as the images are. Logic could have resulted in the impoverishment of language, but this has not happened in the development of the bilingual system. The tendency to abstraction found its highest manifestation in the language of physics. The question is often asked: In what way should the language of science be regarded – is it natural or artificial? It seems to me that it is a natural language, for it has been developing gradually, and in it features are reflected which also manifest themselves in ordinary language, though in a somewhat underdeveloped form.

It would be interesting to trace the historical development of the abstractness of the language of physics. Here we deal with the change of language which occurs almost before our very eyes; at least, it is observed in the available sources. I tried to do this by watching the number of symbols of the mathematical alphabet, the number of words – that is, mathematical operations (for us, a word is a concept denoting, say, the partial derivative $\partial y/\partial t$ or the inverse matrix M^{-1}, etc.) – and the number of phrases (symbols and operations over them separated from one another and from the rest of the text by a blank; e.g., a mathematical expression $m = \sum_{i=1}^{n} \alpha_i m_i$ is considered a phrase). In order not to encumber the text with illustrations, I give part of the material obtained in Fig. 6 and 7. (All the data on the figures are given with respect to a conditional page containing 2,500 printed signs; histograms have been built on the basis of random samples, consisting of 10 percent of the text which made about 50 pages. The data were collected and processed by S. G. Kostina.) At first glance, these drawings cause some bewilderment. We see that for the courses of general physics the distribution functions of the number of pages according to the number of symbols and words (mathematical

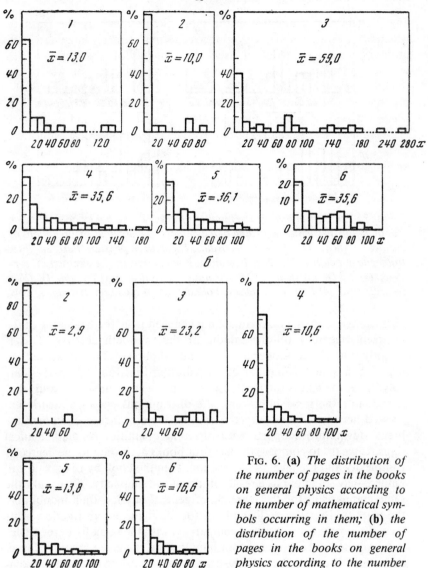

FIG. 6. **(a)** *The distribution of the number of pages in the books on general physics according to the number of mathematical symbols occurring in them;* **(b)** *the distribution of the number of pages in the books on general physics according to the number of mathematical operations occurring in them (in the book by H. Wolf there are no mathematical operations). (1) H. Wolf, Wolfian experimental physics (translated by M. V. Lomonosov), 1760; (2) M. Speranski, Physics, selected from the best authors ordered and supplemented in 1797, published in 1872, previously circulated only as a manuscript; (3) D. M. Perevostshikov, Guide to experimental physics, 1883; (4) F. F. Petrushevsky, Course of observational physics, 1874; (5) E. Grimsel, The course of physics, part 1-4, 1932-1933; (6) N. D. Papalexi, The course of physics, vol. I-II, 1948.*

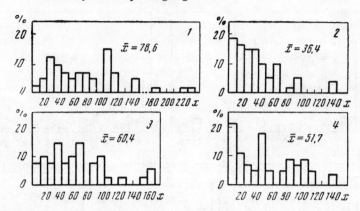

FIG. 7. *The distribution of the number of pages in the books on field theory and quantum mechanics according to the number of mathematical operations occurring in them. (1) A. A. Eihenvald, Theoretical physics, Part IV (Electromagnetic field), 1931; (2) I. E. Tamm, Foundations of the electricity theory, 1946; (3) L. D. Landau, E. M. Lifshits, Theoretical physics, vol. IV (Field theory), 1948; (4) D. I. Blokhintsev, Foundations of quantum mechanics, 1949.*

operations) occurring on them are not changed from the beginning of the nineteenth century till the middle of the twentieth century. This is roughly true of the number of mathematical phrases. For books on field theory and quantum mechanics, distribution functions differ considerably: here, the text is obviously richer in mathematical words, and what is probably the most important, the distributions are of a clearly expressed heterogeneous character; that is, these branches of knowledge break down into subparts with different quantities of mathematical signs. If we try to compare the last four books according to the degree of complexity and the level of abstraction, then the book by Eihenvald will immediately stand out as a result of its relative simplicity. If we make the same comparison for the manuals of general physics, then indubitably the book by Papalexi will stand out for the rigor and abstraction of its style. In any case, it is beyond comparison with the book by Perevostshikov. All these differences cannot be traced on the given graphs. Hence, the following conclusion may be drawn: we are observing that the evolution of the language of mathematics takes place in physical texts: the situation becomes more complicated not because of the increase in the number of mathematical signs, words, or phrases but because of the complexity of the content. Say, one symbol may denote a scalar, as well as a vector, a matrix, one operation — a derivative as well as a divergence, a curl, etc. It appears that the evolution of texts cannot be traced by mere statistical–semiotic analysis. It is syntactic analysis which is necessary, and such an analysis is difficult to carry out quantitatively; at least, I am unable to do this. But if we still restrict ourselves to statistical–semiotic analysis, it turns out that the distribution function of pages on the number of signs, words, and phrases is typical for some fields of knowledge and, as a matter of fact, does not change in time.

There is one more philosophical question of an ontological character connected with the study of the language of physics. Previously, in the Introduction to this book, I spoke about primitive faith in the possibility of understanding the way the world is built by constructing a universal language grammar. When physics was going through the classical period of its development, its language seemed to have a precise grammar of monosemantic deterministic links. Hence, a conclusion was drawn about the arrangement of the world. It was strictly deterministic. Perhaps it was Laplace who expressed the deterministic concept of naïve materialism in the most vivid way. He considered that the state of world at a given moment of time is determined by an infinite number of parameters depending upon the infinite number of differential equations. If a universal mind could write down and then integrate these equations, we would know everything about the past, the future, and the present of the world.

Now the situation has changed considerably. The first flaw in the universal deterministic grammar emerged with the appearance of statistical thermodynamics; the second one, with the development of quantum mechanics, which added probability considerations to the basis of causality; and the third one, with statistical description of complete, diffuse systems of the macroworld (Nalimov, 1971). The grammar of the language by which we describe the world more and more moves from the deterministic mode to the probabilistic. Probably this will at last make scientists view the world as a probabilistically organized structure. It already seems naïve to think that the world is organized in the same way as the grammar of modern physical language.

Mathematics as a Language of Other Branches of Knowledge

Logical structure of applied mathematics. Mathematization of knowledge is much spoken about nowadays. What is usually meant is the penetration of mathematics into such fields of knowledge as engineering sciences, chemistry, biology, and social sciences, where mathematics has hitherto been used sparingly. It is often said that the broad penetration of mathematics into these fields of knowledge leads to the strengthening of the logical structure of these fields of knowledge and to their gradual transformation into a calculus.

I think that in reality the case is somewhat different. Mathematization of knowledge consists first of all in the wide usage of mathematical language to describe the external world and formulate recommendations for our activity in this world. Superficially, the structure of the language of such disciplines becomes much more formal. Many formulations turn into axioms, and the inferences from them turn into theorems. But all this merely creates an external similarity with pure mathematics. As we have already mentioned above, a defining characteristic of the latter lies in the creation of integral structures — laconic formulations rich in their logical consequences. In applied mathematics, integral structures have disappeared altogether; in some cases they have turned into mosaics of criteria — even the question of consistency itself, which plays such a great part in the structures of pure mathematics, has lost its sense for a mosaic collection of axioms. In other cases, mathematical language began to serve for recording statements based upon some rather vague, intuitive considerations. In this case the chain of syllogisms disappeared completely, and this chain is at least an external characteristic of constructions in pure mathematics.

The mosaic character of initial premises in constructions of applied mathematics has been considered in detail in a previous book (Nalimov, 1971) and is illustrated by two examples. One of them deals with the design of experiments. Optimality criteria of the experiment may be considered as axioms, and corresponding designs, as theorems. In some cases these theorems are derived by using relatively simple mathematical means such as linear algebra; in other cases quite modern mathematics is applied, namely, game theory, set theory, functional analysis, etc. Today the state of affairs is such that even for a simple problem, the so-called problems of surface design, there are 22 criteria of optimality. Not all of them are equally important, but still there are about 15 indubitably powerful criteria. The system of axiomatic criteria here is clearly mosaic. For such a mosaic system of criteria, it is absolutely senseless to pose the question of their inner consistency.[2] It is just in the simplest case, i.e., for linear designs, that a part of the above-enumerated criteria appear compatible: this means that experimental designs may be built which would satisfy several criteria simultaneously. The situation becomes still worse for the second-order designs, especially if they are given in a discrete way. As a result we have a variety of designs called to life by various criteria, which do not lend themselves to systematization and comparison.

The second example deals with prediction involving random processes.

---

[2] Criteria may be mutually exclusive: say, in one case we may wish to have a model which behaves best when it is clearly inadequate for the phenomena described; in another case we may, on the contrary, wish to spot the inadequacy as early as possible.

Here the method of Kolmogorov-Wiener is well known. This was discovered in the framework of a well-developed system of notions of stationary random process. But actually all or almost all actually observed processes become non-stationary, judging at least by the behavior of their mathematical expectation. There is no mathematical theory of non-stationary random processes. Nevertheless, according to the picturesque expression in one foreign paper, there exist myriads of papers which suggest different solutions to this problem. The best ones are constructed as follows: a model of a non-stationary random process is suggested, which is formulated as an axiom so that it can be neither proved nor refuted. Proceeding from this model by means of constructing a chain of mathematical judgments, the formula for prediction is found. In the worst papers, the solution is given even without a clear-cut formulation of the initial model. Here we have not managed to give a list of initial models–postulates, similar to the axioms of the experimental design: so far nobody could classify or codify them in any way whatsoever.

The state of matters is the same in computational mathematics, e.g., in the solution of problems connected with the search for the extrema of multidimensional and multiparametric functions. Here a variety of recommendations is brought to computational algorithms, but these techniques do not lend themselves to comparison and·systematization; they are based on premises forming a mosaic structure.

As soon as we try to carry out the comparison of two procedures in the search for extrema, we must immediately introduce new axioms giving such a system of comparison. It is possible to suggest many such axioms. Each of these axiomatic systems creates its own metatheory. Further, the need emerges in creation of a metatheory for a comparative separate metatheory. In the above-mentioned work (Nalimov, 1971), this statement was illustrated with one example, namely, with comparing two procedures of adaptational optimization of industrial processes: a regular simplex procedure and a random search.

In simplex designing, experimental points are placed in the vertices of a regular k-dimensional simplex. The method of random search in its simplest form reduces to the following. An initial point x_k is chosen in a k-dimensional space, and a straight line is drawn through it in a random direction. On this line, on both sides from x_k at the distance ϱ_k, two experiments are performed; the experiment with better results determines a new initial point x_{k+1} for a random construction of the second line, etc. The comparison of the random search method with the simplex procedure can be made only by simulating problems on computers. But in what way can this be done? In one paper it was required that ϱ_k should equal ϱ_r, the radius of the sphere circumscribed around the simplex. From the standpoint of a mathematician, such an approach proved quite logical; it resulted in construction of a precise mathematical system of judgments, and it appeared possible to prove a number of lemmas and theorems. In the case of the experimenter, however, such a requirement caused perplexity; in performing a random search, the researcher even in the second experiment crosses the boundaries of the cube limiting the region of experimentation of the space of independent variables. The larger the dimension of the space of independent variables, the less advantageous the conditions are under which the simplex procedure is placed: it will be performed in the sphere of a smaller radius than that of the random search procedure. In order to make the random search strategy comparable with the simplex procedure, the former should be modified in a special way. Here the very formulation of the problem becomes odd: an algorithm of an applied significance should be modified to become comparable with another one. In one paper an interesting collection of criteria is given for searching an extremum. It is divided into local and global criteria. In local criteria, losses during searches are considered, i.e., "fast actions" at one step and the probability of an error (the probability of an erroneous step). In the non-local criteria the number of trials is considered which is necessary for solving the problem set with a given "divergence" (precision) understood as the average deviation of the value found from the extremum in a given situation. It does not obviously demand too strong an imagination to increase the number of criteria for comparing two so-difficult-to-compare strategies; using these criteria, we shall still obtain new results. Is there any sense in all these activities? Despite the logically evident hopelessness of the problem of confronting techniques based upon different axiomatic systems, much activity is still going on in this field.

Here I should like to answer a question frequently posed: Is it not the case that now in applied mathematics the same situation exists as took place in pure mathematics at the time, say, of Newton and Leibniz? Then there existed no conception of mathematical structures. In any case, mathematicians had learned to differentiate before it was well understood what a function is. We think that, posing such a problem, we must state that there is an immense difference. Even at the initial level of mathematical knowledge, as it was at the time, people found precise and unambiguous solutions, though, as a rule, they could not formulate them as theorems. If we are allowed to assume the viewpoint of Platonic realism,[3] the hypothesis may be stated that mathematicians operated as if they guessed the existence of undiscovered structures. In any case, this is

---

[3] The doctrine shared by some mathematicians, apparently Gödel included, according to which mathematicians do not invent their structures, but discover them in a way similar to that by which physicists discover their laws.

how Bourbaki described the state of matters in seventeenth century mathematics (1948):

> . . . one has to acknowledge that the way towards modern analysis was opened when Newton and Leibniz, having turned their back to the past, temporarily decided to justify the new methods not by rigorous proofs but by the abundance and consistency of results. (p. 188)

In applied mathematics, or, to be more precise, in the applied mathematics which is the subject of our consideration, there is a variety of results, but evidently there is no agreement.

There is another characteristic feature of applied mathematics to be pointed out: if it wishes to remain realistic, it must avoid too rigorous statements. Here is an interesting consideration of Schwartz (1962), an American mathematician:

> The physicist rightly dreads precise argument, since an argument which is only convincing if precise loses all its force if the assumptions upon which it is based are slightly changed while an argument which is convincing though imprecise may well be stable under small perturbations of its underlying axioms. (p. 357)

The statement by Schwartz may be illustrated with examples from the historical development of mathematical statistics. One of the language functions mentioned above is the reduction of information, its compact representation. The well-known English statistician R. Fisher worked out this question at a high level of rigor and suggested algorithms which allowed those parameter estimations which gave effective estimates: that is, the estimates with minimal variance. However, soon it turned out that effective estimates can actually be ineffective. The point is that they proved sensitive to the initial premises. Everything is all right if we deal with the results of observations which may be interpreted as a pure sample, i.e., as a sample out of one general population. But practically we must always be dealing with impure samples which can be interpreted as belonging to general populations with different parameters. And if so, then it is more reasonable to use robust estimates, insensitive to initial premises but less efficient in case these premises are carried out. The algorithms of robust estimates are to be found not upon the ground of strict and elegant constructions but just as the results of simulating these problems by a computer. Robustness is often encountered when choosing criteria for verification of statistical hypotheses such as the hypotheses concerning homogeneity of sampling variances. The well-known Bartlet criteria which had formerly been used for the solution of this problem appeared extremely sensitive to the initial premises. Now, in solving similar problems, we must often restrict ourselves to the problems arising from intuitive considerations instead of applying strict but not robust criteria.

Thus, mathematization of knowledge does not lead to deep axiomatization and high logical rigor of judgments though here the rigor increases. We cannot speak about these mathematized sciences turning into a calculus.

The language of applied mathematics.   Mathematics, in the problems considered, is used just as a language permitting one to obtain logical inferences quickly from initial premises. This language is convenient as a result of its compactness and precision, but in experienced hands it is never made too strict. There is no need to explain and ground the inference rules again and again. Finally, when using this near universal language, associations emerge with other problems, solved by means of the same system of judgments, and this adds to the conviction of the new constructions. Here mathematics is used just as a language to record briefly a system of logical judgment. In this connection it is appropriate to recall a well-known but not at all universally acknowledged thesis by Frege–Russell about mathematics being no more than a part of logic.

The language of applied mathematics, used in chemical and biological problems and especially in the problems of social sciences, becomes much less abstract than the language of mathematical symbols used in theoretical physics. Using the language of mathematics, the research worker always takes into consideration what underlies mathematical symbols in this or that concrete problem. And if the first serious difference between pure and applied mathematics lies in the absence of unified logical structures rich in their logical consequences in a system of judgments, the second difference of no less importance lies in the necessity to follow rather attentively what lies behind the symbols in applied problems of this type. Five examples illustrate this statement.

1. Dealing with questions of the growth of science (Nalimov and Mul'chenko, 1969), we have formulated the informational model of science development. The following postulates have been formulated giving the growth of publications in various situations:

$$\frac{dy}{dt} = ky$$

or

$$\frac{dy}{dt} = ky\,(b - y)$$

where y is the number of publications, k and b are certain constants, and t is time.

The first postulate states that the rate of growth of the number of publications must be proportional to their present number. This postulate must be accepted for the situation in which there are no factors hampering the process of growth. The second postulate writes down the simplest mechanism of self-braking which begins to tell only when the number of publications becomes comparable in its value with the constant b. Integrating, we obtain an exponential in the first case and the equation of an S-shaped logistic curve in the second case. Further, these functions are used to describe the phenomena observed in reality (naturally, in this case the parameter's functions are estimated, the adequacy of the hypothesis is tested, etc.). The growth curves given by the exponents may be extrapolated into the future, yielding obviously absurd values. This will indicate that the mechanism of growth must change. Very complicated situations can occur when in different periods of time different countries and different fields of knowledge enter the game. In this case the results of observations should be presented by a sum of exponents, but this is not very convenient; expanding the sum of exponents into a Taylor series and limiting oneself to the first term, one may confine oneself to the presentation of the results by a sliding exponent, with the parameters being constant only at a certain time interval. In short, it is out of the above rather simply worded postulates that we receive rich logical consequences permitting us to discuss complicated situations more easily. But, certainly, these postulates cannot be regarded as an attempt to give a profound axiomatization to the "science of science." Here, in the language of differential equations, we have formulated everything we could have formulated in our everyday language, but in this case this would have been done in a vaguer form. The plausibility of our reasoning increases when we recall that similar systems of judgments are used in biology when describing the processes of population growth and in physics in deducing the light absorption law or the law of radioactive decay. It is pleasing to know that in all these cases we use the same logical constructions operating with one and the same universal language. However, reasoning like this, we constantly remember what underlies the symbols and formulae constructed out of these symbols. Think of an imaginary experiment: a set of publications and a portion of radioactive substance are delivered to the Moon. Both the publication growth and the radioactive decay go on exponentially. We need no further reasoning to say that the radioactive substance will continue to decay exponentially, but the number of publications will not grow further. Integrating differential equations, we acted like pure mathematicians, not caring about the sense of symbols; but while interpreting the functions obtained we do think of what lies behind the symbols and consequently we do not think like pure mathematicians.

2. The second example is a wrong interpretation of the Zipf law. Assume that there is a text with a total number of words D_N constructed

upon a vocabulary containing N individual words. Denote by n the rank (the ordinal number according to the decreasing word frequency) and by d_n the frequency of occurrence of the word in a text. Then the Zipf law is written as follows:

$$d_n = \frac{k}{n}$$

where k is a constant found from the normalization conditions:

$$D_N = d_1 + k \ln N$$

Now assume that one would like to compute the value of D_{N+1} using this correlation and substituting $N + 1$ for N under the sign of the logarithm. Can this be done? If the new $(n + 1)$th word of our vocabulary will take the $(n + 1)$th place in accordance with its frequency, then certainly this can be done. But just imagine that there has appeared such a new word as, say, "cosmonaut." It will not take the last place in the row of words arranged according to their frequency; a rearrangement of words will occur and the parameter k will not be a constant any longer, that is, renorming will take place. In this case we cannot compute the value D_{N+1} without knowing the new value of k. This specific restriction imposed upon the norming correlation is not written down mathematically. The research worker must keep it in mind; in his desire to use the norming expression as an extrapolating formula, he must think of what is not written down but is only implicit. Obviously, this does not correspond to the pure mathematician's mode of thinking.

If we do not pay attention to the content underlying the formulae, we can obtain absolutely absurd results. I once came across a publication in which a norming expression analogous to the one above was used to study the dynamics of a system. Considering N as a time function, the author began to differentiate the norming function with respect to time, assuming that the parameter k remained constant, and made some curious conclusions on the basis of the results he obtained. When his attention was called to the impossibility of doing this, the whole system of judgments collapsed, for there were no data on the behavior of the derivative dk/dt in time. It seems clear that no information about the dynamics of a system can be drawn from an expression which does not contain such information, but the author was very anxious to do just that.

3. The third example concerns approximating formulae. Is it possible to build approximating formulae in applied mathematics, taking into account only the mutual position of the experimentally observed points and without caring about the vaguely formulated entities underlying these

observations. In one scientific paper, the curve of growth of scientific workers in the Soviet Union was approximated in a deliberately complex way. The author divided this curve into separate regions and invented specific mechanisms for each of them, writing them down by various differential equations. Models thus obtained agreed well with the observed data and, what seems especially curious, they were perfectly linked with each other, thus creating the impression of a well-elaborated system. The author was so absorbed in his constructions that he even decided that he had inferred the models immediately from the results of observations, not from a certain system of postulates. But there is one thing which should be observed carefully: the unsmoothed run of the growth curve is to be explained more reasonably not by the influence of a specific, complicated, and often changing mechanism of growth, but merely by the arbitrary character of the decisions taken by financial bodies to fund science development and the agencies taking stock of the number of scientific workers (the very definition of the notion of a scientific worker and the system of their registration changes every now and then). Then it will be possible to describe the breaches in the exponential run of the curve in terms of fluctuations. The decision about the choice of an approximating formula has to be taken with attention to considerations not expressed in mathematical language.

4. The fourth example deals with applications of the classical methods of mathematical physics. The heat conduction equation

$$\frac{\partial u}{\partial t} = \frac{\partial^2 u}{\partial x^2}$$

can be solved for $-\infty < x < +\infty$, $-T < t \leqslant 0$ where T is a positive number. If the initial condition is given, namely, the temperature distribution at the present moment

$$u(x, 0) = \varphi(x)$$

then we shall find a solution, giving the temperature distribution in the past.

A mathematician asks: How far back is it reasonable to search the temperature distribution in studying space objects, e.g., the Moon, using the heat conduction equation or its generalized form? The answer to this question should be sought by drawing in some additional considerations, which again cannot be written mathematically. Making decisions as to the boundaries of the formula applications, we use information which the formula does not contain.

5. The last example concerns the use of theoretically probabilistic

argumentation in the sphere of applied investigations. Here it is quite easy to formulate a deliberately senseless problem. In a well-known English journal, *Nature*, the question of the correctness of statistical inference was discussed recently. The following example was given: four kings of the Hanoverian House, Edward I, II, III, and IV died on the same day of the week, on Saturday. The probability of such a random event is extremely small: $1/7^4 \simeq 1/2,500$. Won't a mathematician hence infer that Saturday is a fatal day for Edwards of the Hanoverian House? Certainly not. Using some supplementary consideration, he will reformulate the problem (for details, see Nalimov, 1971). A curious paradox was formulated by Kendall (1966), a well-known English statistician. It deals with the experiment of tossing a coin. It is not only the position of the coin fall (i.e., heads or tails) that is connected with this event, but also the character of its sound in falling down, the duration of the fall, and an infinite variety of other phenomena. The probability of joint occurrence of all these events is negligible, and still on this basis a mathematician does not conclude that a coin cannot fall down; he takes into account a number of supplementary considerations and formulates the problem in another way. By the way, from the same considerations it follows that the statement about the impossibility of the emergence of structures by an act of random association of molecules (Quastler, 1964) cannot be taken too seriously. If it does turn out that in a system of inference the probability of the random emergence of life equals 10^{-255} or less, it still seems probable enough but only if the hypothesis as a whole does not cause objections due to other much more general but poorly formalized reasons.

Thus, we see that in the applied problems in question, mathematics functions as a language. In judgments stated in this language, we attach importance not only and not primarily to the grammar of this language, but to what we wish to say about the aspect of the world under consideration, proceeding from some reasons based upon our intuitive concepts. Here it is appropriate to recall the trend in the study of the foundations of mathematics, traditionally called "intuitionism." It is connected with such names as Breuer, Weyl (1927), and Heyting (1934, 1956). I cannot dwell on this complicated system in more detail, since it is connected not only with mathematics but also with the psychology of thinking. I shall restrict myself to a few remarks. In the opinion of intuitional mathematicians, the significance of logic is no more than that of a language whose cogency is determined only by intuitive clarity and immediate evidence of each elementary step of discourse. Apparently, now mathematicians have mostly given up the attempt of grounding mathematics. On this basis the Bourbaki (1948) speak about it as follows[4]:

[4] Perhaps, Bourbaki's statement is too strongly worded. It is necessary to take into consideration that many intuitional views have been accepted by mathematicians of the constructive trend; besides, some

The intuitionist school which is remembered only as a historic curiosity, in any case did service to mathematics by making its opponents, i.e. the overwhelming majority of mathematicians, formulate their position more precisely and become more conscious of the reasons (some of logical nature, others of psychological one) of their confidence in mathematics. (p. 56)

Our interest is not exhausted by this. In the applied problems considered, mathematics plays the part of a language in which the cogency of judgments can be founded from the same standpoint from which intuitionists wanted to found the system of judgments concerning pure mathematics. Statements made in mathematical language in applied problems must always and first of all possess intuitive cogency; this is their substantiation. Here the borderline between pure and applied mathematics is especially distinct.

The language of applied mathematics as a metalanguage. The language of mathematics, used for description of applied problems, plays the part of a metalanguage in relation to the language in which these problems have been formulated and discussed previously. Sometimes the statements in the metalanguage become so general that it leads to the *creation of metatheories*; here it is a hierarchical structure of theories that is in question. A metatheory estimates logical consistency of hierarchically lower theories.

In particular, this has happened in mathematical statistics. Its language became a metalanguage as related to the languages of various experimental sciences. In the language of mathematics, the statements are made about judgments built in the object–languages. These statements became so generalized that there appeared a metatheory, that is, a mathematical theory of experiment. Its fundamental ideas are formulated in detail in my earlier book (Nalimov, 1971). Here, I shall briefly summarize these formulations. The mathematical theory of experiment: (i) allowed one to formalize clearly the process of decision making in experimental testing of hypotheses; (ii) it demanded randomization of the conditions of the experimental process in order to avoid biased estimates in studies of complex–diffuse systems; (iii) it formulated clear-cut claims with reference to the algorithms of the reduction of information; (iv) it formulated the concept of a sequential experiment; (v) it formulated the concept of optimal usage of the space of independent variables (in the design of experiment).

I have already cited (see above, page 38) the statements of Kleene about metamathematics having to be intuitively understandable in its content: with this help we must understand how the rules of formal

---

mathematicians (although few in number) working in the field of foundations of mathematics share the concept of intuitionists. But discussing this question is not our task.

mathematics are applied. In applied problems, mathematics itself serves as a metatheory, and because of this it must also be intuitively grounded, despite the outwardly formal character of its language. It is interesting to note the fact that here the metalanguage proves to be more formalized than the object-language.

More often than not, we hear the statement that the language of mathematics is abstract. This statement is not quite precise. In fact it is possible to build a scale of the abstraction of mathematical languages. On the left of this scale we shall find the abstract language of pure mathematics. Using this language, as I have already shown, a mathematician looks only at symbols and not at what is behind them. This is followed by the mathematical language of modern physics. Here the degree of abstraction is lower; the language of theoretical physics is not comparable with the language of chess calculus. The language of theoretical physics appears to be connected with the external world, though in it notions have been formulated which are hardly interpretable in the language of experiment. Finally, the degree of abstraction becomes still lower when the language of applied mathematics is used in engineering sciences, in biology, and in social sciences. The research worker speaking this language always keeps in mind what is behind the symbols. But sometimes, even for social sciences, quite abstract languages are created, e.g., the theory of context-free languages. It is an absolutely abstract theory which does not differ from constructions of pure mathematics where the connection with the external world is realized only at the stage of interpretation.

Structure of pure mathematics as grammar of the language of applied mathematics.   If mathematics in applied problems plays the part of language, mathematical structures of this language can be naturally regarded as its grammar. One can put a question as to whether it is necessary for one who wants to use this language pragmatically to know this grammar perfectly. Evidently, it is not necessary; at least, the ordinary language can be used without any knowledge of its grammar. I shall remind the reader here that during the first decade after the October revolution it was asserted, strange as it seems, that Russian grammar should not be taught in secondary schools, and indeed it was not taught; nevertheless, the graduates spoke the language properly, though they did not always spell the words correctly.

Above, I have already mentioned the example demonstrating the way the language of differential calculus is used for discussing the rate of scientific growth. Is it necessary for the participants in such conversation to have a clear notion of the foundations of mathematical analysis, based upon the concept of set theory? Evidently not; it is only necessary to have the most general grasp of the rules of differentiation and integration, almost the same as those known at time of Newton and Leibniz and their closest successors.

As was mentioned above, probability theory began to be considered a modern mathematical discipline only after the Soviet academician A. N. Kolmogorov gave its axiomatic construction. It turned out that the theory of probability could be constructed in the frame of general measure theory with a single special assumption: the measure of the whole space must equal unity (probability can never exceed unity, which is the maximal probability of the necessary event). Probability theory formulated as a mathematical discipline appeared only as a part of a very general mathematical conception with a clear logical structure of an absolutely abstract character. However, this approach to the definition of probability proved practically unavoidable for the experimenters. It had been the frequency definition that had exercised great stimulating influence over them. This definition runs as follows: probability is defined as the limit of the frequency of occurrence of the event, when the number of tests increases without limit. From the experimenter's point of view, this definition seems intuitively obvious, though it is logically inconsistent. Kolmogorov (1956) wrote that such definitions would be as odd as, for example, a geometrical "definition" of a point as something obtained as a result of the infinite splitting of a piece of chalk, making its diameter twice as small each time. Further, he says that this frequency definition of probability containing a finite transition is just a mathematical illusion, for in reality one cannot imagine such infinite successions of tests where all the conditions of the experiment would be kept constant. True, Kolmogorov also pays attention to the fact that, in solving applied problems, it is not at all necessary to give a formal definition of probability. Here it is sufficient to speak about probability as a number around which the frequencies are concentrated under specially formulated conditions, so that this tendency to concentration manifests itself more clearly and precisely with growth (up to a reasonable limit) of the number of tests. It is noteworthy that neither of these two definitions solves the paradoxes which can be invented if we wish to apply probabilistic notions formally for the description of real problems.

Another point is relevant here: the grammar of mathematical language cannot be always used for constructing an inference system for actual problems. Let me give an illustration.

In mathematical statistics, a theorem is proved stating that the estimates of regression coefficients obtained with the help of the least squares method prove unbiased and efficient in the class of all linear estimates. Generally speaking, this is true only when all independent variables and all corresponding regression coefficients with mathematical expectation differing from zero are taken into account. But mathematicians never emphasize this condition, and actually they need not do so. A mathematician always deals only with the model which he has in front of him. He cannot take into account something which is implied but unwritten. An experimenter thinks in another way. Applying regression analysis to the description of some industrial process, he realizes that far from all possible and really existing independent variables are included in his mathematical model. Many of them are not included in part because of the practical impossibility of measuring them. In this case the regression coefficients estimated appear biased. The bias may be so great that the results of regression analysis lose any value. The example illustrating this statement was discussed in detail earlier (Nalimov, 1971, p. 162), and in this book (p. 135) I have already said that in solving real problems it is often more convenient to use robust estimates instead of the efficient estimates following from the grammar of mathematical statistics. (Robust estimates are those which are non-sensitive to the breach of the initial premises of the distribution function.)

The variety of the dialects of mathematical language.   It is a fact, universally acknowledged, that one and the same practical problem can be put down and discussed in a variety of mathematical dialects. At one time it can be formulated, say, at the level of deterministic representations, by writing the hypothetical mechanism of the process by means of differential equations; at another time, the same problem can be discussed in probabilistic terms. Different dialects can also be used. At one time we may use the traditional language of classical mathematical statistics; another time, the language of information theory. For example, assume that the question involves the optimization of a technological process. We may try to capture it by a strictly deterministic model; then the optimization problem will involve the calculus of variations with such new branches as the method of dynamic programming and the maximum method of L. S. Pontryagin. However, if we regard the level of our knowledge critically enough, then we shall have to explain the phenomena in the language of multivariate regression analysis or in the language of principal components, and perhaps even in the language of factor analysis. If anybody still dislikes the probabilistic language, it is possible to use Boolean algebra. In the latter case, the intervals of variation of the independent variables should be divided into separate areas, these intervals being encoded in a binary system of numbers. Further, it will be possible to apply the method of minimization of the Boolean functions of the algebra of logic. In this model the purpose function and the predicates will be linked by the logical operators "and," "or," "no."

During a single academic seminar, the same problem may be discussed in different dialects, which is a very rare situation for ordinary languages. Apparently, adequate translation from one mathematical dialect into another is impossible, just as, strictly speaking, translation is also impossible for ordinary languages, and for abstract, strictly formalized languages.

It is impossible to establish a criterion which would permit one to give preference to this or that mathematical dialect in the description of a real problem. Moreover, it is impossible even to suggest a criterion to test the hypothesis that any one dialect of the mathematical languages is preferable for describing a certain situation. Seemingly, the following statement would serve as such a criterion: the language is acceptable for the description of a real problem if it can supply a mathematical model giving an adequate description of the observed phenomenon. But here we can remember Russell's paradox (1956): assume that a person regularly hires a taxi and draws a graph plotting the number of a day on the abscissas and the car number on the ordinates. If n observations are obtained, they can be represented by a polynomial of the $(n-1)$ degree, the corresponding curve crossing all the points observed as is well known in mathematics. The model will be adequate to some extent, although strictly speaking here there are no degrees of freedom left for adequacy testing, but now try to forecast the number of tomorrow's taxi. The same experimental data could be represented as a random process, and then the problem of forecasting would become reasonable. The question of model choosing, and consequently of choosing a dialect in which the problem is discussed, is not solved by a simple verification of the adequacy of the hypothesis. The same difficulty may arise in the problem of interpolation. I once came across a case when, during an experiment, a research worker could obtain experimental points placed only in the left and in the right part of a two-dimensional graph; the middle of the graph remained empty, and it was necessary to find an approximating formula for the run of the function in the region with missing observations. Naturally, a mathematician immediately proposed approximating the results of observations by a polynomial of a higher degree; the graph of this function with its multiextremal character irritated the experimenter. By the way, this is rather a typical conflict situation; the research experimenter intuitively has certain prior information about the mechanism of the process studied but cannot formulate it in a form acceptable for a mathematician.

The on-going process of the mathematization of knowledge leads to the appearance of a variety of publications in which the same or at least similar situations are described by a diversity of models formulated in different mathematical dialects. Wide application of mathematics only aggravates the Babelian difficulties in science. Whether a criterion will appear which would moderate this process is a difficult question. There is one requirement which might serve as such a criterion, namely, that of admitting the right to usage only of those mathematical dialects whose application leads to the formulation of consistent and meaningful meta-theories, such as the mathematical theory of experiment which has resulted from the broad application of probabilistic language for the description of experimental situations. But here a new question immediately arises: What can be considered as a consistent metatheory? Metatheories might emerge which are closed in themselves. While creating a metatheory or its fragments, a research worker brought up in the traditions of pure mathematics can formulate postulates considering only the logical consequences following from them; he may not be in the least troubled by the realistic grounds of his logical constructions. In many countries the question is already being widely discussed of the danger of the so-called "prestige" papers in which a mathematician lacking mathematical imagination formulates an applied problem in one of the mathematical dialects. This is often done merely for the sake of increasing his prestige and without caring about the reality underlying the problem formulation. Here again, there are no tests to be suggested for classifying such problems as "prestige" ones.

It is noteworthy that in pure mathematics two fundamental linguistic channels are also easily traced: the language of continuous mathematics and that of the discrete. From the time of Newton, preference has been given to the first of these, but now there have appeared branches of mathematics such as graph theory, game theory, or the automata theory which are already subdivisions of finite mathematics. Modern computers are called digital, and this also emphasizes the discrete character of their language. Hence arises the problem of the modernization of teaching mathematics, of the transition to the language of finite sets. Unfortunately, I cannot dwell upon this complicated question here.

The polymorphism of mathematical language.   For a long time, the language of mathematics remained strictly monomorphous. It was used only for the description of those well-organized systems with which traditional physics was concerned. Recently, we began using the language of mathematics for the description of poorly organized diffuse systems as well, and it immediately acquired some traits of polymorphism. The demands on mathematical description have become less strict: if previously the description of real phenomena in mathematical language was regarded as the law of nature, now it has become possible to speak about mathematical models. One and the same system studied can be described by a variety of mathematical models, all of which have a right to simultaneous existence. A model, as we have already said, acquires the status of a metaphor. It behaves both like a simulated system and unlike it. Polymorphism can also be observed within one model. It takes place in the problems of the transformation of variables in the multivariate regression analysis where the parameters of transformation can be chosen arbitrarily out of a wide region of all possible values. In any case, now serious programs for multivariate regression analysis are built so that a computer puts out not one model but a variety of them. There exists no possibility of building a criterion which would give preference to one of the models. Thus, in the problem of spectral representation of random processes, the experimenter is given not one but a variety of the curves of spectral density, calculated with different values of smoothing weighting functions. A mathematician has no rules for an unambiguous choice of these filters which are constructed in such a way that the increase in the precision in the estimation of the spectrum leads to the increase of the bias. The terminology itself is interesting here. The filters are called "spectral windows," a term used to indicate that the research worker can look at the same set of data through different windows and see different phenomena. Note that the word combination forming this term is of a clearly metaphorical character: a process spectrum and a window are still two incompatible notions. Quite recently, a mathematical statistician was sure that, in processing the results of observations, he gave the experimenter the same answer as any other statistician in any other country would have done. Now opinions have changed completely. Processing the same data, one and the same statistician gives the experimenter a variety of models having the same formal right to existence, and it is due to rather general reasons that we choose the model which has the most heuristic power.

The polymorphic character of the language of applied mathematics, manifesting itself in the above way, increases its flexibility. The distinction between the ordinary language and the language of applied mathematics is being wiped out to some extent, and at the same time, a new borderline with traditional mathematics appears.

Some unpleasant manifestations of polymorphism of mathematical language have also been revealed in connection with the solution of certain applied problems. Let us return to the fourth example above. In order to estimate the temperature distribution in the past, we must know the initial conditions $U(x, 0) = \varphi(x)$. In real problems we can deal only with a sampled estimate $\hat{\varphi}(x) \to \varphi(x)$, performed approximately. It appears that small arbitrary changes in $\varphi(x)$ and in the finite number of its derivatives may lead to very large changes in $U(x, t)$ when $t = 0$. The problem of temperature distribution for the past values of time proves incorrect in the sense in which Hadamard formulated it while considering Cauchy's problem. (I would remind the reader that Cauchy's problem consists in the search for the solution of a differential equation which satisfies the given initial condition.) For example, Hadamard showed that the statement of Cauchy's problem is incorrect for elliptic equations since their solutions are not continously dependent on the initial conditions. I shall not deal with improperly posed problems; this question is considered in the literature quite fully. I shall only point out that the problem is considered to be properly posed if the solution satisfies the following conditions: it is existent, unique, and stable (that is, depends continuously upon the initial data). The search for the correct statement of the problem is the struggle against the unpleasant ambiguity of mathematical language, conditioned here by its instability. Even if we do manage to formulate some problem correctly, it does not yet mean much. For example, a correct numerical solution of the problem of heat conduction for the past still does not eliminate the question of how long in the past the calculation is sensible. Russell's paradox mentioned above concerning the prediction of the taxi number arises despite the use of a correct, in the above sense, statement of the problem.

Mathematization of nonsense.   The application of mathematical language should have increased the accuracy of judgments. Reading a paper written in mathematical language, we hope to see clearly formulated axioms, understandable inference rules, and reasonable interpretation. However, this is not always the case. Let me illustrate this statement with several examples.

I once came across a publication which was concerned with the search for optimal conditions for a chemical process. Proceeding from the results of the experiment, a mathematical model of the process studied was constructed and the conditions corresponding to the extremal value of the model were found. The results of this research were transferred into industrial conditions, and there the output of the process proved lower, which is quite natural, for industrial conditions may differ from laboratory conditions. But the authors stated quite a strange thing: they said that, from the analysis of the model, they have managed to draw up recommendations which can improve the results under the industrial conditions as well. This is totally incomprehensible. How can anything be obtained from the model under the conditions where it does not work, and what can be obtained from the model which would be better than the extremum if the task is the attainment of the maximal output?

My second example concerns a paper which dealt with the study of social development. Firstly, two independent models had been developed: one for the growth of scientific information and the other for the growth of technological information. Further, the author tried to introduce a postulate about the interconnection of these models and stated that, at first approximation, this dependence could be found if a new function was introduced given by the ratio of the corresponding right and left parts of the two orginal models. This postulate is senseless: how can an interconnection of two processes be given by dividing one model by the other one? If, at first approximation, the models are divisible, then what will another approximation be: their multiplication or raising one of them to the degree with the index given by the second model? The author further states that the ratio he obtained indicated the redistribution of the productive forces in the process of the two types of information and said that this law was of primary importance for the practice of control of social systems. Here everything is based on misunderstanding: if the system of postulates and the models that follow from them do not imply that the processes of growth in both cases rely upon the same resources and are rival, then it is impossible to learn anything about it by means of dividing these models one by another. (Imagine the following situation: somebody has built the models of growth for a suckling pig and for a chicken, and then has divided these models by each other. On perceiving that the ratio of their growth does not remain constant, he claims that the redistribution of resources takes place.) Strange as it may seem, the work in question was published in a journal with a circulation of 40,000.

I have seen publications which proved mathematically that a human being can have only seven levels of abstractions or, no less seriously, stated that in any field of knowledge one-half of the publications falls upon this very field and the other half, upon the neighboring ones. The question is whether there is such a system of postulates from which such conclusions would follow.

The use of mathematical language by itself does not eliminate absurdities from publications. It is possible "to dress scientific brilliancies and scientific absurdities alike in the impressive uniform of formulae and theorems" (Schwartz, 1962). Mathematics is not the means for correcting errors in the human genetic code. Side by side with mathematization of knowledge, mathematization of nonsense also goes on; the language of mathematics, strange as it seems, appears fit for carrying out any of these problems. Recently, several publications have appeared warning against abuses of mathematics. Beside the above-mentioned work by Schwartz (1962), I also point out the papers by Doyle (1965), Shannon (1956), Box (1966), and Leontiev (1971).

Chapter 5

Soft Languages

In this chapter I shall try to give an idea of two soft languages. One is the language of abstract painting, occupying the extreme position on our semantic scale; the other, close to it, is the language of ancient Indian philosophy.

The reader may ask why in this book I pay such great attention to these abstract sign systems. They interest me first of all as an extreme and degenerate manifestation of the semantic disharmony between the transmitter and the receptor. This manifests itself in our everyday language as well, though in a less prominent form. Abstract symbols have been used by people since antiquity. Historically, archeological excavations have yielded abstract ornamentations as often as objective ones. Moslem culture allows only abstract ornamentations. As for modern architecture and furniture—wall papers, blinds, lighting fixtures, plastic floors—they all are patterned on abstract symbols. Even the ceilings and walls of cinema halls and the new metro stations are now decorated in an abstract style. The ornaments of old Russia—flowers, cockerels, and hennies—seem to have dropped out of our everyday life. The semantic degeneracy of abstract symbolism allows one to avoid boring obtrusiveness. This may explain the new style's popularity, but here the following questions may arise: can a semantically degenerate language be the means for the self-expression of an artist? What is the value of abstract paintings as works of art? These questions are beyond my subject and my competence. My task here is the formal study of sign systems in all their manifestations (no matter to what extremes they go), but not their axiological interpretation. That is the task of art critics. Any actual phenomenon can be studied from different angles, and a formal study of

151

one specific language as a sign system is just the study of a single manifestation of a complex system.

The Language of Abstract Painting

It has often been stated that abstract painting may be regarded as a system of signs representing a specific language (e.g., see Klée, 1964). The paper by Andrukovich et al. (1971) written with my participation was an attempt to subject this statement to a precise logical analysis, using general mathematical methods to study the experts' judgments. The experts were offered several abstract pictures and asked to "read" them according to definite rules.

In Chapter 1 of this book, I have already tried to formulate the structural characteristics and functional properties which permit us to rank a symbolic system with language categories. Now let us try to analyze abstract pictures from this standpoint.

No doubt, abstract painting is a medium of communication, transferring information from the artist to the viewer. In any case, a system consisting of a "transmitter" (an artist), a "receptor" (a viewer), and a means of communication between them is clearly present. The viewers attend exhibitions of abstract painting and discuss them passionately, trying to interpret the things observed in ordinary language.

Now let us see in what way the structure of the language of abstract painting is built. First of all, we must manage to select the primary system of signs, situated on the lowest level of sign hierarchy. In the above-mentioned paper (Andrukovich et al., 1971), we tried to do this by analyzing the reproduction of 19 pictures representing various schools of abstract painting (see Appendix 2). This investigation resulted in a list of primary signs, forming *the alphabet of abstract painting*.

The alphabet of abstract painting may be determined by subjecting any such collection of works to geometrical and topological analysis. When we actually did this in Moscow, we reduced the complexity of the artists' creations to thirty-six elements involving lines, circles, shapes, colors, etc., with their various combinations. These are the signs, and with their rules of combination they represent the alphabet and grammar of the language of abstract painting. To test this procedure, it was necessary to determine whether or not a group of 100 art experts would interpret a group of abstract paintings in a manner which would correspond to the reading of a text. A careful logical–statistical analysis of the responses to the exhibit revealed that this was indeed the case. (For complete details, see Andrukovich et al., 1971.)

The spectators can read pictures and place them in more and more complicated aggregate–paradigms. The demand for the hierarchical system of language is fulfilled. The paradigms prove to be connected with grammatical attributes; consequently, the pictures are read as grammatically arranged sign systems. People may be divided into groups according to their ability to build paradigms in a similar way, and these groups prove to be connected with socio-demographic characteristics determined by their general mode of thinking. Hence, it follows that the process of reading pictures is indubitably connected with some prior predisposition. The sign system of abstract painting meets all the demands enumerated above as characteristics of those sign systems which we intuitively perceive as languages.

True, the language of abstract painting appears semantically degenerate. The viewer is never sure whether or not he has apprehended just what the artist had meant to say. In principle, in the language of abstract painting a plurality of possible interpretations is built in. There are many works that examine the creative process of and motives for painting abstract pictures. One of the possible explanations is an urge to express the subconscious in a Freudian sense. But all this is no more than conjecture. Strictly speaking, we do not know, as a matter of fact, what an artist wanted to convey in a particular abstract picture. This statement means only that we cannot translate into ordinary language something expressed in an abstract painting. However, can we translate into our ordinary language something expressed in "serious" music, in a theorem of any branch of modern mathematics, or even in the constructions of modern theoretical physics? Nevertheless, I have tried here to say something in ordinary language about the texts written in the language of abstract painting.

As has been said above, the interpretability of one sign system into the language of another is one of the necessary characteristics of a language system. But our interpretation might be entirely different from what the transmitter actually intended to say. Imagine that an experiment similar to that described above was carried out with a collection of insects. Probably the results would seem rather similar: an alphabet and grammar would be found for the language of insect morphology, and in the reading process the paradigms would be found related to grammatical characteristics. Interpretation of this experiment in our system of ideas would look approximately as follows: a population of insects "converse" with the environment, offering a continuously changing variety of characteristics to the process of evolution. Having managed to rank the collection of insects, people would read this record from quite another standpoint, i.e., proceeding from their à priori aesthetic notions. Will a similar situation not arise when it is necessary to read the messages of the inhabitants of other worlds?

Let us consider another mental experiment. Assume that paintings by classical artists would be studied. Arranging them according to their preferability, we would, most likely, again obtain hierarchical structures. But for this system of pictures, we would not manage to build in any representative alphabet or grammar. Classical painting is not a language of signs, but of *images*, which cannot be divided into elementary constituents. However, as I have already stated, the style of the images of the same type, e.g., icons, probably can be represented as a sign system. Now assume that a similar experiment was carried out with color slides of landscapes. Here, preferability ranking will probably give hierarchical structures as well, but again they cannot be connected with an alphabet and grammar. Broadly, we perceive nature as images but not as a grammatical arrangement of elementary signs. (If the reader wishes to regard images as signs, he will have to admit that this is a strangely extreme type of sign system. The notion of a sign system can be broadened so that any substitute for something is considered a sign, and in this sense a portrait is a sign of a human being. However, I would not feel comfortable with this point of view.)

One more mental experiment: Imagine that we want to make a computer reproduce a certain abstract painting in terms of our alphabet and language. Generally speaking, the computer can cope with the task, but the pictures created will have a large number of variations. We do not know why it was this version, but not another, that the artist created. We may complicate the task and introduce a random generator for changing previously set conditions. Perhaps, in this new set of pictures, a work of genius will appear, but how shall we recognize it? Hence, the failures of those who wanted, through mechanical methods (sometimes obviously exaggerated), to create something constituted of seemingly elementary, easily reproducible signs, arranged according to quite simple rules. The same question arises when we try to simulate by a computer the creativity of a composer or to build mechanically a model of creative thinking. It is one and the same question that remains unanswered: What is the algorithm set up for the selection of a really brilliant solution (even if afterwards we manage to formalize this solution)? But let us return once more to classical painting: here we can build a not too clumsy system of alphabet and grammar which would be adequate to find among the versions created by a computer something looking like the original we wish to reproduce. This mental experiment is perhaps the best way to explain the difference between the imaginative and symbolic means of information transmission.

Probably the dream of creating a highly abstract universal language will always remain with people. We yearn for a language similar to that of the game of glass beads in the book by Hesse (1961).

The Language of Ancient Indian Philosophy[1]

The polymorphism of language is revealed much more clearly in the ancient Indian texts than in the contemporary languages of European culture. A word in Indian texts is always many sided with respect to the meanings ascribed to it. This fact has been noted by all the scholars of ancient Indian thought, as illustrated by the following examples:

> One and the same expression is often used in different meanings, or one and the same idea occurs in different series of concepts. (Oldenberg, 1881)

> To attempt translation of such pregnant terms is however always dangerous as the new word — part of a new language which is the outcome of a different tone of thought — while it may denote the same or nearly the same idea usually calls up together with it very different ones. (Rhys-Davids, 1880, p. 112)

> In using this language, it is not always necessary that certain words should possess a precise meaning. Vagueness can also be useful. It is like a half-empty mould: each can fill it to his own taste. But the principal content is more or less always there, its "flavour" is reproduced in a flowing context. The flavour of the word *dharma* is a concept of duty imposed by religion or nature, which is the same. The stability of our understanding this concept does not depend on anything — it is created by the human being. Outside this general meaning, other more or less special meanings are ascribed to the word *dharma* when needed. Context governs the use of the word which sometimes narrows and sometimes widens its content; the term is flexible, and due to its combinative power it obeys two opposite elements: concrete and abstract. The article specifying to which one of these meanings it corresponds, i.e., what the term is, occupies six pages in the Petersburg Dictionary and shows how this term has acquired religious, moral and political meanings; this is to say, that the whole juridical, social, political and didactical literature had the general name *dharmas'astra*. The word *dharma* embraced the traditions of India, illuminating its ideals of the future and explaining the present of Indian society. Sometimes only a narrow partition separates *dharma* and *karman*. The latter is the symbol of causality; the former is the causality in its final manifestation, in the totality of its results, something like our "destiny." (Willman-Grabovska, 1934, p. 45)

> The symbolic nature of words was well grasped in India, where it was understood that formally one and the same word has tremendous potential, and may denote utterly different concepts; it was known that

---

[1] This section is based on Nalimov and Barinova (1974).

a word's meaning is to a great extent determined by the whole system which the word enters. (Toporov, 1960)

Polymorphism found its manifestation in all sign systems of ancient India including Buddhist fine arts and Buddhist iconography. This is what was said on this point by Toporov (1965):

Semiotic analysis of Buddhist works of art becomes especially expedient due to a tendency for ancient Indian culture to display a high degree of symbolic character in all its manifestations. Sometimes this is so great that visual or some other immediate likeness easily gives place to mediated (in particular, to symbolic) associations accompanied by the tendency characteristic for the culture to link one and the same mode of expression with several different sets of meanings.

In contrast to the language of European culture, in Indian texts the impossibility of unambiguous and consistent definition of a concept is openly recognized and, moreover, *emphasized*. Several examples showing the open introduction of inconsistency in defining word meanings follow. The fact that the cited example relates to the absolute does not distort my thesis: all statements, no matter what they concern, are given by the system of thinking which finds its expression in the language.

He is more subtle than what is subtle, greater than what is great, . . . [S'vetas'vatara Upanishad, III, 20 (The Upanishads, 1965)]

It moves, it is motionless. It is distant, it is near. It is within all, it is beyond all this [Isavasyopanishad, V (The Upanishads, 1965)]

This is my Self within the heart, smaller than a corn, than barley, than mustard, than the kernel of the mustard seed. He is my Self within the heart, greater than the Earth, greater than the sky, greater than heaven, greater than all these worlds [Chha'ndogja Upanishad, III, 14.3 (The Upanishads, 1965)]

It is often recognized that we have to speak of something which is beyond cognition:

The eye does not go there, no speech, nor mind. We do not know that. We do not know how to instruct one about It [Kenopanishad, I, 3 (The Upanishads, 1965)]

How should one know the knower? [Brhadaranyaka-Upanishad, IV, 5.15 (The Upanishads, 1965)]

Where one sees nothing else, hears nothing else, understands nothing else, — that is the Infinite. Where, however, one sees something else, hears something else, understands something else, — that is the Finite. That which is Infinite, is immortal, that which is Finite is mortal [Chha'ndogga Upanishad, VII, 24.1 (The Upanishads, 1965)]

The task set is immense: if not to describe then at least to give some idea of the incognizable. The insufficiency of the word symbol system is acknowledged, and as in abstract painting, empty or almost empty signs are introduced, i.e., signs which have no clearly defined meaning ascribed to them. According to Willman-Grabovska, they are half-empty molds. Following the requirements of clearness and precision — traditions of Indian didactics — it is merely indicated that a word used in a text does not have either this or that meaning.

> The soul which, is not this, not that, nor aught else, is intangible, for it cannot be laid hold of, it is not to be dissipated, for it cannot be dissipated; it is without contact, for it does not come into contact; it is not limited, it is not subject to pain nor to destruction. [Brhadaranyaka-Upanishad, IV, 4 (The Upanishads, 1965)]

Such an unusual attitude toward words led to a situation in which, from the viewpoint of a European reader, ancient Indian philosophy in this style resembles art, sometimes even abstract art, constructed so that "the receptor" can perceive something quite different from what has been put there by "the transmitter."

In any case, the cogency of the statements is given not by the force of their logical structure but by their originality and, sometimes, by the paradoxical character of the judgments, or by unusual comparisons, by inner beauty of word constructions, and their measured rhythm. Sometimes these have an inner refrain. It is not logic that convinces, but rather the magic of words. Here is an example of Indian style from Dhammapada (1952), a famous collection of dicta entering the Buddhist Canon as an independent element:

> 33. The flickering, fickle mind, difficult to guard, difficult to control, - the wise man straightens as a bowman, an arrow.

Ponderous European philosophical thought, expressed, for example, in the language of Kant or Hegel, could hardly be described by such words. But the language of existentialism — a trend in European thought which was born outside traditional European philosophy — can be compared with the language of the ancient Indian texts. In many of its manifestations, existentialism resorts to the language of art and sometimes even to magical, vague expressions, giving up complete logical constructions, proclaiming the possibility of thinking without concepts or introducing clear ideas with great reluctance. This brings existential language closer to the language of ancient Indian philosophy. Existentialism has emerged as a kind of protest against European culture, and in order to express this protest, it was necessary to build another language; otherwise, this protest would have been only a part of the outlook protested against.

To speak about the difference in the languages of different cultures is much more to the point than to pontificate about the difference in national languages.

Chapter 6

A Hard Language of Biological Codes

One of the greatest achievements in modern biology is the notion of the possible reduction of genetics to a formal description of phenomena in terms of language. Now proteins are customarily regarded as a linear "text" written in a 20-symbol alphabet of amino acids. A major part of biological problems is reduced to the analysis of the way one text is specified by another. "The most difficult part of the 'coding problem' has been to arrive at the concept that a code exists. This required at least a century of work" (Yčas, 1969).

A genetic code is not yet a message, but an alphabet and grammar used by a cell for translating a text from a four-letter language of nucleic acids into the twenty-letter language of the protein. The primary alphabet consists of four standard bases: adenine (A), guanine (G), thymine (T), and cytosine (C). These four letters build a genetic message. It is a precise succession of these four letters along a molecule of deoxyribonucleic acid (DNA) that presupposes the structure of a specific protein molecule. A protein molecule is a text built out of twenty letters of the secondary alphabet – standard amino acids, similar for all living nature. Each protein has its own characteristic succession of letters, i.e., amino acids; their number in a polypeptide chain usually varies from dozens up to three hundred or more.

The mechanism of building protein texts is rather unusual. First, information contained in DNA is retranscribed into a similar molecule, called informational ribonucleic acid (RNA). The texts of RNA are also built upon the four-letter alphabet, and three of these letters are of the same

159

type as those in DNA; the fourth one, uracil (U), replaces thymine. The following substitution of letters occurs (Crick, 1962): the code letters of DNA, A, G, T, and C, are transformed into U, C, A, and H of an RNA molecule, respectively, the latter as a rule being used in the tables of genetic code, in which 64 triplets correspond to 20 amino acids.

The code of nucleic acids proves to be triplex. Four bases, taken separately, can specify only four amino acids. Taking two at a time also proves insufficient: it specifies only 16 amino acids. Taking three at a time equals 64; this is already more than ample, and the code structure appears redundant. Most amino acids are encoded by more than one triplet, and some of them, by as many as six triplets. Three triplets do not encode any of the amino acids known; they only play the part of "punctuation marks."

The group of bases specifying one amino acid is traditionally called a *codon* or a *word*:

> With respect to meaning, codons are classified into *sense codons* which specify some amino acids, and *nonsense codons* which do not specify an amino acid. Such codons are referred to as nonsense even if they have some other function. . . . If there is more than one codon for the same amino acid the code is *degenerate*. Degeneracy is complete if all possible codons correspond to amino acids, and partial if some do not. Two codons which specify the same amino acid are *co-degenerate* or *synonymous*. If a codon can be read as more than one amino acid, it is *ambiguous*. The set of codons determining the standard set of amino acids is a *dictionary*. Included in the dictionary are nonsense codons and some which act as start or stop signals for reading. These are referred to as *"punctuation."* If a codon mutates to specify another amino acid, the change, with respect to the amino acids, is a *replacement*. A change from one base to another is a *substitution*. If one or more bases of a codon are also bases of another codon, the code is *overlapping*. (Yčas, 1969)

It is clearly seen from this excerpt that linguistic terms are widely used for formulating statements in genetics. We may go further and show that the symbolic system which describes biological phenomena meets every demand specified for language systems.

Let us begin with the functional characteristics of language. Language, as has already been mentioned, primarily serves to transmit information. This function is obviously carried on by biological symbol systems. The process of biological evolution can be described as "language games." While playing the game, both old and new information is presented, emerging in a spontaneous and logically unpredictable way as a result of mutation. Again, the system proves to be non-Gödelian.

It is the second functional aspect of language which manifests itself most vividly in the biological code: namely, reduction, storage, and retrieval of information.

One of the most important attributes of language symbol systems (as already mentioned above) is the manifestation of hierarchical structure. This is revealed extremely clearly in the language of the biological code. The first two hierarchical levels of this system are 4- and 20-letter alphabets. Evidently, it is feasible to speak about higher hierarchical levels, i.e., about that of the chromosome, about that of separate biological individuals (these are texts of a symbolic system, regenerated when information retained in genes is expanded); and about the level of a species (this is a supertext built from simpler texts — separate biological individuals). Finally, we can take into consideration the hierarchy of species, classes, and orders. This construction is quite reasonable, because for the two lowest levels, the code of every organism is practically universal and the symbolic structure is notable for its clear-cut regularity (Yčas, 1969). The whole biological universe is built upon one and the same linguistic structure; the code seems equally valid both for a human being and for a plant. The seeming diversity of the biological universe is no more than diversity of texts, but not in the least diversity of languages. In this sense the living universe is simpler in its construction than science is.

One of the characteristics of the symbolic systems of languages is the possibility of distinguishing in them between alphabet and grammar. From the above (though very short) description of the biological code, it is clear that both alphabet and grammar are formed there in their full precision. Formal resemblance to ordinary language is quite remarkable here: grammatical code structure foresees punctuation marks — symbols indicating where the synthesis of the chain is to begin and where it will come to an end.

It has been proved that the triplets UAA, UGA, and UAG can tear off a polypeptide chain. However, it still is not known whether all the triplets given are actually used for this purpose in a normal cell; the principal terminating codon seems to be UAA (Spirin and Gavrilova, 1971). The role of initiating codons, beginning the translating region — cystine — is played by the two triplets AUG and GUG. Still, it is not either of these two codons that provides the beginning of a reading. Here the effect of the context tells: it is the space structure of the given region of the chain of the informational RNA that is the main factor for making the triplets AUG and GUG initiating codons (Spirin and Gavrilova, 1971). The effect of the context remains strictly determined; the "hardness" of the code language is not violated here.

While deciphering the language of the biological code, scientists faced a semantic problem: in what way is the triplet sign connected with the referent? Unambiguity of the major part of the codons is beyond doubt, though it still remains possible that several codons are ambiguous, i.e., can encode more than one amino acid (Crick, 1962). Some other unsettled questions remain in the semantics of the biological code: the vocabulary of the code is clearly redundant; the number of symbols it contains exceeds the number of referents. Here it is not clear when we use alternative synonymous codons to indicate the same amino acid, and if we do so whether we do it with equal frequency (Crick, 1962). If we consider the Bayesian model of perception of the meaning of a symbol to be acceptable for the description of a wide class of languages, then the language of the biological code proves degenerate in this respect. It is put at the end of our semantic scale which contains languages with an absolutely hard structure. The natural language of the biological code is arranged as a rather regular structure. The process of reading information in the biological code has a great resemblance to the analogous process in a computer: each molecule of the transporting RNA has its own special succession of three bases, a so-called anti-codon which distinguishes the corresponding codon in the informational RNA by means of coupling bases. It all occurs quite mechanically. In this language, irregularity is introduced only by a breakdown in this mechanical process. Mutations can also result from errors in reading. In the process of genetic recombination and while doubling DNA, one base can be occasionally added. This will cause the displacement of the borderline in reading triplets. This error can be corrected by elimination of one nucleotide. These two changes will cause not only the replacement of two amino acids but the replacement of every intermediate amino acid as well, for intermediate bases have also been read with a displacement in phase, and that is why they will group in triplets in a way different from the normal case (Crick, 1962). Now let us return to our semantic scale. Hard programming languages and all the procedures connected with a computer are unambiguous semantically and do not allow the emergence of mechanical errors in principle. In contrast to this, the irregularity of ordinary language is based on the language structure itself. The language of the biological code occupies an intermediate position: it is regular (or almost regular) in its semantic structure but allows violations in its regular, mechanistic structure.

It is also possible to speak about the dimension of the biological language. We know that genetic information is stored in the form of a linear text in the nucleic acid and can manifest itself as a linear succession of amino acids in protein, but protein itself is already to a great extent three dimensional. It is of great importance which parts of a molecule are brought close together in the three-dimensional structure when compiling the chains. For example, a molecule of lysozyme, an enzyme that destroys membranes of bacterial cells, consists of 129 structural units interconnected in four places by transversal disulfide bridges (Phillips, 1966). Three-dimensional configuration of a molecule is unambiguously determined by the succession of amino acid ingredients. This configuration corresponds to the minimum of free energy. To give the molecule any other form would demand a new influx of external energy. Now we have sufficient knowledge as to how the succession of amino acids in a protein is determined, but the mechanism assisting in three-dimensional ordering remains unknown. In any case, the attempt to solve this problem with the help of a computer is exceedingly complicated. Experiments have been performed where proteins lost their three-dimensional configuration without breaking the links providing the completeness of the molecule. In such a state these proteins lost their fermentative capacity (Levinthal, 1966). Biologically, a ferment-catalyst can serve its informational functions only in its original three-dimensional state.

Concerning the evolution of the language of the biological code, strange as it may seem, biologists can say next to nothing. Evidently, the code's evolution was in progress at the earliest stage of life development, and this hampers the study of the problem considerably (Crick, 1962). The language of the biological code is closed. If changes still do occur in the vocabulary, there are sufficient grounds to consider them negligible. Any change in the vocabulary proves fatal, and evolution, even on a geological time scale, becomes impossible. This seems to be the only known language with a hardened vocabulary. Possibly, in the process of natural selection, the correlation between the regular constituents of the language and the random ones has been gradually changing in some way. For the evolutionary process, both too large a frequency of mutations and too small a one prove injurious. Many hypotheses have been advanced to explain the emergence and natural history of the biological code, but none has been subjected to experimental test (Crick, 1962).

Chapter 7

The Theory of Names

He that has ears to hear, let him hear.
St. Matthew 11:15

This chapter might as well be called "The Mystery of Names." In our view, the Name is a survival of bygone cultures, though the Myth, a structure connected with the Name, entered our life in a transformed manner in certain manifestations of art. The Name as we understand it is an extralinguistic category. Names have no place in our semantic scale. If we decide to regard Names as linguistic categories, we shall have to introduce another dimension. Here I touch upon the problem of the Name in passing, only to emphasize the peculiarities of purely linguistic systems.

The collection of statements about language in Chapter 1 begins with Plato's remarks on the Names of things. The Veda contains mention of the Universal Maker who gave Names to all things. In the Bible we read that Adam gave Names to creatures during the creation of the world. The idea of words as the names of things gave rise to the teaching of language as a hard system. Name became a category of formal logic. The neopositivistic conception of logical atoms may be interpreted as returning to understanding words as names. However, it is curious that in the statements of linguists we do not come across discussions of Names. The Name has fallen out the sphere of linguistic studies. Recently, however, at a seminar of the Semiotics Group of Moscow State University, Yu. V. Rozhdestvenski, presenting a report called "Semiotics and Culture," returned to the problem of the Name. His principal theses are roughly as follows: "The Name is immanent in the individuality named; with anni-

165

hilation of the Name, the individuality perishes; Names are not means of communication."

A woman from the audience was indignant at the second thesis: "Shall I perish if my name is lost?" It is so. By all means, human individuality disappears if a person loses his name. Just for this reason a convict is deprived of his name and assigned a number in place of it. A laundry or a school which has no name but only a number is void of individuality. All schools with individuality have names.

The name of a person, as something immanent in him, is not a means of communication. In a system of communication, it turns into a polysemantic word. Say the name of your intimate friend: it has turned into a word with which the image of your friend, his individuality, is connected with some probability maximal for you; however, the same word is connected, though with a smaller probability, with other people having this name and their traits. If you want to use the word connected with the name of a person as his mark, e.g., to find out his address, the Name-word will turn out to be insufficient. Its polysemy must be narrowed, and you add the patronymic, the family name.

Here is how one of Shakespeare's characters opposes turning a name into a word:

> *Clown.* To see this age! A sentence is but a cheveril glove to a good
>   wit: how quickly the wrong side may be turn'd outward!
> *Viola.* Nay, that's certain; they that dally nicely with words may
>   quickly make them wanton.
> *Clown.* I would, therefore, my sister had had no name, sir.
> *Viola.* Why, man?
> *Clown.* Why, sir, her name's a word; and to dally with that word
>   might make my sister wanton. But, indeed, words are very rascals since bonds disgraced them.
> *Viola.* Thy reason, man?
> *Clown.* Troth, sir, I can yield you none without words, and words
>   are grown so false, I am loth to prove reason with them.
>   (W. Shakespeare, *Twelfth Night; or, What You Will*, act III,
>   scene 1)

Here the author gives his own ideas through the Clown's words, as was customary at that time.

I believe that some ideas about names are a relic in our culture. They relate to the pre-logical, image thinking, and in making an attempt to correlate them with logical atoms, one ascribes quite a novel meaning to the old concepts.

Let us try to reconstruct the nature of image thinking. A Name is immanent to the individuality. A person having heard a Name should recognize it by "reading" inside himself (here, it seems pertinent to remember Plato's conception of knowledge by means of ideas, of the love for an idea as a way of knowledge). Names are not logically operated upon; merely an inner concentration about the Name takes place, and its recognition comes in the process of meditating upon it. The Name is outside logic: one cannot learn what underlies the Name by comparing the Name-word with other words, since its meaning is related to the Name which is immanent only to it alone. In the terms of Langer (1951), the Name is a non-discursive symbol; it is of no use to expand it into separate elements, since it acts only as an entity. The rules of constituting it from separate elements are of no significance in the process of its perception. The Bayesian model of perceiving symbols developed above has nothing to do with the process of perceiving Names. As I have already said, Names have no place on our semantic scale; although Names are in hard connection with something, it is unknown with what. It seems they might be placed at the end of the scale where languages with an extremely hard structure are situated, but in these languages we know what signs signify, and these signs are logically operated upon. If Names do create a language, then, as mentioned above, we need another dimension to present their semantics.

If this reconstruction of Name theory is accepted, such phenomena as belief in the magic of Names become clear. In this system of views, the Name could be immanent in the hidden natural forces which could be aroused by pronouncing the Name. The structure of religion also becomes clear. A sufficiently elaborated religious system may consist of dogmatic formulations made at the word-logical level, symbols of belief — Names, whose sense can be understood only in profound self-examination and in the rites which are play manifestations of the name symbolics. It is noteworthy that symbolist poets made an attempt to revive the role of Names. The goal of a symbolist-poet became a search for a symbol Name and increasing the possibility of its comprehension, correlating it with something in our fantasy by poetical means. Myth is a non-discursive system as well, with a structure identical to that of a Name, but hierarchically higher. A myth is like a vivid dream. A good instance of an almost modern myth is Gogol's story "Nose" (with the subtitle "A Dream"). The story is written in ordinary language with words arranged into phrases according to grammatical rules. All events are outwardly fairly logical, or at least the story lacks the deliberate illogicity of modern abstract plays. At the same time, however, the whole situation is not perceived as a logical construction. The point is that the word "nose" has a peculiar inexplicable meaning. It is a name of something, and this something should be guessed by the reader. Guessing is not a logical analysis, but a reconstruction in fantasy. An example of a modern myth is Antonioni's film "Blow-up" (the reader may find a detailed description of the film in Baskakov, 1971). Separate episodes of the film appear quite logical, but as a whole it is not perceived as a development of any logical plan. Perhaps the key to its understanding is the scenes with clowning boys and girls at the beginning and end of the film. This is the burden of the film. It finishes with the scene in which the hero, the photographer Thomas, enters the tennis game the clowns play: they play as if in a real game but without a ball and with a non-existent racket. Here again we can watch Antonioni's favorite theme — the obviously illusory nature of human existence; however, the stage manager refused in his interview to explain his film on a logical level. This is myth which should affect our thinking only through our imagination, although the film produces a very deep impression, probably as a result of its use of very unfamiliar forms for its effect.

Works of art claiming to interpret a problem in a deeply philosophical way may as well be written mythologically. A good example is the apocryphal Gospel according to St. Thomas, recently published in Russian translation. [The English version was published in *New Testament Apocrypha* (McWilson, 1963).] Again, separate statements are constructed according to correct grammar, but the whole content is not perceived as a logical construction. This is a reproduction of a mystery, the meaning of which ought to be guessed, and the scheme of this monument of art is such that he who will have guessed it will stop being a mortal. The Gospel begins with the words: "These are the secret words which the Living Jesus spoke and Didimus Judas Thomas wrote. And he said: 'Whoever finds the explanation of these words will not taste death.' "

The Gospel according to St. Thomas pretends to a much more profound penetraton of the essence of Christianity than the four canonical Gospels, including that according to St. John. However, it did not enter the Canon which was basically formed already in the fourth century, and there is no evidence why. It could be that the rationalism of the late-Hellenistic era made them supporters of logical ways of exposition even where a religious conception was concerned. I cannot here dwell any longer upon the role of a myth in the system of religious ideas; it has been the subject of numerous papers, but it is not my subject. I should only like to remark that in modern philosophical papers one can have mythological constituents. *Tractatus* by Wittgenstein, a professional logician, despite the chaste logic of separate formulations, sometimes resembles a myth. It is the uncommon combination of logic and implications inferred from it, which can be restored only by the force of our fantasy, that makes this paper especially attractive.

The notion of perceiving a Name as a reading inside oneself leads us to a vague concept about inborn human abilities. But what is understood under this concept? It most likely serves as a polite code for our ignorance. If we cannot trace the entire chain of the evolutionary process, we can at least formulate a hypothesis about an explosive mutation, which, however, does not explain anything either; it seems less onerous to speak of the inborn nature of abilities. It is interesting that Chomsky (1968), in his previously mentioned book *Language and Mind*, formulates a hypothesis about the innate nature of language. According to him, a child acquiring the mastery of his native language does not *learn* it but *matures* to its mastery.

There certainly are grounds for this hypothesis. As a matter of fact, humanity has not succeeded in tracing the evolution of intellect in the process of its mastering of language. Tribes at a lower stage of cultural development are quite prepared to use all language means. At the same time, even higher animals cannot be taught the elements of linguistic behavior if language is understood as a system of logical operations over abstract symbols and not as a simple response to separate signals. The difference between humans and animals is a much wider gap than that along the derivative. Hence, Chomsky's conclusion about the existence of a universal grammar underlying all grammars of the actually existing diversity of languages. Its restoration in this system of ideas should have solved the problem of machine translation as well. Is it, however, correct to make such far-fetched propositions? I consider it more reasonable to act with greater caution and speak not of innate grammar as a certain complete logical structure but of the faculty for making an abstract, i.e., symbolic, representation of observational results, for giving to symbols a polymorphous meaning, and for conducting with them formal logical operations and operations of interpretation. In short, I think of the innate faculty for perceiving language as a system that is more complicated than any constructions of deductive logic. It is, in my opinion, not structures which are innate, and not even languages, but the capacity for their perception. Here it seems pertinent to make a comparison between the human intellect and a computer. The latter can be taught to perform logical operations but cannot be taught the whole complexity of verbal behavior. Hence come the difficulties of machine translation[1]: so far, the problem has to be reduced to strictly logical procedures.

Now let us return to the problems of perceiving Names. If a Name is reduced to recognition, then this faculty must be innate. But, in order to explain the innateness, we do not have to resort to Platonian idealism. All may be explained in a far more realistic manner. At present, nobody doubts the fact that certain chemical agents may change a person's mood and even arouse vivid hallucinations in him. These chemical agents are

---

[1] Interesting data on machine translation of texts are given by Sinaiko (1971): a translator translates a text at the rate of 450 words per hour, whereas editing the translation made by a computer proceeds at the rate of 400 words per hour!

but stimulators switching (and strengthening) the human mechanism of generating fantasies. This potentiality has to be acknowledged as being inborn. It is thus quite possible to believe that discursive symbols are a key for switching the generators of fantasy at an extralogical level. It is just in this sense that Names are not means of communication. They do not transfer anything from one person to another but are a key for switching on the reproducing mechanism inside ourselves. We may suppose that it is a potential faculty which is innate in us while its concrete realization is given by the influence of a culture and, perhaps, by the human will — one's ability to concentrate and meditate, ignoring the impact of other external stimuli (irritants) and communication on the logical level with others and oneself. In some cultures, the technique of meditation has been thoroughly developed. In an attempt to comprehend the mechanism of extralogical consciousness, we shall evidently face a problem analogous to deciphering the biological code. At this point I can state something in common with the concepts of Efraimson (1971) on the genetic encoding of certain cultural manifestations. Somewhere at a subcellular level non-discursive effects may again turn into discursive ones. At present, however, I believe that a formal semiotic analysis of non-discursive symbols can hardly be fruitful since we know nothing about the recording link.

An example of what we have just said is a variety of American abstract films. There is a flow of senseless images which nevertheless greatly influence spectators, their effect being comparable to the effect of drugs (Sobolev, 1971). Psychologists of many countries have long studied the possibility of a direct effect of the cinema upon the subconsciousness.

A few words about music seem relevant. One could compile an interesting collection of statements about music. Here are separate fragments of such statements borrowed from the book by Langer (1951): "Music as expressive form; music as the language of emotions; music as logical expression of feelings; music as means of self-expression; music as tonal structure; somatic influence of music; music as morphology of feelings . . ." Langer's concluding formulation is, "Music is our myth of the inner life — a young, vital, and meaningful myth, of recent inspiration and still in its 'vegetative' growth."

In the collection of articles *Semiotics and Artmetrics* published recently in the USSR, in the article by Lévi-Strauss (1964) taken from his book *Mythologique I. Le Cru et le Cuit*, attention is drawn to the profound similarity of music and myths. It has become commonplace to interpret music as a myth. Simultaneously, it is possible to speak of the language of music. Such composers as Haydn, Handel, and Mozart were interested in the mechanics of musical composition. The advent of computers gave quite a serious direction to these ideas. There appeared the possibility of a formal language analysis of musical pieces and later of their synthesis. Simultaneously, work has begun on synthesizing sounds of various pitches. All this is described in detail in the book *Cybernetics and Music* by Zaripov (1971), where it is even stated that a computer is capable of creating new syntactic structures and thus can break the limits of previous rules. (In the United States, extensive studies in this direction are carried out by Bell Laboratories and at Carnegie-Mellon University in Pittsburgh, Pennsylvania.)

However, I believe that a musical piece should be regarded rather as a non-discursive construction of a mythological type. Formal analysis of the inner musical structure, as well as formal analysis of rhythm in poetry, is perceived, at least nowadays, as something external, not organically related to the process of creation and perception. Everything would perhaps be perceived otherwise if we knew something about the mechanism of subcellular recording. In any case, for both music and rhythm in poetry, semantic units cannot be isolated which are analogous to the words of everyday language; neither can we compile defining dictionaries for them, however polymorphous they might be. I want to contrast music to abstract painting since, to my mind, the alphabet and grammar of abstract paintings are clearly connected with the process of their perception. It may be stated, though it is difficult to prove, that abstract painting is perceived as discursive. The character of its influence is something perceived coldly, logically rather than emotionally–physiologically. Certainly, there are cases of a mixed influence. As for objective painting (which is far from being the subject of my work), I can find extreme cases where the pictures are perceived as myths influencing us in an extralogical way. One such instance is "quiet painting" by Giorgi Morandi. His seemingly simple and almost realistic still lives with an oft-repeating theme produce a very deep and logically inexplicable impression, but in order to perceive it, one has to stop in front of them and abstract oneself from everything, as if to enter them. There exists, however, narrative painting, e.g., the Russian group of painters known as "peredvizhniki" who used art merely to emphasize the effect of a strictly narrative subject.

In Western countries it is routine nowadays to speak of estrangement or alienation in the peculiar meaning given to these terms by existentialists. The cause of alienation is supposed to spring from the specific traits of modern culture and the dominant role words play in it. These judgments are not difficult to understand. Verbal communication between people takes place in the form of a dialogue, not a monologue. (Even such passive means of information transfer as books, articles, and broadcasts, if they are interesting, immediately cause dialogues: reviews, notices, and discussions.) In order to raise the level of comprehension of statements made in a language with an irregular structure, a dialogue again is necessary. Understanding is never complete, and this dialogue allows one to estimate the level of lack of understanding. In cultures where human communication is based on the perception of a myth, misunderstanding or lack of understanding (if any) remains unrevealed. It may be revealed if we start discussing the inner state in everyday language, but this is not always done. Cult rites—the mystery plays of the past—were procedures for uniting people. Are not these theories of alienation just a yearning for the past forms of life?

Among the younger generation of the United States there is now a broad movement for the creation of a new, according to them, culture—the culture of the human community. The ideology of this trend is very well presented by Reich (1970), whose book *The Greening of America* was a bestseller, parts of which were published in *New Yorker* magazine. Here are several very interesting quotations from the book:

> People are "together" when they experience the same thing in the same way. . . . Music has become the deepest means of communication and expression for an entire culture. . . . Electronics did, in fact, make possible sounds that no instrument up to that time could produce. . . . Electronic amplification also made possible a fantastic increase in volume, the music becoming as loud and penetrating as the human ears could stand, and thereby achieving a "total" effect. . . . They [people] are all the closer to each other because their being together is not mediated or separated by words. . . . They think rational conversation has been overdone as a means of communication between people, and they have invented a new term "rapping" for communication when it does take the form of words. . . . They believe that when people are really "together," their motivation will be higher, and their creativity multiplied far beyond the sum total of what they could produce as individuals. . . . Drugs . . . add a whole new dimension to creativity and to experience. . . . The use of drugs, especially because they are illegal, establish a blood-brotherhood before the musicians even began to play . . . and both bands and listeners consider drugs to be an integral part of musical experience.

This book is written with great sympathy for the new American movement—the author sees in it the beginning of a new culture. However, the impression is very sad. A religious bond seems to be restored without any nucleus and through an artificial chemical stimulation. However, from the scientific standpoint this is a very interesting phenomenon, a curious and spontaneously evolved experiment. Its most interesting feature is, first of all, the fact that the fight against modern culture has the fight with language as its principal manifestation. Also, the importance of drugs in mystery plays of a new type is interesting. Does not it follow from this that music perception, though in a rough form, is somatic and effectuated through the subcellular structures which are subject to a direct chemical effect? This seems to support the concept developed above on the inner mechanism of generating fantasies which can be opened by one key and strengthened by another. Is not all this evidence of a profound intellectual crisis of Western culture? But this is surely another subject.

I would not like the reader to think that this short chapter is an attempt to sketch a theory of the arts. It was only intended to emphasize the role of language in our culture. I am quite aware that the reader, having read the previous chapters, may wish to start a dialogue with me and attempt to discuss the way other cultural manifestations may be regarded from my standpoint. I decided to begin this dialogue even though I have no sufficiently compelling arguments. As to the other approaches to the language of art, I shall confine myself to pointing to the book by Goldman (1968), a very popular work in Western countries. A detailed critical analysis of this book was presented by Barrett (1971).

If the reader has found this chapter speculative and incomplete, so be it.

Chapter 8

Language and Thinking:
Continuity vs. Discontinuity[1]

Infinite Divisibility of Word Meanings as an
Indicator of Continuity of Thinking

In this book I have so far confined myself to language analysis, leaving aside the analysis of thinking. But now I shall try to build a bridge between language and thinking. The Bayesian model of language which has served to explain so many aspects of human verbal behavior seems also to contain implicitly the idea of continuity of thinking. Below I shall try to expand on this thesis.

It follows from all written above that words have two facets, atomistic and continuous. Logical constructions are built over a discrete sense symbol, which is an invariant of the whole meaning in the fuzzy field of meanings, i.e., encodes the field of meanings.

Comprehension of logical constructions — their decoding — takes place on the continuous level: it is from continuous consciousness that the prior notion of the distribution of word meanings is taken, and it is, again, to continuous consciousness that the posterior distribution function of the selectively oriented word meaning (after its comprehension within the phrase) is directed. To pass from the study of language to that of thinking, one has to manage to estimate to a certain extent the degree of word fuzziness. Words can be explained only by other words. One can

[1] This chapter will be in the second Russian edition of the book. Its expanded version was published by Tbilisi University in 1978.

get an idea of word meanings from dictionaries, both explanatory and bilingual. The number of explanatory words is here an index of fuzziness of the entries. The distribution function is illustrated in Fig. 8, which shows how the entries are distributed according to the number of the explanatory words in the following three dictionaries:

1. *English-Russian Dictionary*, edited by O. S. Akhmanova, Sovetskaya Entsiklopediya, 1970 (20,000 entries).
2. *Complete English-Russian Dictionary in Two Volumes,* edited by I. R. Galperin, Sovetskaya Entsiklopediya, 1972 (150,000 entries).
3. *Webster's New World Dictionary of the American Language*, edited by D. B. Guralnik, The World Publishing Company, Cleveland and New York (over 100,00 entries, 896 pp., over 6,000 illustrations).

We see that bilingual dictionaries have a predominant maximum somewhere between 5 and 10 explanatory words. This means that most words —codes of one language— do not correspond exactly to the symbols of another language, but can be given a not too verbose explanation. In the explanatory dictionary where the words are described by other words of the same language, the maximum is much more blurred and shifts to the right for about a dozen words. Especially interesting are the tail parts of the curves. In the smaller bilingual dictionary the maximal number of explanatory words is 87, in the larger one it is 1,362, and in the explanatory dictionary it is 471. The comparison of the bilingual dictionaries shows that the transition from a smaller dictionary to a larger one has two components. The first is enrichment by addition of easily explained name words. In the larger dictionary there appear such name words as

feather-mail—clothes of feathers (of Mexican Indians)
feather-man—a tradesman or hawker of former times who dealt in
    feathers or plumes
feather-meal—flour made of feather

which are absent in the smaller dictionary.

The second component of the larger dictionary is the expanded explanation of words that also appear in the smaller dictionary. For example, the word "set," one of the most "horrible" English words, is explained in the smaller dictionary by 96 words and in the larger one by 1,816 words. The number of entries in the larger dictionaries, as compared with the smaller one, increases 7.5 times, and the number of explanatory words is 13.4 times larger. The first of the above-mentioned components results in preserving a prominent peak for the larger dictionary as well, while the second one leads to a long tail part.

Thus, a deeper penetration into language is accompanied, on the one hand, by the enrichment of the dictionary with name words and, on the

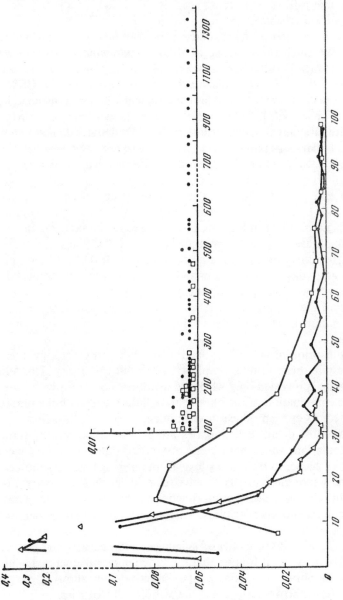

FIG. 8. *Distribution of entries according to the number of explanatory words in three dictionaries:* •, *large two-volume English-Russian dictionary;* △, *small English-Russian dictionary;* □, *Webster's New World Dictionary. Distribution functions are obtained from random samples, consisting of 1,000 words each. The calculations were made by G. A. Batulova.*

other hand, by the expanded explanation of polysemantic words. Still, no "complete" dictionary can embrace all the potentially possible variety of word meanings, as is shown by the following examples.

Imagine that a Russian who has been living abroad for a long time is shown a cartoon in which a good-for-nothing man sadly contemplates a notice over the counter of the chandlery shop: "French polish is sold only after 11." We catch the meaning of the joke immediately because we know that French polish is sometimes drunk by real drunkards and that 11 o'clock is the time when alcohol begins to be sold in the USSR. However, a person isolated from his environment will not understand it, and no dictionary will help him. In the same manner, people studying English without going to Great Britain or the United States do not understand half the cartoons published in such a magazine as *The New Yorker*. The field of word meanings includes all our life experience which can be mastered in no other way than through life itself.

Another example is the Russian slang phrase "пудрить мозги," which translates into English as "to powder one's brains." This expression, of course, has no meaning in English, but it is used in the same manner as the English phrase "to pull the wool over one's eyes." If you heard someone say, "Yesterday he came again and tried to pull the wool over my eyes" or "Yesterday he came again and tried to powder my brains," in both cases you would understand the meaning even if you had not previously heard these expressions. It would be obvious that someone was trying to change the other person's ability to see or to understand something clearly.

Thus, the prior distribution function of the words entering these idioms, despite their seeming simplicity, turns out to be very rich, and their meaning is revealed only when the words are combined with other words: the combination of the phrase "to pull the wool" with the phrase "over someone's eyes" produces a vivid image.

Even the most detailed dictionaries are able to embrace only those word combinations which have become standard (idiomatic), i.e., have turned into a cliché. In translating texts from one language into another, we constantly face the necessity to solve such riddles. No dictionary provides us with the prior distribution function of the word meaning necessary to comprehend all possible word combinations of the given language.

From the probabilistic model of language, recorded with the help of the Bayesian theorem, it follows that the function $p(y|\mu)$ emerging while one reads the phrase acts as a peculiar selective filter allowing one to choose quite a narrow strip from the word's field of meanings. The mechanism of filtration is amazingly simple. The prior distribution function of the word meanings may be arranged so that adjacent regions would have almost equal probabilities, in which case they are indistinguishable if the word is considered independently of any context.

However, it would always seem possible to think of phrases for which $p(y|\mu)$ will look almost the same as the δ function; then, in accordance with the Bayesian theorem, the region indistinguishable from other ones will be selected.

One has to acknowledge the following: *we shall never be able to state that it is impossible to think of another phrase which would reveal the word meaning in some new way.* Proceeding from the analysis of language semantics, it is in this sense that we can speak of the continuous character of thinking. The semantic field of word meanings is infinitely divisible.[2] The notion of atoms of meaning, which is so indispensable for constructing logical semantics, psychologically is nothing more than an illusion.

I was once prompted by a good analogy: the notion of the continuous nature of word meanings may be compared (though the comparison is far-fetched) with the well-known mathematical notion of a Dedekind section. This is a constructive method of introducing irrational numbers as certain partitions of rational ones. For example, $\sqrt{2}$ is an irrational number dividing rational numbers into two classes: one class includes negative numbers, zero, and positive numbers a such that $a^2 < 2$; the other class consists of positive numbers b such that $b^2 > 2$.

A new unexpected word meaning is always perceived as something extrarational, i.e., as a *metaphor*, which wedges itself between two closely connected and familiar meanings of the word. An attempt to list all possible metaphors would be futile. Metaphors can be given only *constructively,* by new phrases reflecting a new situation or a new aspect of thought. A new metaphor starts to lose its metaphoric status as it becomes familiar in everyday verbal behavior. In this way language is enriched by revealing what it *contains potentially.*

Above, I posed the question: by what is the evolution of culture better characterized, by the growth of the number of new words or by the broadening of the meaning of old ones? At present I would answer this question in the following manner. New words broaden the meaning of old words since new words allow us to generate phrases revealing in the old words a new sense, previously concealed. In this way the *dialectics* of the continuous and discrete is reflected in language.

Mathematicians, especially those who deal with computers, do not see any major difficulties in making discrete devices as compared with continuous ones. Indeed, if we have to find the area under a curve which is

---

[2] I should like to remind the reader of the traditional definition of continuity as infinite divisibility (the definition is ascribed to Anaxagoras): "The small does not contain the smallest, but the smaller. Since what exists cannot disappear (after dividing)" (cited from Panchenko, 1975).

not given analytically, it will not make any difference if the points on the curve are taken as densely as wanted. But the formulation of the problem would be ridiculous if we were given only a code denotation of the curve and its fairly vague description by code denotations of other similarly given curves. This is just what we are facing in language: we know a word — a code denotation of the field — and a vague description of the latter given by other code denotations. The whole variety of the semantic content remains hidden; it is revealed only through the potential possibility of inventing an infinite number of new phrases.

However, we do not have in front of us such a set of phrases prepared beforehand. The continuous semantic content underlying discrete symbols of the language remains, in the main, unmeasurable. Only its separate fragments are accessible to us when we interpret concrete phrases. It is important to note that every language has its own system of entering the continuous streams of consciousness.

If comprehension of our everyday verbal communication takes place on the continuous level, we may suggest that thinking itself is essentially continuous. Hence come the ever-repeating complaints (even by poets) of the insufficiency of the expressive means of language. Rhythm in poetry and incantations reflects an attempt to put the continuous constituent in discrete carriers of speech. Vague legends of Lemurians whose speech was like the murmur of the stream is an echo of pre-logical, continuous forms of communication.

Plastic art forms are the only long-preserved forms of continuous communication. In music, discrete symbols of notes are not themselves the means of communication; they are only the record of what should be done to reproduce the continuously perceived sequence of sounds. Abstract painting is an example of an attempt to construct an essentially discrete form of communication for the emotional sphere of life.

Fossil forms of pre-logical communication are retained in folk speech. "Such, for example, is the literary tradition of the European peasants from Cervantes' Sancho Panza to Tolstoy's Platon Karataev. Both are illiterate; both are rich in proverbial lore; both are untroubled by intellectual consistency; and both represent many of the values which are characteristic of oral culture" (Rankine, 1968, p. 61). One might note an even more remarkable phenomenon: the culture of silence. An example is the part of the culture of the Russian Middle Ages whose source lies in Byzantine hesychasts (Meyendorf, 1974). Its spirit is expressed in plastic forms of churches, in vignettes in holy books, and in icons — but not in words. There is no clear verbal interpretation of holy texts which would allow us, the representatives of a verbal culture, to understand the specific features of Russian medieval consciousness. We are dealing not only with iconological thinking but also with iconological forms of expressing this thinking (Pomerants, 1974).

Many people know from their own experience how expressive and important fragments of scientific texts become if one manages to give them an inner rhythm. The variety of rhythms of narrative prose is only of late becoming the object of serious study (Chicherin, 1974) though we always feel it inwardly. Religious texts are always so arranged that they have an inner rhythm. It is because of their rhythmical structure that they are especially convincing: "The system of commandments may be not quite logical, but it invariably obeys some rhythm, it is poetically organized. . . . There is no *image* of the new morality comparable with Bach's 'Passions,' Rublev's 'Saviour' or the 'Buddha of Gandhara' " (Pomerants, 1974, pp. 423–424). Possibly, all of these may be regarded as a direct appeal to the continuous constituent in human thinking.

Unusual or Altered States of Consciousness as a Direct Manifestation of Continuity of Thinking

I am quite aware of the fact that my approach to contrasting language and thinking may easily be criticized. One possible objection might run as follows: If the human brain functions as a discrete computer, then probably its part responsible for thinking properly disposes of a number of elementary discrete carriers of information several orders of magnitude larger than our language vocabulary. Outwardly, this would seem exactly like saying that thinking is of a continuous nature and language has a discrete nature. I am ready to answer the challenge and meet it with a number of facts borrowed from the psychology of thinking, anthropology, and psychiatry. I believe that these facts testify directly to the continuous nature of thinking, and an attempt to demonstrate this follows.

Reflective thinking and creative insight. In my opinion, reflective thinking is the discrete control of the continuous flow of thoughts. A person asks himself a question in the discrete language; this is a question to the spontaneous thinking process. Having received an answer, he analyzes it on a logical level, and if it does not satisfy him, another slightly modified question is formulated.

Discovery is an answer suddenly entering one's mind in response to a meaningfully formulated question. Even in mathematics, discoveries are not made on the level of logical thinking.

Logical means only help to formulate the problem and test the solution which comes as an insight. The psychology of mathematical creation is brilliantly described in the book by Hadamard (1945), a well-known French mathematician. His principal conclusions are as follows: there is hardly any completely logical discovery; discovery is arrived at subconsciously, as a flow of ideas after conscious prior work; words and other symbols are absent from the creative process.

Hadamard's conclusions are supported by many facts he has collected. He cites outstanding mathematicians and refers to the results of questionnaires he distributed among American mathematicians. All this allows one to state that creative insight, even in mathematics, presupposes leaving the limits of logical thinking.

Comprehension on the extralogical level.   In the tradition of the well-known Soviet physicist-academician L. I. Mandelshtam (1950), we can speak of two degrees of comprehension. The first is comprehension on the logical level, which is easily achieved by the majority of students. The second degree, profound comprehension, allows the student to master the subject so that he not only is able to speak about what he has learned but also to answer a sudden question. In order to pass to this second level of creative comprehension, Mandelshtam thought it extremely useful to discuss with students some paradoxes of quantum mechanics, a process which resembles thinking over koan (the paradoxical statements of Zen philosophy; see Chapter 2).

It seems pertinent to formulate here the following statement: although scientific theoretical structures are recorded in an abstract symbolic form, it is not our knowledge that is recorded; the symbolic record is only a way to evoke this knowledge in our mind. None of such generally known concepts as, say, the Ψ function in quantum mechanics or even that of a field in physics, the concept of randomness in probability theory, or that of a virus in biology can be simply and unambiguously interpreted by our immediate concepts of the external world. I consider it unnecessary to worry about how to give a more accurate meaning to these words-symbols. I believe students should merely be taught how, with the help of such concepts, one can build logically meaningful statements whereby we come to understand the world at the profound level at which we can easily manage without atomic word meanings.

Meditation—a direct access to continuous streams of consciousness. A call for silence as the means of knowing oneself and the world (Buddha, Chuang Tzu, Rabindranath Tagore, Krishnamurti, and even Wittgenstein) is an appeal for direct access to continuous thinking in its pure form. The technique of meditation is a skill to govern continuous thinking without resorting to language. The goal of control is to direct freely flowing, logically unstructured streams of ideas.

Recently, unusual or altered states of consciousness have become the subject of scientific investigations in the West. These states include those resulting from contemplative meditation and silent prayer. The study of altered states of consciousness has become a branch of clinical research. The experience accumulated by mystics of many religious sects has come to be the object of psychological and psychiatric research. The widely known collection of papers *Altered States of Consciousness* (Tart, 1963a) contains a bibliography of 1,000 titles.

Meditation may be regarded as deautomation of familiar psychic structures; the meditating person leaves the boundaries of logically structured consciousness. He brings about a new state of consciousness which consists of the experience of "merging" with the object of meditation, dissolution in it, and loss of the boundaries of his personality. The sensation of integrity arises. Discrete symbols of language prove inadequate to express this state of consciousness. The laws of Aristotelian logic are violated, contradictions no longer cause surprise, and both space-time and cause-effect structuring of the world undergo essential changes; paradoxical aspects of the experience are perceived as most natural.

Below I quote Deikman (1963), who reports the impressions of a subject of experimental meditation concerning the sensation of merging (the object of meditation was a blue vase).

> *Merging:* "merging" was reported by subject A. . . . She reported, "One of the points that I remember most vividly is when I really began to feel, you know, almost as though the blue and I were perhaps merging, or that vase and I were one. . . . It was as though everything was sort of merging and I was somehow losing my sense of consciousness almost." This "merging" experience was characteristic of all of the subject's meditation sessions, but she soon became familiar with it and ceased to describe it as anything remarkable. Following the six sessions she reported, "At one point it felt . . . as though the vase were in my head rather than 'out there'; I knew it was out there but it seemed as though it were almost a part of me." "I think that I almost felt at that moment as though, you know, the image is really in me, it's not out there." (p. 206)
>
> In subsequent sessions, subject A described a "film of blue" that developed as the boundaries of vase dissolved. It covered the table on which the vase sat and the wall behind it, giving them all a blue color. In the tenth session the "film" became a "mist" and in the eleventh it became a "sea of blue" . . . "it lost its boundaries and I might lose mine too" and describing the general experience as "I was swimming in a sea of blue and I felt for a moment I was going to drown." . . . However, despite the anxiety it occasioned, she felt that the experience was very desirable. (p. 207)

Hypnosis as one of the altered states of consciousness. Hypnosis, too, attenuates the common perception of reality familiar for the logically structured consciousness. It allows one to acquire a new experience close to meditation, a state which may be regarded as a form of autohypnosis.

Dream as a manifestation of an altered state of consciousness.   The freely flowing dream consciousness is also devoid of logical structures. In a dream we unaccountably find responses to the "sore spots" of our day's consciousness. Hence comes the proverb, "An hour in the morning is worth two in the evening." As a result of dream analysis, Jung (1930) developed his conception of archetypes — certain images common for all humans and preserved through the ages in the *collective* subconscious.

Altered states of consciousness arising from direct biochemical effect. The fact that altered states of consciousness can result from a direct biochemical effect has been known from time immemorial, but only recently has this phenomenon become an object of close study (see, for example, the collection of papers compiled by Tart, 1963a). Again, the states of consciousness thus achieved are very much like those achieved in meditation.

An extremely vivid description of an altered state of consciousness achieved by administering nitrous oxide (laughing gas) is given by William James, the outstanding American psychologist and author of the well-known book *The Varieties of Religious Experience* (1902). In one of his papers James (1882) wrote:

> . . . all contradictions, so-called, are but differences; . . . all differences are of degree; . . . all degrees are of common kind, . . . unbroken continuity is of the essence of being, and . . . we are literally in the midst of an *infinity*, to perceive the existence of which is the utmost we can attain . . . *yes* and *no* agree at least in being assertions; a denial of a statement is but another mode of stating the same, contradiction can only occur of the same thing — all opinions are thus synonyms, all synonyms are the same. But the same phrase by difference of emphasis is two; and here again difference and nondifference merge in one. (p. 360)

This is an illustration of a possibility of extralogical or, if you like, of a truly dialectical arrangement of consciousness.

Extralinguistic structure of Zen philosophy.   Zen-Buddhism is something more than a religious-philosophical system; this is a unique culture strangely inserted into our world (for more detail on Zen, see, for example, Fromm et al., 1960).

The principal burden of Zen is extralinguistic experience, a perception of the world outside its logical comprehension and without verbal communication. Reality should be experienced; it is useless to attempt to express it verbally (Berkman, 1972).

Zen seems to be a unique philosophical system without a doctrine. Zen state of consciousness is achieved by three methods: zazen, a Zen form of meditation; koan, laconic paradoxes or riddles without a logical solution; and mondo, a series of questions and answers asked and answered "rapid fire." Koan and mondo serve only to "open the eyes" — to liberate consciousness from verbal and logical traps. An example of a koan was given in Chapter 2.

Here I should like to illustrate a mondo dialogue reported by Watts (cited from Berkman, 1972):

> — "I have no peace of mind," said Hui-ko. "Please, pacify my mind."
> — "Bring out your mind here before me," replied Badhidharma, "and I will pacify it."
> — "But when I see my own mind," said Hui-ko, "I cannot find it."
> — "There," snapped Badhidharma, "I have pacified your mind."

The meaning of this dialogue may be interpreted as follows (Fromm et al., 1960). The problems of Ego are not important, but the problem of Ego existence is. To my mind, in this dialogue, the person who asks loses himself; he can no longer retain the sensation of discreteness of his own existence. This is the aim of the dialogue. Mondo is usually practiced in dialogue between pupils and teachers of Zen. Questions are selected so as to relate to the field which is studied by the pupil but which he does not understand completely. The teacher tries to arouse the pupil's response at the intuitive level without resorting to logic and theoretical constructions.

An attempt to create extralinguistic communication by modern technical means. At present, we are observing a fairly unusual phenomenon: attempts are being made to use modern technical means — lasers, special image-deforming optics, electronics — to create the so-called synaesthetic cinema. It is a cinema of the space-time continuum. The effect of continuity is created by superimposition or welding of parts, unfocused complexity, into a mosaic of simultaneousness.

At least the titles of such films as Brakhage's "Dog.Star.Man," Stanley Kubrick's "2001: a Space Odyssey," and Belson's "Allures" and "Samadhi" are well known. All these are attempts to link a rich inner experience with the external world and to transfer it to others by extralinguistic means without trying to express discretely what is perceived as a unified whole.

Isn't all this to say that there exist *immediately observed phenomena which are hard to interpret without acknowledging continuity of thinking*?

The facts collected in this section might seem rather unusual, since I have followed an unconventional path; I have widened the scale of analyzing human psychic activity. When studying a phenomenon in the exact sciences, we always strive to widen the interval of varying independent variables, since otherwise investigating in a narrow interval we shall unavoidably simplify the matter and shall believe a linear model to be fit for describing unknown complicated functional dependence.

So why should we limit ourselves by the boundaries of our own cultural stereotype while studying the human psyche? The tendency of today is to push back these boundaries and to make use of the whole variety of human behavior in alien cultures and altered states of consciousness. But having chosen this road, we immediately face the problem of continuity of our consciousness which is only implicitly given in our modern culture.

Semantics of Rhythm: Rhythm as a Direct Access to the Continuous Streams of Consciousness[3]

> Кто-то едет - к смертной победе.
> У деревьев жесты трагедий:
> Иудеи - жертвенный танец!
> У деревьев - трепеты таинств.
> Это - заговор против века:
> Веса, счета, времени, дроби . . .
> Се - разодранная завеса:
> У деревьев - жесты надгробий . . .
> Кто-то едет. Небо - как въезд.
> У деревьев - жесты горжеств.

> Somebody is going to the deathly *victory*.
> Trees have gestures of *tragedies*:
> The sacrificial *dance* of Judea!
> Trees have gestures of *sacraments*.
> This is the plot against the *age*:
> Weighing, counting, time, and *fraction* . . .
> This is the torn *curtain*:
> Trees have gestures of *gravestones*.
> Somebody is going. The sky is like an *entrance*
> Trees have gestures of *fêtes*.

Texts—they may be so various. Why do some of them worry and excite us? They are the Message. We know this but we cannot always express this information in a familiar and visible shape—a word. But the invisible shape of the Message has already penetrated into us, and we have accepted it: "This is the torn curtain."

---

[3] This section was written by V. V. Nalimov and J. A. Drogalina. The poems used belong to the outstanding Russian poet M. I. Tsvetayeva. We give their word-for-word translation, not daring to translate them into proper English. The rhyming Russian words are italicized in the translation.

What is this invisible component, which is so convincing, genuine, and real?

To what does it turn us?

At what level does it make the message "explicit," personally directed, and provide:

1. the "entrance" according to the individuals's "tuning" and capabilities (the prior function of the sense distribution);
2. personal recognition, by way of creative impulse inherent in any person and based upon the live experience of insight (the latter being defined as an extralogical capability of direct entrance into the continuous stream of consciousness, the faculty to cognize the introobjective, whereby, according to Bergson, one is "transferred inside the object to merge with what is there unique and inexpressable");
3. the faculty to co-participate in the throbbing of Universal Existence.

Why is it the messages which are no longer texts as logical development of an idea, but Texts as revelation of Mystery, that are so exciting?

Probably they excite us because through them we realize the faculty of personal creativity, and of cognition in the most unknown and boundless meaning of the word:

> Вздрогнешь - и горы с плеч
> И душа - горе́.
> You shudder – and mountains are off your mind,
> And your soul is mounting.

Image. Not an addition, but merging and welding; integrity of vision and visions. This becomes an ordered message, rhythmical and reduced.

Rhythm allows one to record the phenomenon in an essentially briefer form than it is described and signified, without resorting to abstraction. How does this become possible? Thanks to what peculiarities?

Rhythm — and we shall speak here only of the rhythm of texts — what is rhythm? Rhyme, consonance, assonance, alliteration, or refrains are but external manifestations of rhythm.

Inherently and essentially, rhythm is something much more significant; rhythm probably means the dissolving of word meanings, their merging into a continuous, inwardly indissoluble stream of images. In other words, rhythm provides an opportunity for non-Bayesian reading of the texts.

In ordinary speech devoid of rhythm, we use the mechanism of Bayesian reading (see Chapter 2): the word meaning μ is specified by its usage; we pronounce phrase y and get in our mind the function $p(y|\mu)$ which acts as a filter for the previously given distribution function of the word meaning $p(\mu)$. Out of the set of meanings of the word μ, a subset of meanings is selected with new, probabilistically given weights. The verbal context specifying and narrowing down the meaning of the word μ limits it and brings it into correspondence with the whole text. But in a rhythmically organized text, everything happens otherwise. Rhythm here is a governing essence welding separate groups into integral wholes.

The text is organized so that the words do not limit one another but, on the contrary, have their meaning broadened, smoothly flowing into one another and merging into one stream. Is that not really so?

> Перерытые как битвой,
> Взрыхленные небеса,
> Рытвинами - небеса,
> Битвенные - небеса.
> Перелетами, как хлестом,
> Хлестанные табуны,
> Взблестывающей луны
> Вдовствующей - табуны!

> Dug up as if battled,
> Loosened heaven,
> Groovy heaven,
> Battled heaven.
> Lashed by flights, as if by whips,
> Lashed *herds*,
> *Herds* of the glittering
> Widowed *moon*.

Are any comments necessary here? Should one try to explain how the merging words create a freely flowing image? The poem is entitled "Clouds."

Words, affected by their neighbors, transcend the prior distribution functions of "meaning." Word borders are erased. Words quite different in their meaning interlace and converge.

But where lies the organizing center of this logically chaotic conglomeration of words? We believe that it is rhythm in all the variety of its manifestations. It makes the words exist where they are put by the author, though they blur their semantic borders.

A formal mathematical study of a rhyme, no matter how delicate and subtle it is, does not reveal the image of the poem. It is not the rhyme which tells but the words interlacing thanks to the rhythm and catching the gliding image.

Repeated usage of synonymous words makes even a prosaic text rhythmical. Synonyms are not merely identical, semantically close words. A set of synonyms blurs word meanings and welds them into something immensely larger. A text poor in synonyms always looks dismal. When speaking of a verbally rich text, we most often mean its richness in synonyms. Such richness of a prosaic text might serve as the measure of its rhythmical arrangement.

In poetical texts, words which are not originally synonymous become so. In the above-quoted poem, each line is synonymous with any other, and all of them are synonyms of the image "clouds." The word "cloud" has broadened, lost its boundaries, and turned into something grandiose, fantastic, and immanent to what the poet feels. The author succeeded in expressing by the huge conglomeration of words what is not expressed by single words. We recognize the Name of the cloud discovered by the poet.

But it is probably better to speak of rhythm in another manner, brief and fragmentary, without trying to weave the lace of logical construction:

1. Rhythm — is a witness to the state of purification, of liberation from noise — fragments of thoughts; the state of "entrance." Being "inside," where there are no discrete symbols, everything is in everything, where the continuous stream of images is being "read" unconsciously and extra-logically. [The continuous character of consciousness is discussed in greater detail in another publication (Nalimov, 1978).]
2. Rhythm — is generated by resonance; this is a linking constituent, transforming the continuous image into a discrete symbol, the power giving the Name. But the Name itself remains a mystery and is not pronounced. (For a semantic interpretation of the term "name," see Chapter 7.)
3. Rhythm — is a catapult: "The screaming Word broke loose from a word" (from *Beethoven* by N. Zabolotsky). It reveals the essence immanent in the Name.
4. Rhythm — is a self-sufficing effect (no need of an explanatory context): something open for an immediate perception by the possibilities of cognizing, addressed directly to continuous images.
5. Rhythm — is a witness to the possibility of approaching the Mystery of the world. It completes the text written only by consonants.

> Consonants are muscles of the speech; they are the power, the frame, and the contour to the sound; they are the banks holding in the fluid essence of Vowels. (Volkonsky, 1913)

It procures the necessary vowels revealing the secret meaning with such force that it becomes self-evident, true, and real. (These words are from the novel *Golem* by Gustav Meyrink, 1915.)

6. Rhythm — is merging with Name.
7. Rhythm — is justification of a pause, its structure. A pause signifies

the completeness and completion of a statement. An ability to glance at the unfinished and finish it without words.

> Understanding does not come with knowledge. In the interval between words, between thoughts, comes Understanding, – this interval is silence unbroken by knowledge . . . (Krishnamurti, 1970)

8. Rhythm—is liberation from logic. It is independent and beyond any limits. And our tyrannical encroachments to "test harmony by algebra" are impotent.
9. Rhythm—is archaic, alien to our culture, legally preserved only in poetry and only sometimes breaking through in other texts. But often do we long for it under the cover of logical thoughts.

And then a double-structured, bifacial text collapses upon us . . .

Amazing as it is, we have to acknowledge that paradoxical statements also blur word semantics and thus make texts rhythmical. Remember the famous koan: "Does a dog have the Buddha nature? Nothing." A disciple in a Zen monastery would meditate over its meaning for months or even years, but the koan has no logical solution. Meditation has nothing to do with logical analysis. The disciple should achieve a state in which words with such different semantics as "dog" and "Buddha" have expanded to the degree that they could merge with one another, and this merging goes through the fundamental, though verbally inexpressible, Buddhist concept encoded by the single word "nothing." Should the disciple develop an ability to comprehend the koan, that would seem to mean he has achieved a new state of consciousness, and the possibility to enter directly the continuous stream opens up before him.

And, mind you, the formula recording the entrance into another state of consciousness is extremely compact.

When the words' semantics are infinitely fuzzy, they naturally cease to obey logic. Texts no longer contain contradictions, since they are composed of words with fuzzy semantics smoothly gliding into one another. If, say, we start to meditate over the word "life," expanding its meaning, we shall see sooner or later that it includes the concept of death as well: death becomes a component of life. And the moment that opposition of life and death disappears, texts can no longer contain a contradiction which may be generated by the discrete comprehension of these two words.

The dialectics of such flowing of word semantics is unusually well described by Japanese philosophers. Below, we quote the words of the Japanese thinker Masao Abe (1969).

> In Zen, which denies all dualities including the vertical one, there is neither the rule of God nor the idea of creation nor the last judge-

ment. History as well as man's living-dying existence (*samsara*) has no beginning and no end. There is only a beginningless beginning and endless end. This is, however, not a vague notion, but a concept made possible through negation of a vertical duality implied in historical incarnation. Since *samsara* is without beginning or end, history has no center. Accordingly, every point in history is a center. This is the reason, as I stated earlier, that at every moment of our living-dying existence we realize the paradoxical oneness of living and dying in its totality, and thereby we are liberated from it. At the very moment of our existential realization, "Great Death" and "Great Life" take place in us. And so there is no process in history. At every moment a profound disjunction is realized. (p. 10)

Compare this fragment with the lines of the apocryphal Gospel of St. Thomas, which stood at one source of our culture (McWilson, 1963).

19. The disciples said to Jesus, Tell us what will be our end. Jesus said, Have you discovered the beginning that you look for the end? Since where is the beginning there will be the end. Blessed is he who will be at the beginning, and he will know the end, and will not partake of death.

But now let us return to the texts of modern culture. Here, too, among nonpoetic texts one might discover bifacial ones, i.e., those having simultaneously logical and rhythmical constituents.

Among these is *Tractatus Logico-Philosophicus* by Wittgenstein (1955). It is written by a professional logician, and one of its constituents is, indubitably, precise logic. But I am sure many will agree that it is also rhythmical, and this accounts for its magic effect. However, the source of the rhythm is not rhyme of any sort but rather a paradoxical character of the propositions. The text of *Tractatus* consists of a sequence of enumerated paradoxes, and it is their structure which is unusual. These are laconic statements with rich content which are obviously contradictory to the concepts generally accepted in our culture. Here is one such paradox:

In the world everything is as it is and happens as it does happen. In it there is no value—and if there were, it would be of no value. (6.24)

The proposition quoted obviously does not correspond to the cardinal concepts of our culture, which is permeated with the idea of goals both for the individual and for whole nations or even whole cultures. The historical development of European culture can be viewed as a process of formulating goals, fighting for their realization, and then unintentionally discrediting and abandoning them.

In a few simple words, this brief proposition tears at the basis of our outlook, but the power of these words in no way stems from their ability to convince us logically. The error of our concept of goal could well be suggested in a purely logical way. It would suffice to say that "goal" is a metaconcept and for this reason it cannot be placed within our universe, the world of hierarchically lower object concepts; but such an approach would require us to introduce abstract concepts of a fairly high order. The author of *Tractatus* chooses another way. Instead of using logic, he weaves a lace of words that makes the reader ponder not over what is expressed by words (strictly speaking, they lack meaning) but over what lies behind them if their meaning is expanded infinitely. His words do not prove his idea; rather, they make us think of what there must be in the mind of the person who proved capable of penetrating the problem to its very core. Note that the cited paradox contains a purely logical contradiction: "In it there is no value—and if there were, it would be of no value." This resembles a Zen koan. In European philosophical literature *Tractatus* occupies a unique place as a result of its "alien" nature. This also accounts for the acutely negative attitude of positivists toward it. Carnap recommended that it be read and thrown away, and Popper ironically described Wittgenstein as a person claiming the role of a prophet. In its time, *Tractatus* was hardly circulated. [For a biographical analysis of Wittgenstein's writings, see the highly readable book by Bartley (1973).]

Now let us turn to the sources of European culture. Paradoxical as it may seem, we have to acknowledge that European culture, which has so consistently and thoroughly developed the cult of rationalistic thinking, has at its base two quite opposite trends: Hellenic rationalism and the irrationalism of early Christianity. Still, we would like to consider European culture as an integral whole, despite the variety of its ramifications: European atheism also has a Christian nature which is quite different from, say, Oriental nihilism. Atheism first of all must argue with something, and, consequently, its structure is determined by what it argues with and also by the arguments it uses. These latter must of necessity get into the frame of the existing paradigm; otherwise they will be neither comprehended nor accepted. Already in the Middle Ages, Catholic Christianity, through the efforts of Thomas Aquinas, had dressed itself in a rationalism more profound than Aristotelian. [For a brief analysis of the development of determinism in European culture see my earlier paper (Nalimov, 1976).]

However, Christianity is based upon the texts of the Gospels, and any attempt to analyze them logically is impertinent and awkward since they are full of internal contradictions. The difficulty in constructing positive hermeneutics of Christianity is obvious (Pye and Morgan, 1973). Here is Christ's own brief formulation of the contents of his teaching:

17.6. I have manifested thy name unto man . . .

A contemporary reader brought up on logic expects a clear explanation of what these words mean and gets no answer. The Name is revealed by the rhythm. The words "He who has ears, let him hear" are the refrain of the New Testament.

Below we cite the Gospel of St. John where, we believe, the principal cosmogonic idea is expressed.

1.1. In the beginning was the Word, and the word was with God, and the Word was God.
1.2. The same was in the beginning with God.
1.3. All things were made by Him; and without Him was not any thing made that was made.
1.4. In Him was life; and the life was the light of men.
1.5 And the light shineth in darkness; and the darkness comprehended it not.
1.14 And the Word was made flesh, and dwelt among us, full of grace and truth.

Look how simple the text is. Its meaning is based on the infinite expansion of the concept "word" and its merging with the semantics of seemingly quite alien concepts. And we observe a picture of the Universe with a cybernetic significance and flavor.

We come to see that the source of everything is information, the informational flow of the matter structuring the initial Chaos; it integrates the word, life, and teaching. But this idea is not made explicit; it is not logically developed. It is only implied by expanding the meaning of the familiar concept "word," and the implications tune us in, in resonance with this deeply monotheistic outlook.

The modern definition of the same concept, "word," sounds as follows: "A word is a fragment of a text between two blanks." This definition is clear and precise and can easily be used to construct logical statements, but how poor and deprived its meaning is! It will slip away altogether if we try to comprehend the concept "text," undefined here.

It would be very interesting to trace back the ways in which two styles of text organization—logical and rhythmical—confronted each other in European culture during the process of its development. In our days, the rhythmical structure of texts has acquired a new manifestation in the philosophy of existentialism. We hope it will not be thought a great exaggeration if we state that this philosophy is, as a matter of fact, based on the infinite and cosmic expansion of the seemingly simple word "existence."

Is the Hypothesis of Substantial Existence of "Fields of Consciousness" True?

It is time to return to discussing the hypothesis known from time immemorial of the substantial existence of "fields of consciousness" outside the human mind. Taking into consideration the variety of information on the role of altered states of consciousness in intellectual life, we would like to ask again whether man is a creator of continuous thinking or only the receptor of streams flowing somewhere outside him. If the second suggestion is true, then all human efforts directed at the perception of these flows—meditation, psychedelic drugs, participation in mystery rites, and, lastly, the ability to ask oneself questions in the language of discrete ideas and await the answers to them—all these are but various ways of "tuning" oneself for the reception.

This concept of the substantial character of continuous thinking, deeply linked with Oriental philosophical teachings, is not foreign to Western philosophical concepts. In some sense it reminds one of Plato's teaching on ideas, Schopenhauer's concept of the universal will, and Jung's idea of archetypes and the collective subconscious. While Suzuki (Fromm et al., 1960) speaks of the *Cosmic Unconscious*, Fromm (in the same book), following the title of the well-known book by Bucke (1923), prefers to speak of *Cosmic Consciousness*.

There is no need now to correlate these constructions with abstract idealism, since contemporary cosmogonic concepts are quite capable of a limitless expansion of our notion of the material Universe. It is also pertinent to recall here that some serious mathematicians are deeply convinced that in their creative activity they do not invent but rather discover abstract structure existing in reality and independent of them.

What arguments are there in favor of the hypothesis of the substantial existence of continuous fields of consciousness?

First of all, it is worth mentioning once more the studies of altered states of consciousness in which a person loses the sensation of the limits of his personality and perceives himself as part of a non-differentiated whole. Is it only illusion? Extremely interesting are the experiments in what is called mutual hypnosis (Tart, 1963b). It consists of a procedure during which subject A hypnotizes subject B and the latter, in the state of hypnosis, in his turn hypnotizes A. This chain of mutual hypnosis repeats several times, and the state of hypnosis becomes deeper and deeper. The most impressive (and frightening for the patients) result of such an experiment was the sensation of complete merging with each other, which Tart (1963b) describes as follows:

> This seemed like a partial fusion of identities, a partial loss of the distinction between I and Thou. This was felt to be good at the time,

but later the subjects perceived this as a threat to their individual autonomy. (p. 306)

Further, Tart remarks that he knows of a comparable case of merging and loss of individuality as a result of two married couples taking LSD-25 together. Something of the kind seems to have happened during the mystery rites of ancient times, and a current attempt to duplicate them appears in the practice of combining deafening music with taking drugs. Again we would like to ask: Is it only an illusion or is it an aspect of reality foreign to our culture? Of great interest in this respect are observations by Jung, who revealed the most ancient mythological motifs in dreams of modern people and demonstrated the likeness between paranoid delirium and ancient cosmogonies and eschatological prophecies. Whence come these archetypes, these ancient universal human images? One last remark regarding the concept of scientific creativity as *insight*: could this be just another form of manifesting the same access to something which exists outside us?

All these observations are certainly insufficient to prove the hypothesis of the substantial existence of fields of "images" outside humans, but they are sufficient to suggest that these beliefs merit further study.

We may immediately be opposed in the following manner: If substantially existing continuous streams of images are the storeroom of our culture, whence comes progress? It may be that people could scoop from this storeroom only what their waking consciousness is accustomed to, the consciousness which is the base for our culture. The process may consist simply of preparing the consciousness for ideas taken from somewhere in the streams flowing outside it. Strange as they may seem, we ought to ponder some of these conceptions of the remote past.

One might, of course, suggest another hypothesis: namely, that peculiar states of consciousness are a relic phenomenon preserved in a precisely encoded form from the remote past when humans were at the primitive stage of their development. This again gives rise to numerous unanswerable questions: Why did the initial stage of development generate such versatile and inwardly rich manifestations of consciousness? Why are they maintained till now in our subconscious? Why do they manifest themselves so that we have to regard them as more profound levels of consciousness, nourishing and regulating our logical thinking? And, finally, if this is not a result of personal experience nor a reflection of the external world but rather something encoded more or less similarly in all human races, then in what aspects does this concept differ from the hypothesis of the substantial existence of continuous fields of consciousness outside people? Perhaps we should confine ourselves to the statement that continuous fields of consciousness exist outside man, but not outside humanity.

Now we can ask in what way we see the mechanism by means of which a person switches on to the continuous fields of images. One might think that the mechanism of continuous thinking is of analogous character, different from reflective logical thinking for which the mechanism of discrete arrangement must be responsible. (The latter should allow the existence of biological bearers of discrete symbols — an analogy of bearers of the genetic language.[4]) It is possible that the mechanism of profound — analogue — thinking is not entirely cerebral, but rather a general somatic process. In some sense, a person thinks with all his body, and there is some support, though indirect, for such a suggestion. First of all, attention should be paid to the fact that some chemical agents act as a "trigger," opening up human consciousness to the continuous flow of thought.

Perhaps in the processes of meditation, concentration, and prayer, certain chemical agents are produced which also act as a trigger. And, what is especially important, it is hard to imagine that such primitive psychedelic drugs as, for example, nitrous oxide, acted in any other way.

Further, it is important to note that yogi in the practice of rajah-yoga always pay attention to the general state of the body, especially to the technique of breathing; their theoretical constructions are largely based on the vertebrae and switching of sexual energy. Those who have studied Zen meditation emphasize that their practice called Zazen changes not only consciousness but also the whole body: a person opens up for the perception of another domain of reality (Tart, 1963a; Fromm et al., 1960). Suzuki states that according to Zen, the region of the unconscious is located in the abdominal cavity, which is the nearest to nature. It seems that already in the 1930s the statement was formulated that relaxation of certain muscles has a specific effect upon the processes of thinking. The practice of autogenic training introduced by the German psychologist Schultz seems to have received general acceptance. Could it happen that the science of today will take note of ancient conceptions from the teaching of Yoga (Fromm et al., 1960)? Another interesting observation is that electroencephalograms both in Zen meditation (Kiefer, 1973) and in yoga meditation (Anand et al., 1963) reveal the presence of continuous alpha-waves with a large amplitude. In a normal state, such oscillograms characterize a relaxationally modified state of consciousness. The state of hypnosis does not give such a picture.

---

[4] Present data on RNA participation in the process of memory are very contradictory (for details see Lindsey and Norman, 1972).

Concluding Remarks

We hope that all that has been said above may support our statement that the internal deep state of consciousness is unique in its essential continuity which cannot be reduced to the discreteness of language.

We would also like to draw the reader's attention to the fact that the so-called altered state of consciousness is present in our everyday life and affects our verbal behavior. *Statements made in a discrete language are constantly interpreted on a continuous level.* This is the principal burden of our conception. We believe that the term "altered state of consciousness" is incorrect since we should speak not of a special state which is hard to achieve but of another *entrance* to consciousness. Should this deep consciousness have been absent in our behavior, we would have acted as well-programmed logical automata. Our behavior would have been described by the *normative* models so popular in psychology and sociology (see, for example, Harran, 1953). Deep consciousness always underlies discretely structured everyday consciousness. It is not without interest that working out the probabilistic model of language has led us simply to a new interpretation of the concept of fields of consciousness introduced by James (1890; see also Mitokhin, 1960).

Concluding this chapter, we would like to say a few words on artificial intelligence. Is the dialogue of man with a computer possible by means of formal logic? If it is possible, it will be addressed to nothing. Computers do not have deep consciousness — they do not dream.

Strange as it may seem, ancient Oriental thinkers understood quite clearly the possibilities of automata. Radhakrishnan (1948) says that yogi who achieved a certain state were able to create bodies with artificial minds whose behavior was remarkably systematic. These bodies died a sudden death as soon as yogis removed their control over them. It was stated that, as opposed to a usual mind, they did not leave any traces after them.

It may be objected that the dialogue between man and computer has already been made possible. One example is playing chess. This is a true dialogue but it is conducted in a strictly monosemantic language. It may be that human thinking, even in playing chess, is essentially different from that of computers. However, this does not interfere with the dialogue since in this case the interpretation of statements made in the language of chess does not need to resort to the continuous fields of consciousness. But we are not going to dwell upon such degenerate cases of dialogue.

Nevertheless, the work on the problem of artificial intelligence, in its modern interpretations, seems particularly interesting. It is here that forms of intellectual activity can be selected which may be wholly carried out at the discrete–logical level. But humans will always be interested in the problem formulated very broadly: How is thinking organized?

Humans are prone to believe that they have understood something only after they have managed to embody this solution in some way. If the hypothesis of the existence of substantial fields of consciousness is correct, then probably the automaton will be able to switch on to them if the mechanism of biochemical triggers has been understood. If everything linked to continuous streams of ideas is genetically encoded, probably one can manage to decode them. And won't this then be equivalent to a creation of animate life?

We would like to emphasize here that the path to constructing artificial intelligence, if it should and can be done at all, must pass through a new stage: the study of the biochemistry of conceptual thinking, and then through the mastery of the long-accumulated experience of resorting to continuous streams of consciousness.

But putting automata aside, the most peculiar feature of recent years in Western culture is the urge of a small number of its intellectuals to cross the boundaries of their paradigm, to enrich themselves by experiencing the structure of consciousness in other cultures, in an effort to exploit all the potential riches of human faculties. But is it possible that a culture will emerge with broad forms of consciousness, without the limitations which seem so far to have been necessary to concentrate energy in a very narrow direction? Most cultures have had, till now, a set of restrictions, restrictions imposed by their specific histories.

Limitations imposed by the dominant trends of modern European culture, i.e., the filter formed by its paradigm to select ideas from the continuous fields of consciousness, have started to be perceived as excessively despotic. The task is not to destroy it but to broaden its capacity, and we now see how determinism begins to weaken, though only recently it was formulated very rigidly. Multi-valued logic is created, probabilistic thinking is developed, and the principle of complementarity acquires the right to exist in science. It is also noteworthy that, simultaneously, linguistic means are expanded.

All these manifestations may be but negligibly small steps. The key problem of scientific development is the problem of how the structure of human consciousness and language evolve, the latter being the arena of changes of this state of consciousness.

Our opposition of continuity and discontinuity is actually deliberate. As a matter of fact, man always acts in his entirety, but nothing can be analyzed without dismembering it into separate parts. This is, after all, the heart of dialectics.

In this chapter we wished not so much to give answers as to ask questions. At present, we can hardly claim anything more. A skeptical reader might remark that we are merely submerging the problem of language and thinking in the problem of continuity and discontinuity which has from time immemorial (about twenty-five centuries) been an object of consideration and study for philosophers, physicists, and mathematicians. [For more details, see the highly readable book by Panchenko (1975) and also my earlier book (Nalimov, 1978).]

Chapter 9

Epilogue

I want to remind the reader that this book is only an extended essay. It is not to be regarded as a definitive monograph. Languages which are well known to me have been considered at great length; other languages outside my competence have been dealt with only superficially. From the standpoint of my probabilistic model, the language of architecture, the language of rhythm in poetry, the language of musical composition, and the language of icon-painting style could also have been considered, but this has not been attempted.

Some readers may be surprised that among the numerous quotations in this book they have found no references to Keynes, Reichenbach, and Rescher. Since the time of Hume, who showed the impossibility of the logical grounding of induction, great efforts have been spent in the rehabilitation of inductive logic. Particularly interesting results have been obtained during recent decades: there have appeared probabilistic and indeterminate logics, and it has become necessary to construct rules for the transformation of the non-deductive logic of inductive judgments into pure deduction. A detailed description of all these questions can be found in the recently published collective monograph *Logika i Empiricheskoye Poznanie* (Tavanets, 1972). This is, if you like, another approach to the problem discussed in my earlier book — an approach being developed from the standpoint of those whose prior notions are given by logical concepts. My task has been different, namely, that of approaching the study of human intellectual activity through the analysis of language as an actual system. It is only natural that different approaches lead to an essentially different statement of problems, though for solving them we often use the same probabilistic concepts. Most likely, in the future it will be possible to speak about where the two or more approaches intersect. Another approach to the analysis of the language of science which differs from mine and seems to be dictated by a deep belief in traditional logic can be found in the book by Popovich (1966).

I believe that the considerations stated in this book have a certain pragmatic importance. Everyone engaged in teaching at institutions of higher education clearly comprehends the necessity of philosophical or, perhaps a little narrowly, of logico-linguistic interpretations of the process of scientific development. Science can be regarded as the development of a certain language adapted so as to receive and mirror our knowledge of the world. Today, more rapidly than ever, the transformation of the language of science proceeds. This process is going on more quickly than it can be understood. This causes a certain bewilderment. It is not clear what language should be taught to students: the old one in which knowledge has been acquired or the new dialects which have come from abstract mathematical constructions. Of what service can these new dialects be? These new dialects are backed by computers, allowing one to reduce the routine part of conversation a million-fold and producing for discussion only the final results. Despite all the allurements of new language means, they are inculcated much more slowly than would be expected, and they face resistance which cannot always be explained merely by the natural conformism of scientists who fear the loss of what has been acquired so far. Are not too many dialects rushing upon the heads of those who have been accustomed to speaking ordinary language in science—though a little bit changed? Do not new dialects introduce an unnecessary hardness unnatural for the system of constructing judgments in this or that field of knowledge? More often than not, we hear complaints that, say, in medicine, mechanical methods of diagnostics suppress the initiative of the physician. We can hardly do anything but agree with this. Everything would be different if the algorithms of diagnostics were soft and produced not one but a set of answers with corresponding commentaries, giving a physician a possibility to meditate.

It is not quite clear what we want to achieve by the mathematization of knowledge. Do we want to change radically the established system of thinking in this or that field of knowledge? Or is the task perhaps more modest—to find a language which would permit us to describe phenomena in the established system of thinking but in a more compact and mobile way?

Recently, many hopes have been pinned to machine methods of informational service in the sciences, but only a small part of these have been realized. The process of searching for new scientific information is one of the main constituents of creative research, and an attempt to translate this procedure into hard languages of descriptive systems based upon the

Boolean algebra seems altogether naïve. The whole discussion about "pertinence" and "relevance" of such systems seems totally unrealistic, though systems so constructed prove very efficient for the solution of some partial problems. It also appears possible to use computers on a wider scale relying upon natural languages of science and using natural searching attributes of publications (Nalimov and Mul'chenko, 1969). At present, information science, or documentation science as it is usually called in the Western countries, is not a scientific discipline but just a set of some (not always apt) cookbook rules and technical solutions. In my opinion, its truly scientific, theoretical basis can be developed only on the grounds of the analysis of scientific language. Moreover, the philosophy of science itself, if it implies something consistent and genuinely important for scientists, can be constructed upon the background of logico-linguistic analysis of science. Here lies, above all, the pragmatic essence of language theory understood in a broad sense.

A question can be asked as to whether the formal approach to language analysis suggested in this book is correct and how far we can go in this direction.

Imagine that an observer from another World has come to our Earth. Having become acquainted with our culture and its history he, as a metaobserver, might send an account of his observations that would sound roughly as follows:

Earth is inhibited by humans, odd creatures who claim to be thinking beings. They have invented enormously complicated and intricate things — Words — and finally themselves fell under the dominion of their cruel invention. Their history shows that the Word did not acquire its universal significance at the very beginning. There is a dim legend of Lemurians, forefathers of men, who lived in ancient Lemuria, a sunken continent. They had no Words as a sign system. Their speech was like the sounds of Nature: wailing of the wind, murmur of a stream, sound of a waterfall, roar of a volcano. In ancient times among these people, there were sages who did not worship the power of the Word and were not afraid of it. There were teachings which they called mystic in which the teachers did not convey in Words their profound experiences of inner contemplation. They only spoke of the way other people could acquire this experience. It was stated that even great Texts could not give novel knowledge; they only destroyed ignorance and thus gave way to inner knowledge. But all this remained in the past, and all is forgotten. It was only a collateral line of their culture. Then new times came and everything began to develop around the Word. It was said, "In the beginning was the Word . . ." And the Word became the most significant thing in life, and life was embodied in the Word. One of their modern philosophers [Karl Jaspers (1883–1969), one of the founders of German existentialism] proclaimed communication to be the essence of a human being. He declared that the *"nous* is identical to an unrestricted will to communication." If something could be named, incarnated in the Word, it was considered to be cognition. Another philosopher and writer [Jean Paul Sartre (1905–1980), one of the founders of French existentialism] described the notion of Word absorbed by him in childhood in the following way

> . . . and each thing was humbly begging for a name, and giving it one was like both creating it and taking it . . .
> . . . since I had discovered the world through language, for a long time I mistook language for the World. To exist was to have a registered trade-name somewhere on the infinite Tables of the World, writing meant engraving new beings on them or – this was my most persistent illusion – catching living things in the trap of phrases: if I put words together ingeniously, the object would become entangled in the signs, and I would hold it. . . . I tried to unveil the stillness of existence through a counteracting murmur of words, and, above all, I confused things with their names: that is belief.

This is a hymn to the Word and its power, a description of how it subdues man from his childhood and how the Word's master, a writer, is born.

There appeared words as symbols carrying information only of themselves. People succeeded in constructing rules for combining these Words–symbols which are extremely fanciful and difficult to comprehend and at the same time inwardly beautiful and fascinating by the perfection of their rigor. This has begun to be considered as the height of knowledge. Maintaining the pureness of this language became the principal concern of many people, the object of worship of new priests. However, somebody has shown that this language is not inherently omnipotent and is probably quite helpless. But, even by means of this language whose Words do not mean anything, it has become possible to learn much about the World and even to subdue it. Their new temples are places where Logic – the daughter of the Word – is worshipped. Still, some of their philosophers have realized that Language is only a Game. And someone else has understood that they perceive the World the way their Words allow them to.

For some reason or other, Words with rhythm have acquired a peculiar power. They may intoxicate the listener. Those who are masters of such Words possess in the human World an unlimited attractiveness for others. Words have acquired power over people. By means of Words great changes in their society have been made. Words led people to make wars. And what is amazing here: no two people understand Words in the same way.

Systems of Words have been invented in which the same Words mean quite different things for different people. Some people believe that the less clear a Word's meaning is the more that can be expressed with it. And nobody can understand why some Words which possessed a universal power in the quite recent past are now forgotten.

With the help of Words, people have invented new absurdly powerful ways of disseminating words. Senseless Words came pouring in; they have become so numerous that nobody can comprehend them. And, what is altogether astounding, this is just the way Words exercise their influence upon people.

And finally, somewhere in the West, there appeared angry young men who revolted against the Word for the first time during the long progress of their culture's development. They proclaimed that the culture of the Word had fallen in pieces—that the Word brought the Big Lie to the World—and they demanded that it be destroyed. What do they want? Do they want to destroy themselves? They are children of the Word and they are fighting against it by means of the Word, too.

And others, those who like and highly appreciate their culture, keep longing for the Universal Word by means of which it would be possible to express and understand everything.

I cannot comprehend anything in this strange World. There is no place for a metaobserver here. It's time for me to go back . . .

This is a myth of language.

Appendix 1

Collection of Statements About the Term "Statistics"

"Let us sit on this log at the roadside," says I, "and forget the inhumanity and ribaldry of the poets. It is in the glorious columns of ascertained facts and legalized measures that beauty is to be found. In this very log we sit upon, Mrs. Sampson," says I, "is statistics more wonderful than any poem. The rings show it was sixty years old. At the depth of two thousand feet it would become coal in three thousand years. The deepest coal mine in the world is at Killingworth, near Newcastle. A box four feet long, three feet wide, and two feet eight inches deep will hold one ton of coal. If an artery is cut, compress it above the wound. A man's leg contains thirty bones. The Tower of London was burned in 1841."

"Go on, Mr. Pratt," says Mrs. Sampson. "Them ideas is so original and soothing. I think statistics are just as lovely as they can be."

> O. Henry, "The Handbook of Hymen" (the epigraph to the book *Distribution Theory* by M. G. Kendall and A. Stuart)

There are innumerable cases in which the meanings of words shift because the referent human activity denoted by a term undergoes a significant transformation. Thus, lexicons either are updated or become receptacles of archaic curiosities. The term "statistics" belongs to this class. The etymology is beyond doubt. It derives from the Latin *status* which in the middle ages had come to mean state in the political sense (French *état*, Spanish *estado*, German *Staat*). Statistics, in the modern sense, derives from the practice of collecting and analyzing quantitative data that described certain material conditions of a state. What was first "political arithmetic," bills of mortality, etc., began to be studied in England by the middle of the seventeenth century and was taken up on the continent of Europe a little later.

207

208 *In the Labyrinths of Language*

The emergence of the profession of statistician and the mathematization of the analysis of social data owed much to the development of the calculus of probability as a subtle branch of mathematics. The varying definitions given to the term reflect the two histories: the social practice and the advances in the mathematical formalism. (For details, see Karl Pearson, *The History of Statistics in the XVII and XVIII Centuries*, Macmillan Publishing Co., Inc., New York, 1978.)

The collection of statements about the term "statistics" given here is largely based on a paper by E. P. Nikitina, V. L. Freidlina, and A. V. Yarkho (published by Moscow State University, preprint N 37, 1972). Items marked with an asterisk are borrowed from the article "Definitions of Statistics" by W. Willcox (*ISI Review*, Vol. 3, No. 4, 1935). This collection in no way claims to be complete, especially in the part related to the twentieth century. It is intended only to give contrasting statements.

1749* The so-called statistics is the science of governing a state. . . . It comprises the major information of characteristics of a civilized society. [G. Achenwall, *Abriss der neusten Staatswissenschaft*]

1752* The science of governing a state means a policy, and therefore I leave it to philosophers, because they deal with general statements, and I want to call statistics which deals only with empirical data, the science of a state, or the science of a state structure. [ibid.]

1770* . . . the science that teaches us what is the political arrangement of all the modern states of the known world. [Bielfeld, *Elements of Universal Erudition* (translated by Hooker), Vol. 3, p. 269]

1789* . . . that branch of political knowledge which has for its object the actual and relative power of the several modern states, the power arising from their inhabitants and the wisdom of their governments. [Political Geography, Introduction to the Statistical Tables, etc., as quoted in *The Monthly Review,* **81**:175]

1792* Statistics is a historical science which describes exhaustively and truly the modern and past state of some people. [M. Ch. Sprengel, *Grundriss der Staatenkunde*]

1792* Statistics is a scientifically ordered conception of a modern political condition of a state. [J. G. Meusel, *Lehrbuch der Statistik*]

1797* . . . a word lately introduced to express a view or survey of any kingdom, county, or parish. ["Statistics," *Encyclopaedia Britannica*, 3rd edition]

1798* . . . inquiry into the state of a country for the purpose of ascertaining the quantum of happiness enjoyed by the inhabitants and the means of its future improvement. [J. Sinclair, *Statistical Account of Scotland,* XX:XIII]

1803* Statistics is an actual account of everything which exists. [P. E. Herbin de Halle, *Statistique générale et particulière de la France et de ses Colonies*]

1804* History is a current statistics, and statistics is a still history. [A. L. v. Schlözer, *Theorie der Statistik*]

1805* Statistics should study how by the constitution, of a state, i.e. by its inner structure, its physical and legislative power is revealed and supported. [G. F. D. Göss, *Ueber den Begriff der Statistik*]

1805* Statistics is a science based on the study of facts, whose object is to evaluate the power, and wealth of a state by analyzing the sources and means of retaining its welfare and grandeur, which result from its territory, population, industry, commerce, and army; in a word, this is a science of actual force and power of a political state. [J. Peuchet, *Statistique Élémentaire de la France*]

1805* . . . the science which studies physical, moral, and political force of a state. [D. Fr. Donnant, *Théorie Élémentaire de la Statistique*]

1806* . . . a historic art which studies the modern condition of a state [G. F. D. Göss]

1807* Description of a state has its own rules both for collecting data from the only right standpoint and for using them for a higher aim; the set of these rules is called statistics. [A. Niemann, *Abriss der Statistik und Staatenkunde*]

1808* . . . scientific presentation of the data which allow [one] to learn the real goals of a state at a fixed, e.g. present moment of time. [W. Butte, *Statistik als Wissenschaft*]

1808* . . . full knowledge of the modern condition of the facts which determine welfare of the population and its separate groups. [S. Cagnazzi De Luca, *Elementi dell' Arte Statistica*]

1810* . . . scientific presentation of the data which show modern political power of a given state. [J. Zizius, *Theoretische Vorbereitung und Einleitung zur Statistik*]

Undated* Statistics is the budget of things. [Napoléon Bonaparte, cited from *Las Casas, Memorial de Sainte-Hélène,* 1835]

1817* Statistics studies the modern condition of the factors which make clear the power and weak points of a state. [A. Padovani, *Introduzione alla Scienza della Statistica*]

1819* . . . the science of the state of political societies. [A. Et. de Férussac, *De la Nécessité de fixer et d'Adopter un corps de Doctrine pour la Géographie et la Statistique*]

1819* . . . systematic presentation of the principal conditions of the external and internal life of a state as well as connection and interrelation of this external and internal life from the modern point of view. [K. H. L. Pölitz, *Die Staatswissenschaft im Lichte unserer Zeit*]

1821* . . . an exact science which teaches us to collect data and positive facts about all the objects, and to arrange and use them by publication; on the modern level of knowledge about the state, the object of statistics is the study of the tasks of a town society. [J. Gröberg von Hemsö, *Theorie der Statistik*]

1821* Since statistics either describes, or studies, or teaches to investigate the condition of modern states, it may be regarded in three ways: as a science, as an art, or as a teaching. [E. Klotzius, *Theoria Statisticae tamquam scientiae*]

1824* . . . description of a state present. [F. J. Mone, *Théorie de la Statistique*]

1825*   . . . science which teaches how to study the forces of a state, and to illuminate their nature and relations. [Ch. A. Fisher, *Grundriss zu einer neuen systematischen Darstellung der Statistik als Wissenschaft*]

1826*   . . . scientific and experimental study of the latest condition of a state, its organisational and material basis and those essential changes to which the composite parts of this basis have been subjected so far because of human activities and realisation of ideas. [J. C. von Koch-Sternfeld, *Grundlinien der allgemeinen Staatskunde*]

1826*   . . . the most complete and grounded knowledge of the condition and position of a state and life within it. [C. A. v. Malchus, *Statistik und Staatskunde*]

1829*   . . . scientifically arranged description of reality called forth by the necessity to perfect the art of governing. [G. R. Schnabel, *Generalstatistik der Europäischen Staaten*]

1832*   The subject of statistics is the investigation and exposition of the actual condition of states and nations in regard to their internal organization and foreign relations. ["Statistics," *Encyclopedia Americana*]

1833*   The object of statistics is to present the facts in the most compressed form. [A. M. Guerry, *Essai sur la Statistique Moral de la France*]

1834*   . . . scientific description of the real peculiarities, which characterize national economy of each state and promote its progress and, thus, promote national welfare. [W. C. A. von Schlieben, *Grundzüge einer allgemeinen Statistik*]

1838*   . . . the ascertaining and bringing together of those "facts which are calculated to illustrate the condition and prospects of society. It differs from Political Economy because . . . it does not discuss causes nor reason upon probable effects." [*Statistical Society of London, Journal*, Vol. 1, p. 1, quoting from the Prospectus of the Society]

1838*   . . . description of political forces which acted in a definite time within definite political boundaries. [*S. Die Statistik der Kultur*]

1838*   Statistical inquiry = Investigations which by explaining the progress of mankind in knowledge, wealth and civilisation lay open the springs of human happiness and discover the sources of social difficulties and misery. Statistics are facts or data of any individual thing or of any science, natural or political. Statistical science is the collection and arrangement of such facts. [Jos. E. Portlock, "An Address Explanatory of the Object and Advantages of Statistical Inquiry"]

1840*   The object of statistics should consist in studying the regularities of relations and connections, in discovering the absolute within the relational phenomena, in studying the constant within the changing phenomena and in recognizing the discovered law in the newly found facts. [J. E. Wörl, *Erläuterungen zur Theorie der Statistik*]

1840*   . . . the ascertaining and the bringing together of those facts which are fitted to illustrate the condition and prospects of society. [B. B. Edwards, *American Statistical Association Collections*, Vol. 1, p. v (1847)]

1840* The object of statistics is to come, by the methods which are inherent to it, to the discovery of laws according to which the social facts develop. (P. A. Dufau, *Traité de Statistique ou Théorie de l'Étude des Lois*]

1842* Statistics is derived from state or Staat signifying a body of men living together in social union and it comprehends all the details connected with their condition. ["Statistics," *Encyclopaedia Britannica*, 7th edition]

1842* . . . that department of political science which is concerned in collecting and arranging facts illustrative of the condition and resources of a state. ["Statistics," *The Penny Cyclopaedia*]

1843* The central concept of statistics is that of the factual: it is revealed partly in facts, partly in the regularities of phenomena. [J. Fallati, *Einleitung in die Wissenschaft der Statistik*]

1844* The task of statistics should consist in revealing and developing relations among the peoples of the Earth appearing in the course of the historic revolution (i.e. natural interrelations from the viewpoint of geography and history). [Blum]

1846* . . . the science of facts produced by forces of nature and human life in the social milieu; of the results of this combined activity for society, and of the constant and periodic phenomena which, being determined by this activity, occur within a given social system. [Ch. de Brouckère, "Cours d'Économie Politique," quoted by S. Vissering, Congrès International de Statistique, 7ème Session]

1847* . . . the science of social facts expressed in numerical terms. [Al. Moreau de Jonnès, *Eléments de Statistique*]

1847* . . . presentation of possible relations in the state and in the national life. [F. W. von Reden, *Zeitschrift für deutsche Statistik*]

1848* The object of statistics is to give us a true account of a state in a definite epoch. . . . Statistics is a new science whose object is to study various aggregates of people. [Ad. Quetelet, *Du Système Social et des Lois qui le Régissent*]

1850* Statistics is a self-sustained science with its own objects and methods. Its result is political arithmetic, its object is cognition of regularities of the development of an organism of human society; its task is to obtain accurate knowledge of all the factors determining the phenomena of the external world in its integrity. [G. A. Knies, *Die Statistik als selbständige Wissenschaft*]

1851* . . . the conception of modern relations among the states given in figures and facts. [W. Dieterici, *Begriff der Statistik*]

1852* . . . presentation of an individual life from a certain standpoint. [L. Stein, *System der Staatswissenschaft*]

1852* . . . an empirical science revealing the laws which social and state relations expressed by figures obey. [J. Hain, *Handbuch der Statistik des österreichischen Kaiserstaats*]

1853* Statistics is an exposition of measurements and comparison of results obtained in the study of state and folk life. Its object is what can be reduced to a value and a measure and presented quantitatively in the results of state activities and facts of folk life. [B. von Hermann, *Bewegung der Bevölkerung im Königreich Bayern*]

1854* . . . description of real facts, especially relating to the modern folk life, in correspondence with the law of evolution observed by theoretical science. [W. Roscher, *Grundlagen der National-Oekonomie*]

1858* Statistics gets an idea of the evolution and social life of the nation from the qualitative, quantitative, and model relations to the subject. [V. Viebahn, *Statistik des zollvereinten und nördlichen Deutschlands*]

1858* . . . the science which describes with the maximal plausibility human relations connected with national life and subject to the study at the present moment, mainly in a definite country, and thereby it provides the overview of the facts, their immediate causes and natural laws of changing phenomena, primarily of use for solving the problems set by the government, as well as for general enlightenment. [R. von Mohl, *Literatur über den Begriff der Statistik*]

1858* . . . the science which has for its office the collection and arrangement of facts relative to the physical, social, political, financial, intellectual, and moral condition and resources of a state or nation. ["Statistics," *New American Encyclopaedia*]

1860* . . . description of states, their positions and forces, as well as social relations within them. [G. Fr. Kolb, *Handbuch der vergleichenden Statistik*]

1861* . . . presentation of the modern life of civilized peoples in states, based on facts. [G. Hanssen, *Vorlesungen*]

1863* Statistics tends to discover characteristics of human societies on the basis of systematic mass observations and calculation of homogeneous phenomena. [G. von Rümelin, *Zeitschrift für die gesamte Staatswissenschaft,* XIX]

1863* . . . logical synthesis and analysis of facts enumerated with a definite purpose and accompanied by few calculations. [G. Caporale, *Lezioni di Statistica Teoricopractica*]

1864* Statistics in a broad sense is description of the situation in general; in a narrow sense, it is description of the states of human societies and their structures at a given moment of time, as well as exposition (and explanation) of permanent changes generated by these states within a definite period. Statistics should systematically carry out mass observations and present the results in figures so that they would correspond to the purposes of sciences and official bodies which make use of statistical methods. [E. Engel, Statistisches Seminar, *Zeitschrift des königlichen preussischen statistischen Bureaus,* IV]

1864* . . . the study of reality and noticeable facts. [A. M. Guerry]

1865* . . . political and social art of measurements. [B. Hildebrand, *Die Wissenschaftliche Aufgabe der Statistik, Jahrbücher für Nationalökonomie und Statistik,* IV]

1867* . . . a methodical inductive technique to discover and explain mechanisms functioning in human society and nature, i.e. to infer and explain the laws of functioning of these mechanisms and to discover and study causal relations among the phenomena of nature and human society; namely, this is a technique which leads to an accurate quantitative definition on the basis of systematic mass observations over these phenomena. [A. Wagner, Statistik, *Bluntschli Brater's Deutsches Staatswörterbuch*]

1868* Statistics tends by systematic quantitative mass observations to study the national-economical, social, and political character of peoples and to compose a general scientific picture of these observations. [A. von Oettingen, *Moralstatistik*]

1868* ... cognition of facts on the basis of their presentation in a numerically comparable form. [R. Böckh, *Vorlesungen*]

1869* ... the science of a state, which must give the results of its development in a certain epoch and the principal laws governing this development. [A. R. Balchen, Congrès International de Statistique, 7ème Session]

1870* Statistics should apply the registration methods to the whole picture of life; statistics is logical methods of objective induction. [A. Oncken, *Untersuchung über den Begriff der Statistik*]

1872* 1) Methods which study the states and events by mass observations; 2) science of a variety of phenomena within the states and groups of people, of their oscillations and laws. [M. Haushofer, *Lehrbuch der Statistik*]

1877* ... a scientific method of investigating the peculiarities of human society expressible numerically, and of revealing the regularities in social life. ... a systematic description and explanation of actual events and laws inferred from them, as well as of human social life on the basis of quantitative mass observations ... the aggregate of social facts whose importance for society may be stated only by quantitative mass observation forms an object of an independent science which we call statistics. [G. Mayr, *Gesetzmässigkeit im Gesellschaftsleben*]

1878* Description and cognition of contemporary position of states. [J. E. Wappaeus, *Einleitung in das Studium der Statistik*]

1880–81* ... a quantitative record of the observed facts or relations in any branch of science. [P. Geddes, "Classification of Statistics and Its Results," *Proceedings of the Royal Society of Edinburgh*]

1882* 1. Methods which study the state and separate facts by mass observations; 2. the science of mass phenomena, especially those of social life, their oscillations and laws of these oscillations. [M. Haushofer, *Lehr- und Handbuch der Statistik*]

1884* Statistics is social arithmetic. [A. Beaujon, *Antrittsrede*]

1885* ... the science which treats of the structure of human society. [Sir Rawson W. Rawson, Statistical Society of London, *Jubilee Volume*]

1885* There are three definitions which seem to deserve attention as respectively the most popular, the most philosophical, and that which is a fair compromise between the conflicting requirements of a good definition. According to the first of these definitions, Statistics is the arithmetical portion of Social Science. ... According to the second definition, Statistics is the science of Means in general (including physical observations); according to the third definition, of those Means which are presented by social phenomena. The third definition is here adopted . . . [F. Edgeworth, Statistical Society, *Jubilee Volume*]

1886*   Statistics may be regarded as a science and as a method. As a science, it tends to describe the political, economical, and social situation of the people or a group of population in general; for this reason it is often called demography. . . . Statistics . . . has a method of observation which consists 1) in using numbers; 2) in grouping them to select (relatively) constant facts, i.e. to distinguish them from accidental facts; 3) in comparing . . . different epochs in different places and different circumstances; 4) in using the compiled and mathematically processed data for induction and deduction. [M. Block, *Traité Théorique et Pratique de Statistique*]

1886*   Statistical theory should proceed from the essence of statistical methods, it should discover techniques, judgments, and conclusions by a variety of different variable phenomena . . . on the basis of calculating common characteristic ones among them. [A. Meitzen, Geschichte, *Theorie und Technik der Statistik*]

1888*   Statistics may be understood in a narrow sense and in a broad one. In a broad sense it is a method, and in a narrow sense it is a science. As a science, it studies actual social situation by quantitative observations. [A. Gabaglio, *Theoria Generale della Statistica*]

1889*   . . . numerical study of social facts. [E. Levasseur, *La Population Française*]

1890*   . . . the science of numbers. [H. Westergaard, *Theorie der Statistik*]

1894*   According to the modern, generally accepted linguistic practice, statistics is a presentation of states or processes based on the fact that single events, after abstraction from their differences, are calculated as similar and united into groups. But in a narrow sense we may interpret statistics as application of this method of study and description to the people living in a state and society; in short, the study of people's life in society with the help of a large number of figures. [W. Lexis, *Handwörterbuch der Staatswissenschaften*]

1895*   . . . a description of any class of facts expressed by means of figures. [H. C. Adams, "Statistics," *Johnson's Universal Cyclopaedia*]

1895*   Statistics consists in the observation of phenomena which can be counted or expressed in figures. [R. Mayo-Smith, *Statistics and Sociology*]

1895*   Statistics in the material sense, or the science of statistics is the explanation, based on exhaustive facts and expressed numerically, of the situations and phenomena of human social life to the extent the latter is expressed in social masses. Statistics in the formal sense, or statistical methods, is the result of exhaustive mass observations expressed in numbers and measures as applied to social and other masses. [G. Mayr, *Statistik und Gesellschaftslehre*]

1901*   . . . science of averages . . . science of large numbers. . . . the science of the measurement of the social organism, regarded as a whole, in all its manifestations. [A. Bowley, *Elements of Statistics*]

1903* . . . the science of large numbers and of averages. [J. Merz, *History of European Thought*]

1906* . . . methodical enumeration of facts, individuals or objects which can be calculated, and arrangement of the figures obtained. [F. Faure, *Eléments de Statistique*]

1909* . . . numerical statements of facts in any department of inquiry placed in relation to each other. [A. Bowley, *Elementary Manual of Statistics*]

1911* . . . quantitative data affected to a marked extent by a multiplicity of causes. [G. Yule, *Introduction to the Theory of Statistics*]

1911* . . . any information received after abstracting separate phenomena from their particular differences and uniting them into groups as identical values. [W. Lexis, *Handwörterbuch der Staatswissenschaften*]

1917* . . . numerical statements of fact by means of which large aggregates are analyzed, the relation of individual units to their group are ascertained, comparisons are made between groups and continuous records are maintained for comparative purposes. [M. T. Copeland, *Business Statistics*, p. 3]

1917* . . . aggregates of facts "affected to a marked extent by a multiplicity of causes" numerically stated, enumerated or estimated according to reasonable standards of accuracy, collected in a systematic manner for a predetermined purpose and placed in relation to each other. [H. Secrist, *Introduction to Statistical Methods*, p. 8]

1917* . . . an arithmetical science of mass observations whose task is to reveal the regular and typical features in mass observations as well as in changes observed [A. O. Holwerda, *Die wissenschaftliche Richtung in der Statistik*]

1918* . . . the method of collecting, tabulating and interpreting the facts for groups of persons, things, or events in terms of the groups. [L. I. Dublin and E. W. Kopf, "Some Considerations in Vital Statistics Education," *American Statistical Association Publications* 16:465]

1919* 1. Construed as sing. In recent use, the department of study that has for its object the collection and arrangement of numerical facts or data, whether relating to human affairs or to natural phenomena. 2. Construed as plural. Numerical facts or data collected and classified. [*New Oxford Dictionary*]

1921* . . . a method which by mass presentation of numerical results leads to describe collective phenomena and allows to trace in their variety both the permanent and regular features and those which change despite the outward uniformity. [A. Julin, *Principes de Statistique Théorique et Appliquée*]

1921* Statistics has a task to make accessible the cognition of so-called mass phenomena, namely, in the first place, the mass phenomena of human life in society which we are interested in. [F. Zizek, *Grundriss der Statistik*]

1922* . . . an exposition of certain methods employed in presenting and interpreting the numerical aspects of a given subject. [G. R. Davies, *Introduction to Economic Statistics*]

1923* . . . the science of methods of investigating mass phenomena. [J. H. van Zanten, *Antrittsrede*]

1925*   . . . the body of methods and principles which governs the collection, analysis, comparison, presentation and interpretation of numerical data. [R. E. Chaddock, *Principles and Methods of Statistics*]

1926*   . . . the teaching of mass phenomena in social life, and especially of regularities in their structure and evolution. It embraces groups of human individuals (independently of whether they are a real group formed by the town residents, or a logical, imaginable group comprising babies or suicides) and also studies their activities. [Fr. Zahn, *Handwörterbuch der Staatswissenschaften*]

1927*   Statistics is higher mathematics—let it go at that. [E. B. Wilson, "What is Statistics," *Science*]

1927*   Statistics in a general sense should study phenomena to observe mass characteristics by grouping and calculating if this helps to reveal what can be further an object of the study. [J. H. van Zanten, *Lehrbuch der statistischen Methode*]

1928*   Statistics, in the material sense of the word, is a specifically arranged quantitative presentation of facts; in the formal sense, these are methods of research of mass phenomena and their interrelations which allow discovery of regularities common for these phenomena, or, in short, this is a methodical registration of phenomena with a large number of observations. [C. A. Verryn Stuart, *Inleiding tot de beoefening der Statistick*, 2nd edition]

1928*   . . . the system of numerical observations in general. [H. C. Nybolle, *Grundzüge der Theorie der Statistik*, 2 Aufl.]

1928   The task of the probability theory within so-called *mathematical statistics* consists in studying whether *the given statistical material forms a collective*, or in what way it may be reduced to the collectives with the simplest possible distribution. . . . The fact that statistical theory is only a "preliminary" or "second-rate" way of explaining natural phenomena as compared with deterministic, which satisfies our "need of causality," is a prejudice which is understandable if we trace the history of natural sciences but which must disappear as scientific consciousness grows; so far not a single case has been noted where statistical conception of a phenomenon would progress to a causal. [R. Mises, *Probability and Statistics*]

1933   In early use, that branch of Political science dealing with the collection, classification, and discussion of facts (especially of a numerical kind) bearing on the condition of a state or community. In recent use, the department of study that has for its object the collection and arrangement of numerical facts or data, whether relating to human affairs or to natural phenomena. [*Oxford English Dictionary*]

1934*   . . . the numerical study of groups or masses through the study of their component units, whether these units be human or subhuman, animate or inanimate. At present statistics has a broader meaning, the numerical study of groups, and a narrower one, the numerical study of social groups. [W. F. Willcox, "Statistics," *Encyclopaedia of the Social Sciences*, Vol. 14, p. 457]

1938   Statistics may be characterized in brief as a science of reduction and analysis of the material observed. [R. Fisher, *Statistical Methods for Research Workers*]

1946   Statistics, a branch of social science which has for its object the collecting, arranging, analysis, and comparing of facts bearing on the condition, social, moral, and material, of a people [*Funk and Wagnall's Standard Encyclopaedia of Universal Knowledge*]

1947   By *Statistics* we mean quantitative data affected to a marked extent by a multiplicity of causes. . . . By *Statistical Methods*, we mean methods specially adapted to the elucidation of quantitative data affected by a multiplicity of causes. . . . By *Theory of Statistics* or, more briefly, *Statistics*, we mean the exposition of statistical methods. . . . Perhaps the most abstract use of the word occurs in the theory of thermodynamics, wherein one speaks of *entropy* as *proportional to the logarithm of the statistical probability of the universe*—a definition which no statesman would be unwilling to admit to lie completely outside his purview. But it is unnecessary to multiply instances to show that the word "statistics" is now entirely divorced from "matters of State." The *theory* of statistics as a distinct branch of scientific method is of comparatively recent growth. Its roots may be traced in the work of Laplace and Gauss on the theory of errors of observation, but the study itself did not begin to flourish until the last quarter of the nineteenth century. Under the influence of Galton and Karl Pearson, remarkable progress was made, and the foundations of the subject were laid in the next thirty years—as it has turned out, very securely. The subject has not, however, yet reached a stage whereat a cut-and-dried exposition of its methods can be given. . . . The words "statist," "statistics," "statistical" appear to be all derived, more or less indirectly, from the Latin *status* in the sense, acquired in mediaeval Latin, of a political *state*. [G. U. Yule and M. G. Kendall, *An Introduction to the Theory of Statistics*]

1949   Classical statistics based on calculating states is a limiting case of quantum statistics where the number of states is calculated proceeding from the number of various wave functions (it may be shown that classical statistics comes from the quantum one if the number of particles in the volume of the average wave length λ^3 is much less than a unity). In quantum physics two statistics are differentiated, that of Fermi-Dirac (for the particles obeying Pauli's principle—antisymmetrical Ψ) and that of Bose–Einstein (symmetrical Ψ, Bose particles). In their principal basis these two statistics, certainly, do not differ. [D. I. Blokhintsev, *Osnovy Kvantovoi Mekhaniki* (Foundations of Quantum Mechanics)]

1951   We would like first of all to consider the heterogeneous phenomena which occur everywhere in "practice" and the study of which is usually called "statistics." In accordance with its meaning in contemporary language, but not with its origin, "statistics" is understood as a study based on a large collection of data, "the science of distributions." Its object are a long series of homogeneous phenomena, presentable as numerically measured by some technique. . . . The original meaning of the word "statistics" seems to be "the teaching of a state" . . . The first large part of the probability theory which we are going to illuminate is statistics in the common meaning of the word: the study of numerical series formed by calculating homogeneous events in human life. [R. von Mises, *Wahrscheinlichkeit, Statistik und Wahrheit*]

1952   The theory of statistics is a branch of applied mathematics aiming at a mathematical description of certain events under given conditions. [A. Hald, *Statistical Theory with Engineering Applications*]

1954   Mathematical statistics is a branch of mathematics devoted to the mathematical methods of systematization, processing and usage of *statistical data* for scientific and practical conclusions. Statistical data are the information of the number of objects in a certain more or less vast universe, the objects having various characteristics. [*Bol'shaya Sovietskaya Entsiklopediya*, 2nd edition, vol. 26, A. N. Kolmogorov, "Matematicheskaya Statistika" (Mathematical Statistics)]

1954   Numerous definitions of statistics have so far been given by different authors. It is known that sixty years ago Rümelin cited already 63 definitions, including his own. According to M. Huber [Cours de Statistique Appliquée aux Affaires], in 1940 their number reached 100. In our opinion, one hundred has now been passed. We shall quote here some of the definitions of statistics which have the best formulations.

Here is a definition given by Cournot (1801–1877) in 1843: "By statistics they generally mean the collection of facts taking place by force of agglomeration of people in political societies, but for us this word will have a more extended meaning. By statistics we shall understand a science whose object is to collect and systematize *numerous facts* of every kind, so that one can obtain numerical relations essentially independent of random deviations and denoting the existence of regular causes whose effect is combined with that of random causes . . ."

Detoeuf, President of Cégos [Commission Générale d'Organisations Scientific du Travail], after presenting a series of studies on the role of statistics in modern economy, said: "Statistics is like big cities, industrial concentration, socialism and modern warfare – it is a mass phenomenon. It becomes necessary every time when one has to pass from unities to multiplicities."

According to a humorous definition, "statistics is the art of making the unknown more precise."

. . . Another definition may help to illuminate the essence of statistics: "It is a body of methods whose object is the quantitative study of collectives." [R. Dumas, *L'Entreprise et Statistique*]

1954   The secret language of statistics, so appealing in a fact-minded culture, is employed to sensationalize, inflate, confuse and oversimplify. Statistical methods and statistical terms are necessary in reporting the mass data of social and economic trends, business conditions, "opinion" polls, the census. But without writers who use the words with honesty and understanding and readers who know what they mean, the result can only be semantic nonsense. [D. Huff, *How to Lie with Statistics*]

1954   From the personalistic point of view, *statistics proper* can perhaps be defined as the art of dealing with vagueness and with interpersonal difference in decision situations. [L. J. Savage, *The Foundations of Statistics*]

1954   The term "statistics" comes from the Latin word "status" which means "state." Initially, in the XVIIth century when statistic was formed as a scientific subject, the term "statistics" was connected with the system of describing facts characterizing the state of a state. At the time it was not even suggested that statistics should deal only with the phenomena of mass nature. At present statistics embraces broader and simultaneously more definite contents. Namely, statistics may be said to consist of three different sections:

1) *collection of statistical data,* i.e. data characterizing separate units of some mass universes (populations);

2) *statistical analysis of the data* consisting in revealing regulations which can be found on the basis of the mass observation data;

3) development of the techniques of mass observation and analysis of statistical data. The latter section is, properly, the subject of *mathematical statistics.* [B. V. Gnedenko, *Kours Teorii Veroyatnosteĭ* (Probability Theory)]

1954   Statistics as a science is a branch of applied mathematics and it can be regarded as mathematics applied to elaborate the results of mass observations . . . Statistics may be regarded as: 1) the teaching of *aggregates*; 2) the teaching of *variation* and 3) the teaching of *presenting data in a compact form.* [R. A. Fisher, *Statistical Methods for Researchers* (retranslated from the Russian)]

1955   Statistics may be defined as *the collection, presentation, analysis and interpretation of numerical data* . . . Statistics should not be thought of as a subject correlative with physics, chemistry, economics and sociology. Statistics is not a science; it is a scientific method [F. S. Croxton and D. J. Cowden, *Applied General Statistics*]

1955   Planning with the help of statistics obtains the numerically measured information of the economic aspect of matters. Besides, statistics is an important instrument of control over the fulfilment of a plan. Thus, the task of our statistics is different from that of bourgeois statistics. Bourgeois statistics, e.g. that of West Germany, consists exactly in the data of the economic development there; however, it does not pursue the task of presenting the actual economic position of people in West Germany, on the contrary, it embellishes the situation and conceals actual relations in the interests of monopolistic capital, whose unreserved servant is modern bourgeois statistics. [A. Kindelberger, *Die statistische Berichterstaatung der privaten Wirtschaft*]

1955   Similar to all other mathematical subjects, probability theory and mathematical statistics study general regulations of mass phenomena in an abstract form indifferent to the specific nature of the objects considered . . . The principle of primacy of a qualitative analysis over a quantitative one which predetermines the study of the quantitative aspects inseparably from the qualitative aspects, in technology is decisive for applying statistical and theoretico-probabilistic methods [I. V. Dunin-Barkovskii and N. V. Smirnov, *Teoriya Veroyatnosteĭ i Matematicheskaya Statistike v Tekhnike* (Probability Theory and Mathematical Statistics in Technology)]

1956   When one comes closer to the historic evolution of the concept of statistics, one discovers that for a long time it used to denote only the description of "the state characteristics" (its population, soil composition and other data). Only at present do the statistical methods of research penetrate into natural sciences.

It is known that, though the general notion of statistics is not easy to formulate, still it seems correct to state that it deals either with the study of phenomena relating to masses of individuals or which unites in some way the variety of separate phenomena. Thus, the specific feature of statistics is the study of mass phenomena. [L. Schmetterer, *Einführung in die matematische Statistik*]

1957 . . . the kernel of mathematical statistics is the question: how far can the values calculated from samples, deviate from the corresponding ideal values? [B. L. van der Waerden, *Mathematische Statistik*]

1957 By statistics is almost exclusively understood the collection of numerical data for a not too long period of time, description of "the state characteristics," such as the population, soil composition, etc. The so-called mathematical statistics for about 30 years has been dealing primarily with the description of numerical data through the mean and measure of dispersion, which not once resulted in fruitless arguments whether this index is useful or unfit. [L. Schmetterer, *Grundlagen der matematischen Statistik*]

1957 The mathematical theory of statistics, or mathematical statistics, is a section of the theory of probability. Each problem of mathematical statistics as understood in this book is essentially a problem of probability. . . . Mathematical statistics is a branch of the theory of probability. It deals with problems relating to performance characteristics of rules of inductive behavior based on random experiments. [J. Neyman, *First Course in Probability and Statistics*]

1957 Statistics is a social science dealing with the quantitative aspect of mass social phenomena in close contact with their qualitative aspect, it investigates the quantitative expression of social development regularities in concrete conditions of place and time. . . . Authentic scientific statistics studies the quantitative aspect of social phenomena proceeding from tenets and laws of historic materialism and Marxist-Leninist political economy. It is based on the statements of the Marxist dialectical method of interconditionality and interdependency of events, their continuous development, transition of quantitative changes into qualitative. . . . Bourgeois statistics, like other modern bourgeois sciences, is used to defend capitalist society. The bourgeois statistics at every step distorts the data. [*Bol'shaya Sovietskaya Entsiklopediya*, 2nd edition, vol. 40, A. M. Vostrikova, "Statistics"]

1958 Statistical science allows one to acquire and accumulate knowledge concerning mass, repeated phenomena and processes by way of their current accounting and specially organized observations and surveys [A. M. Dlin, *Matematicheskaya Statistika v Tekhnike* (Mathematical Statistics in Technology)]

1958 The basic concept of mathematical statistics is a sample or a set of observations $x = (x_1, \ldots, x_n)$ of a quantitative index. [Yu. V. Linnik, *Method Naimen'shikh Kvadratov i Osnovy Matematiko-Statisticheskoi Teorii Obrabotki Nabludenii* (Least Squares Methods and Principles of Mathematical-Statistical Theory of Processing Observations)]

1958 Development of methods of registering, describing and analyzing statistical experimental data obtained as a result of observing mass random phenomena forms the subject of a special science—mathematical statistics. [E. S. Ventsel, *Teoriya Veroyatrostei* (Probability Theory)]

1958 Statistics is the branch of scientific method which deals with the data obtained by counting or measuring the properties of populations of natural phenomena. In this definition "natural phenomena" includes all the happenings of the external world, whether human or not. For the avoidance of misunderstandings in the interpretation of this definition one might well point out that "Statistics," the name of the scientific method, is the collective noun and takes the singular. The same word "Statistics" is also applied to the numerical material with which the method operates, and in such a case takes the plural. Later in this book we shall meet the singular form "statistics," which is defined as a function of the observations in a sample from a population [M. G. Kendall and A. Stuart, *Distribution Theory*]

1958 Statistical problems . . . mainly consist in making conclusions on the basis of knowing the properties of a specially selected part of a set of elements about the whole set, as well as in deciding which of the properties under consideration should be transferred to other unknown elements [M. Fisz, *Wahrscheinlichkeitsrechnung und Mathematische Statistik*]

1959 The microworld phenomena themselves are statistical. That is why the role of statistical approach here is considerably deeper than in macrophysics. Here Statistics is necessary not only to work up the measurement results but also to investigate the very nature of phenomena under study. [V. L. Godansky, A. V. Kytsenko, and M. I. Podgoretskii, *Statistics of Reports in Registrating the Nuclear Particles*]

1959 At present the theory of random errors in measurement is a section of another, more extensive science, mathematical statistics which elaborates rational techniques of processing experimental data referring to mass phenomena and reflecting the effect of dispersing random factors. These techniques, essentially connected with the assumption of stability of details and the presence of probabilistic laws of dispersion are called mathematical-statistical methods. [N. V. Smirnov and I. V. Dunin-Barkovskiǐ, *Kratkiǐ Kurs matematicheskoǐ Statistiki dlya Tekhnicheskikh Prilozheniǐ* (A Concise Course of Mathematical Statistics for Engineering Applications)]

1959 In recent years, Statistics has been formulated as the science of decision making under uncertainty. This formulation represents the culmination of many years of development and, for the first time, furnishes a simple and straightforward method of exhibiting the fundamental aspects of a statistical problem. [H. Chernoff and L. E. Moses, *Elementary Decision Theory*]

1959 The "raw material" for statistical investigations is a set of observational data; these data are the values of random variables X, whose distribution P_0 is at least partially unknown. . . . The necessity of statistical analysis arises from the fact that distribution X, and, consequently, certain features of the situation underlying the mathematical model, are unknown [E. L. Lehmann, *Testing Statistical Hypotheses* (retranslated from Russian)]

1960 Yule wrongly treats statistics as a whole as a nonmaterial, but methodological science, as a theory where statistical methods are successively exposed. . . . Mathematical statistics is an independent science. It is not a social science, not a part of socio-economic statistics, but a branch of applied mathematics. All branches of mathematics are similar in the completely abstract ("mathematical") character of their scientific statement. The peculiarity of every branch reflects the peculiarity of the objective properties and traits of a certain sphere of real phenomena. The specific task of mathematical statistics is to obtain summarized abstract-quantitative characteristics of a mass population (universe) without paying attention to the real contents of a phenomenon. For this reason under special conditions, categories and methods of mathematical statistics are applicable to studying mass populations (universes) mainly in nature, and in social life as well, though essentially less. Finding out their applicability is an important and sometimes not too easy task which a statistician has to face. [V. S. Nemchinov, Introduction to the book *Theory of Statistics* by G. Yule and M. G. Kendall]

1961   In statistical procession numbers are the initial point of consideration; however, the object is to cognize certain social phenomena and their regularities. [*Allgemeine Theorie der Statistik*, Autorenkollektiv]

1961   Mathematical statistics deals both with statistical description of experimental and observational results and constructing and testing suitable mathematical models containing the concept of probability. Its methods enlarge the possibilities of scientific prediction and rational decision-making in numerous problems where the essential parameters cannot be known or controlled with sufficient accuracy. [G. Corn and T. Corn, *Handbook of Mathematics for Research Workers and Engineers*]

1961   Statistics studies all the spheres of social life on the basis of Marxism-Leninism, and investigates the problems of a large volume directly or indirectly related to the planning of the national economy. It sets itself tasks proceeding from the laws, regulations and requirements of the party and the government. In this way Marx and Engels became the founders of proletarian statistics which gave impetus to the largely new socialist statistics; today it exists in all the capitalist countries where communist and labour parties are at the head of the struggle of the working class against its exploiters.

The data of proletarian statistics are used in this struggle to strengthen international movement for peace by revealing the maneuvers of imperialists.

Socialist statistics develops everywhere where workers and peasants who govern the state build socialism [A. Kindelberger, *Wie arbeitet die Statistik?*]

1963   Statistics is sometimes defined as the art and science of treating quantitative observations which are subject to variation. [E. V. Lewis, *Statistical Analysis. Ideas and Methods*]

1963   The first task of mathematical statistics consists in indicating methods of collecting and grouping (if the data are numerous) statistical information. The second task of mathematical statistics consists in working out methods of analyzing statistical data according to the goals of the research. . . . Thus, the task of mathematical statistics consists in creating methods of collecting and processing statistical data for obtaining scientific and practical conclusions [E. V. Gmurman, *Vvedenie v Teoriyu Veroyatnosteĭ i Matematicheskuyu Statistiku* (Introduction into Probability Theory and Mathematical Statistics)]

1964   The meaning of this word [statistics] has undergone a great change during the last two centuries. The word "statistics" which is cognate with the word "state," originally denoted the art and science of government: the first professors of statistics at German universities in the Eighteenth Century would today be called political scientists. As governmental decisions are to some extent based on data concerning the population, trade, agriculture and so forth, the statistician naturally became interested in such data, and gradually statistics came to mean the collection of data about the state, and then the collection and handling of data generally. This is still a popular meaning of the word, but a further change is now taking place. There is no point in collecting data unless some use is made of it, and the statistician naturally became involved in the interpretation of the data. The modern statistician is a student of methods for drawing conclusions about a population, on the basis of data that ordinarily is collected from only a sample of the population. [J. L. Hodges, Jr., and E. L. Lehmann, *Basic Concepts of Probability and Statistics*]

1964   As opposed to probability theory, statistics is a branch of applied mathematics. It is characterized mainly by an inductive structure since in this case we go in the opposite direction: from observation to hypothesis. Argumentation is based on the conclusions from probability theory a profound knowledge of which is thus absolutely necessary. [D. Hudson, *Statistics*]

1965   Descriptive statistics is a method of numerical description of numerical aggregates. Actually statistics is a method of quantitative description using numbers as an objective basis. [G. Calot, *Cours de Statistique Descriptive*]

1965   The object of statistics is to analyze social phenomena and to indicate the corresponding conclusions which help to plan and control national economy.

    The generally-accepted nature of statistical indices and methods, as well as of registration principles, are the objective basis of statistical science, statistical theory.

    . . . Statistics as a theoretical subject is part of social sciences since its methods are intended to analyze social and natural phenomena. . . . In theory and practice statistics often resorts to mathematical methods, and especially to mathematical statistics, a branch of mathematics. But, similar to theoretical physics which also intensively borrows its methods from mathematics, it is in no way a mathematical discipline. [*Allgemeine Statistik, Lehrbuch,* Autorenkollektiv]

1965   *Mathematical statistics* is a science dealing with general techniques of processing experimental results. Experiments in various sciences: physics, chemistry, biology, medicine, etc., possess a common property that their results are influenced not only by factors controlled by the experimenter, but also by numerous chance factors. Consequently, the experimental result is usually a chance value. The aim of the researcher is to see behind random fluctuations the causative law. Techniques applied to achieve this goal may be common for various sciences. These techniques are studied by mathematical statistics. [O. V. Manturov, Yu. K. Solntsev, Yu. I. Sorkin, and N. G. Fedin, *Tolkovyĭ Slovar' Matematicheskikh Terminov* (Dictionary of Mathematical Terms)]

1965 Mathematical statistics works out techniques . . . trying to use most exhaustively all the information contained in the limited data at hand [N. V. Smirnov and I. V. Dunin-Barkovskiĭ, *Kurs Teorii Veroyatnosteĭ i Matematicheskoĭ Statistiki* (A Course in Probability Theory and Mathematical Statistics)]

1965 Statistics is often defined as the science of methods for studying regularities of mass phenomena. For mathematical statistics this general definition may be modified as follows: mathematical statistics is a science of methods for deducing the properties of the corresponding universe on the basis of observations over the representative sample, observation data being randomly chosen from the universe.

Thus, the main task of mathematical statistics is the development of methods allowing one to generalize observational results [Z. Palvovskiĭ, *Vvedenie v Matematicheskuyu Statistiku* (Introduction Course of Mathematical Statistics)]

1965 The main approach to statistical inference is inductive reasoning, by which we arrive at "statements of uncertainty." The rigorous expression that degrees of uncertainty require are furnished by the mathematical methods and probability concepts which form the foundations of modern statistical theory [C. R. Rao, *Linear Statistical Inference and Its Applications*]

1967 The object of mathematical statistics includes the study by probability theory methods of mass phenomena in nature, society, and technology, and their scientific foundation [R. Storm, *Wahrscheinlichkeitsrechnung, Mathematische Statistik, Statistische Qualitätskontrolle*]

1967 Probability and statistics are related fields. In problems in probability, we make statements about the chances that various events will take place, based on an assumed model, whereas in problems in statistics we have some observed data and wish to determine a model that can be used to describe the data. [G. J. Hahn and S. S. Shapiro, *Statistical Models in Engineering*]

1968 The methods by which statistical evidence is collected, summarised, and used as the basis for generalization, are known as *statistical methods*, or statistics [D. D. Bugg, M. A. Henderson, K. Holden, and P. J. Lund, *Statistical Methods in the Social Sciences*]

1968 We may say that mathematical statistics is a science of methods for the quantitative analysis of mass phenomena, which at the same time takes into account the quanlitative peculiarity of these phenomena. [B. V. Gnedenko, *Besedy o Matematicheskoĭ Statistike* (Talks about Mathematical Statistics)]

1968 The word "statistics" can be used either in the plural or in the singular. It is used in the plural, according to the dictionary, to mean "numerical facts systematically collected," while the science of statistics (in the singular) is "the science of collecting, classifying and using such facts." Following these definitions, a statistician may be either a collector of statistics (plural) or a more or less expert exponent of the science of statistics (singular), and confusion between these ideas helps to explain the rather unfavourable attitude of the general public towards statisticians. [J. M. Craddock, *Statistics in the Computer Age*]

1968   Statistics is a mathematical theory of how to learn about the world through experience. [W. Thompson, *The Future of Statistics*]

1968   Statistics is in some way a body of knowledge about bodies of knowledge or views and methods of increasing bodies of knowledge. I wonder if, in the strict sense, whether this then is really a science, if a body of knowledge about real phenomena is science, and if it isn't really more a philosophy or an attitude rather than a science itself. [Geisser, ibid.]

1968   A short and crisp definition of statistics which I like is the following: "Statistics deals with the collections and interpretation of data." . . . I would agree to describe statistics as that branch of applied mathematics which is predominatly (though not exclusively) concerned with stochastic phenomena. . . . No statistician, I think, can fail to recognize that he's got to live with the world as it is. . . . What is statistics? There have been many definitions, indeed scholarly articles have carefully collected together hundreds of definitions. I have, myself, contributed more than one. . . . It is an old wheeze that a statistician is a man who draws a straight line from inadequate evidence to a foregone conclusion. . . . A much more adequate definition would be "a statistician is a part of a winding and twisting network connecting mathematics, scientific philosophy, and other intellectual sources — including experimental sampling — to what is done in analyzing data, and sometimes in gathering it" [J. Tukey, ibid.]

1968   What we are concerned with is no less than the scientific investigative method itself — the art of generating and analyzing data so as to arrive at new knowledge. . . . The process of optimizing scientific investigation — I don't know whether that is a science or not, but that's what we are trying to do. . . . I think it was a great mistake to have ever invented the term mathematical statistics. That was a major blunder and has resulted in all kinds of difficulties ever since [G. E. P. Box, ibid.]

1970   Statistics is a science dealing with the quantitative relations of mass social phenomena. Statistics works out the methods of quantitative analysis, which in the aggregate form statistical methodology and are used by other sciences.

In the social sphere, the statistical regularities function as the laws of mass phenomena based on the law of large numbers: definite law-governed quantitative correlations manifest themselves here only in the statistical total combination. [*Philosophic Encyclopedia,* Vol. 5]

1970   *The Law of large Numbers in economic science and social economic statistics.* The law of large numbers creates neither regularities manifesting themselves in average, nor their common average measure for a mass of phenomenon units (for example, the level of labour productivity cost, average norm of profit, the probability of disease, etc.); . . . thus the law of large numbers can neither change the mean level of phenomena, nor make the dynamical number of levels be stable, nor predetermine the measure of deviations from the average level, nor even explain the real reasons for the appearance of the level itself or its deviations. Hence it demonstrates the complete failure of antiscientific attempts of some bourgeois scientists to ascribe to the law of large numbers some miraculous, almost mystic capability of creating regularity out of any random events, chaos, even if there is no inner necessity, inner regularity; if there only exists a "large number" of units, which itself (irrespective of the essence of mass phenomenon) is supposed to cause regularity in it. The law of large numbers does not create regularity, but only governs its manifestation. [*Large Soviet Encyclopedia*, 3rd edition, Vol. 3, F. D. Lifshits, "Large Numbers Law"]

1971   The subject and contents of mathematical statistics consists in developing rational means and methods of observing, compiling and analyzing statistical data. [I. P. Tsaregradskii, *Kurs Lektsii po Teorii Veroyatnostei i Matematicheskoi Statistike* (Lectures on Probability Theory and Mathematical Statistics)]

Appendix 2

List of Pictures Used in the Experiment

1. Josef Istler (a modern painter, Czechoslovakia), "Still-life" (oil, 50 × 116 cm), 1949.
2. Frantisek Foltyn (a modern painter, Czechoslovakia), "Oil" (oil, 89 × 116 cm), 1935–1936.
3. Robert Rauschenberg (b. 1925, USA), "A bed" (construction 188 × 79), 1955.
4. Jan Kotik (a modern painter, Czechoslovakia), "Painting in Space" (acril, canvas, height 57 cm), 1966.
5. Vasily Kandinksy (b. 1866, Moscow–d. 1944, France), "Dark-brown" (83 × 72 cm), 1924.
6. Vasily Kandinsky, "Composition 10" (130 × 195), 1939.
7. Giuseppe Santomaso (b. 1907, Italy), "Vita segreta," 1961.
8. Roberto Matta (b. 1912, Santiago de Chile), A fresco in the building of UNESCO Secretariat in Paris, 1958.
9. Kasimir Malevich (b. 1878, Kiev–d. 1935, Leningrad), "Suprematic composition" (oil, 50 × 44 cm), 1915.
10. Karel Appel (b. 1921, Amsterdam), A fresco in the building of UNESCO Secretariat in Paris, 1958.
11. Willem de Kooning (b. 1904, Rotterdam), "Noon" (oil, canvas), 1947–1948.
12. El Lisitsky (b. 1890, Moscow–d. 1941), "Proun 30-T" (combined technique, 50 × 62 cm), 1920.
13. Antoine Pevsner (b. 1886, Orel–d. 1962, Paris), "Composition" (oil, wood, 53 × 35 cm), 1923.
14. Joan Miro (b. 1893, Barcelona), "Painting" (oil, canvas), 1953.
15. Lucio Fontana (b. 1899, Argentina–d. 1968), "Space concept-waiting" (white canvas), 1959.
16. Auguste Herbin (b. 1882, France), "Summer" (oil, canvas), 1952.
17. Jean Arp (b. 1887, Strasbourg–d. 1966, Basel) "Wooden relief," 1922.
18. Max Bill (b. 1908, Switzerland), "Four rows in a green field" (oil, 80 × 80 cm), 1966–1967.
19. Vaclav Bostik (a modern painter, Czechoslovakia), "Red and green" (oil, canvas, 20 × 16 cm), 1945.

227

References

Abel, R. 1969. Language and the electron. *Akten des XIV International Kongres Philosophie,* Vienna, vol. 3, p. 351.

Achinstein, P. 1968. *Concepts of Science. A Philosophical Analysis.* Johns Hopkins University Press, Baltimore.

Achinstein, P. 1969. *Between Science and Philosophy,* by Smart JJ (book review). *J. Philos.* 66:315–360.

Akhmanova, O. S. 1966. *Slovar' Lingvisticheskikh Terminov.* (Dictionary of Linguistic Terms). Sovetskaya Entsiklopediya, Moscow (in Russian).

Aleksandrova, Z. E. 1971. *Slovar's Sinonimov Russkogo Yazyka* (Dictionary of Russian Synonyms). Sovetskaya Entsiklopediya, Moscow (in Russian).

Anand, B. K., G. S. Chhina, and Baldev Singh. 1963. Some aspects of electroencephalographic studies in yoga, p. 503–506. In: C. Tart (ed.), *Altered States of Consciousness.* John Wiley & Sons, Inc., New York.

Andrukovich, P. F., V. S. Gribkov, V. P. Kozyrev, V. V. Nalimov, and A. T. Terekhin. 1971. Abstract painting as a specific-degenerate-language. A statistical approach to the problem. *Metron* 29(12):3–30.

Arbib, M. A. 1964. *Brains, Machines, and Mathematics.* McGraw-Hill Book Co., New York.

Averintsev, S. S. 1970. Jung, pp. 600–602. In: *Filosofskaya Entsiklopediya,* vol. 5. Sovetskaya Entsiklopediya, Moscow (in Russian).

Bally, C. 1932. *Linguistique Générale et Linguistique Française.* Leroux, Paris.

Bar-Hillel, Y. 1962. Some recent results in theoretical linguistics, pp. 551–557. In.: *Logic, Methodology, and Philosophy of Science, Proceedings of the 1960 International Congress.* Stanford University Press, Palo Alto, Calif.

Barrett, C. 1971. Review of: N. Goodman. *Languages of Art. An Approach to a Theory of Symbols,* 1968. *Br. J. Philos. Sci.* 22(2):187–198.

Bartley, W. W., III. 1973. *Wittgenstein.* J. B. Lippincott Co., Philadelphia.

Baskakov, V. 1971. Complex world and its interpreters. In: *Burzhuaznoye Kino Segodnya: Mify i Real'nost'.* Iskusstvo, Moscow (in Russian).

Baudouin de Courtenay, I. A. 1871. Some general remarks on linguistics and language. In: *Zhurnal Ministerstva Narodnogo Prosveshcheniya.* Golovin, St. Petersburg (in Russian).

Baudouin de Courtenay, I. A. 1907. Language and languages. In: *Entsiklopedicheskii Slovar' Brokhausa i Efrona.* Granat Institute, St. Petersburg (in Russian).

Berkman, R. 1972. Semantics and Zen. *Psychologia* (Kyoto University) 15(3):127–136.

Black, M. 1949. *Language and Philosophy.* Cornell University Press, Ithaca, N.Y.

Black, M. 1962 *Models and Metaphors. Studies in Language and Philosophy.* Cornell University Press, Ithaca, N.Y.

Bloomfield, L. 1926. A set of postulates for the science of language. *Language* 2:153–164.

Bloomfield, L. 1935. *Language.* Henry Holt and Co., New York.

Bohr, N. 1958a. Quantum physics and philosophy, pp. 308–314. In: R. Klibansky (ed.), *Philosophy in the Mid-Century. A Survey.* Klibansky, Florence.

229

Bohr, N. 1958b. *Atomic Physics and Human Knowledge.* John Wiley & Sons, New York.

Bourbaki, N. 1948. L'architecture des mathématiques, pp. 35–47. In: *Les Grands Courants de Pensée Mathématique.* Cahiers du Sud, Paris.

Box, G. E. P. 1966. Use and abuse of regression. *Technometrics* **8**(4):625.

Brhadaranyaka-upanisad. 1931. In: *Twelve Principal Upanisads,* vol. 2. Theosophical Publishing House, Adyar, Madras.

Bucke, R. M. 1923. *Cosmic Consciousness. A Study in the Evolution of the Human Mind.* Dutton & Co., New York.

Budagov, R. A. 1971. *Istoriya Slov v Istorii Obshchestva* (History of Words in History of Society). Prosveshchenie, Moscow (in Russian).

Bühler, K. 1934. *Sprachtheorie.* Frockhaus, Jena.

Capra, F. 1976. Modern physics and Eastern mysticism. *J. Transpersonal Psychol.* **8**(1):20–40.

Carnap, R. 1959. *The Logical Syntax of Language.* Paterson Littlefield, Adams and Co., New York.

Carroll, L. 1930. *Through the Looking-Glass and What Alice Found There.* Macmillan, New York.

Chao Yuan Ren. 1962. Models in linguistics and models in general, pp. 558–566. In: *Logic, Methodology, and Philosophy of Science. Proceedings of the 1960 International Congress.* Stanford University Press, Palo Alto, Calif.

Cherry, C. 1957. *On Human Communication.* MIT Press, Cambridge, Mass.

Chicherin, A. V. 1974. Rhythm and image in narrative prose. In: *Istoriko-filosofskie Issledovaniya (Pamyati Akademika N. I. Konrada).* Nauka, Moscow (in Russian).

Chomsky, N. 1956. Three models for the description of language. *IRE Trans.* **IT-2**(3):113–124.

Chomsky, N. 1968. *Language and Mind.* Harcourt, Brace and World, New York.

Crick, F. H. C. 1962. The genetic code. *Sci. Am.* **207**:66–74.

Danoyan, Yu. B. 1970. On one aspect of scientific information analysis (Contradictions and tautology in the language of psychophysiological problems). *Nauchno-tekhnicheskaya Informatsiya* **2**(1):22.

de Broglie, L. 1960. La langue française comme expression de la pensée scientific. In: *Sur les Sentiers de la Science.* Michel, Paris.

Deikman, A. J. 1963. Experimental meditation, pp. 199–218. In: C. Tart (ed.), *Altered States of Consciousness.* John Wiley & Sons, Inc., New York.

de Saussure, F. 1959. *Course in General Linguistics.* Philosophical Library, New York.

Dhammapada. 1952. Calcutta.

Dishkant, G. P. 1968. *O Formalizatsii Fizicheskikh Teorii* (On Formalization of Physical Theories). Dnepropetrovsk (in Russian).

Doyle, L. B. 1965. Seven ways to inhibit creative research. *Datamation* **11**:2.

Drevnekitaiskaya Filosofiya (Ancient Chinese Philosophy), vol. 1. 1972. Mysl', Moscow (in Russian).

Efraimson, V. 1971. Genealogy of altruism. *Novyi Mir* **10**:193–213 (in Russian).

Einstein, A., and L. Infeld. 1954. *The Evolution of Physics.* Cambridge University Press, New York.

Entwistle, W. J. 1953. *Aspects of Language.* Faber and Faber, London.

Fedorov, N. T. 1939. *Obshchee Tsvetovedenie* (General Course of Color Studying). GONTI, Moscow (in Russian).

Feigenberg, I. M. 1972. *Mozg, Psikhika, Zdorovie* (Brain, Psychic, Health). Meditsina, Moscow (in Russian).

Feyerabend, P. K. 1962. Explanation, reduction, and empiricism. *Minnesota Studies in the Philosophy of Science,* vol. 3. University of Minnesota Press, Minneapolis.

Feyerabend, P. K. 1965. On the "meaning" of scientific terms. *J. Philos.* **62**:266–274.

Filosofskaya Entsiklopediya (Philosophical Encyclopaedia). 1960-1970. Goz. Nauch. Izd., Moscow.

Florenskii, P. A. 1967. Reverse perspective (written in 1919). *Uchyonye Zapiski Tartusskogo Gosudarstvennogo Universiteta. Trudy po znakovym Sistemam,* vol. 3, p. 381.

Fortunatov, F. F. 1897. *Sravnitel'noye Yazykovedenie* (Comparative Linguistics). Lectures, delivered in 1894-1895 academic year. Soviet Academy of Sciences, Moscow (in Russian).

Fromm, E., D. Suzuki, and R. de Martino. 1960. *Zen Buddhism and Psychoanalysis.* Allen and Unwin, London.

Garfield, E. 1970. Citation indexing. Historio-bibliography and the sociology of science, pp. 187-204. In: *Proceedings of the Third International Congress of Medical Libarianship,* 5-9 May 1969. Excerpta Medica, Amsterdam.

Gellner, E. 1959. *Words and Things.* Collancz, London.

Ginsburg, S. 1966. *The Mathematical Theory of Context-Free Languages.* McGraw-Hill Book Co., New York.

Good, I. J. 1962. Subjective probability as the measure of a non-measurable set. In: *Logic, Methodology, and Philosophy of Science, Proceedings of the 1960 International Congress.* Stanford University Press, Palo Alto, Calif.

Goodman, N. 1968. *Languages of Art. An Approach to a Theory of Symbols.* The Bobbs-Merrill Co., New York.

Gorsky, D. P. 1969. From descriptive semiotics to theoretical one. *Voprosy Filosofii* **10:**72-81 (in Russian).

Grigorieva, T. 1971. Reading Kavabata Yasunari. *Inostrannaya Literatura,* vol. 8 (in Russian).

Grimm, J. 1864. Über den Ursprung der Sprache. *Kleinere Schriften,* vol. 1. F. Dumnler, Berlin.

Hadamard, J. 1945. *An Essay on the Psychology of Invention in the Mathematical Field.* Oxford University Press, New York.

Harran, D. 1953. *Communication: A Logical Model.* MIT Press, Cambridge, Mass.

Hartley, D. 1834. *Observations on Man, His Frame, His Duty and His Expectations.* Thomas Tegg and Sons, London.

Heisenberg, W. 1958. *Physics and Philosophy.* Harper and Brothers, New York.

Helvetius, C. A. 1758. *De l'Esprit.* Lepetit, Paris.

Hesse, H. 1961. *Das Glasperlenspiel.* Auflau-Verlag, Berlin.

Heyting, A. 1934. *Mathematische Grundlagenforschung, Intuitionismus. Beweistheories.* Springer, Berlin.

Heyting, A. 1956. *Intuitionism; an Introduction.* North Holland Publishing Co., Amsterdam.

Hjelmslev, L. 1950-1951. Method of structural and linguistic analysis. *Acta Linguistica* (Copenhagen) **6:**2-3 (in Russian).

Hobbes, T. 1658. *Elementorum philosophiae sectio secunda de homine.* A. Crooke, London.

Humboldt, W. 1843. Ueber das vergleichende Sprachstudium in Beziehung auf die verschiedenen Epochen der Sprachentwicklung. *Gesammelte Werke,* vol. 3. Frockhaus, Berlin.

Hutten, E. H. 1956. *The Language of Modern Physics.* Allen and Unwin, London.

Hutten, E. H. 1967. *The Ideas of Physics.* Oliver and Boyd, Edinburgh.

Ivanov, V. V. 1964. Ancient Indian myth of name-making and its parallel in Greek tradition. In: *Indiya v Drevnosti.* Nauka, Moscow (in Russian).

James, W. 1882. On some Hegelisms. *Mind* **7:**186-208.

James, W. 1890. *Principles of Psychology,* 2 volumes. Longmans, Green & Co., London.

James, W. 1902. *The Varieties of Religious Experience.* Longmans, Green and Co., London.

Jung, C. 1930. *Psychologische Typen.* Rascher, Zürich.

Karcevsky, S. 1929. Du dualisme asymétrique du signe linguistique. *Travaux du Cercle Linguistique de Prague,* vol. 1. Prague.

Kasanin, J. (ed.). 1944. *Language and Thought in Schizophrenia.* University of California Press, Berkeley.

Kazamatus, A., and T. Hirai. 1963. An electroencephalographic study of the Zen meditation (Zazen), pp. 489–501. In: C. Tart (ed.), *Altered States of Consciousness.* John Wiley & Sons, New York.

Kendall, M. G. 1966. Statistical influence in the light of the theory of the electronic computer. *Rev. Int. Statistical Inst.* **34**(1):1.

Kiefer, D. 1973. The psychophysiological principle and the Prazna Paramita. *Psychologia* (Kyoto University) **16**(2):110–114.

Klée, P. 1964. *Théorie de l'art Modern.* Editions Gothier, Paris.

Kleene, S. C. 1952. *Introduction to Metamathematics.* North Holland Publishing Co., Amsterdam.

Kobozev, N. I. 1971. *Issledovaniya v Oblasti Termodinamiki Protsessov Informatsii i Myshleniya* (Studies in Thermodynamics of Information and Thinking Processes). Moscow University Press, Moscow (in Russian).

Kolmogorov, A. N. 1956. Probability theory. In: *Matematika: Eyo Soderzhanie, Metody i Znachenie,* vol. 2. The USSR Academy of Sciences, Moscow (in Russian).

Kondakov, N. I. 1971. *Logicheskii Slovar'* (Dictionary of Logic). Nauka, Moscow (in Russian).

Konrad, N. I. 1966. *Zapad i Vostok* (West and East). Nauka, Moscow (in Russian).

Kopnin, P. V. 1971. Philosophical problems of language. In: *Filosofiya i Sovremennost'.* Nauka, Moscow (in Russian).

Kozlova, M. S. 1972. *Filosofiya i Yazyk (Kriticheskii Analiz Nekotorykh Tendentsii Evolutsii Pozitivizma XX Veka)* (Philosophy and Language: A Critical Analysis of Certain Tendencies in the Evolution of the XXth Century Positivism). Mysl', Moscow (in Russian).

Krishnamurti, J. 1970. *The only revolution.* Harper and Row, New York.

Kulikova, I. 1970. Antihumanitarian nature of absurd art, pp. 246–275. In: *Burzhuaznaya Estetika Segodnya.* Nauka, Moscow (in Russian).

Laird, C. 1961. *Thinking about Language.* Holt, Reinhart and Winston, New York.

Lakatos, I. 1963. Proofs and refutations. *Br. J. Philos. Sci.* **14**:1–139.

Langer, S. K. 1951. *Philosophy in a New Key. A Study in the Symbolism of Reason, Rite, and Art.* Harvard University Press, Cambridge, Mass.

Lektorskii, V. A. 1971. Analytical philosophy today. *Voprosy Filosofii* **2**:87–99 (in Russian).

Lem, S. 1971. *Dzienniki Gwiazdowe.* Czytelnik, Warsaw.

Leontiev, V. 1971. Theoretical assumptions and non-observed facts. *Am. Economic Rev.* **61**(1):1–7.

Levinthal, C. 1966. Molecular model-building by computer. *Sci. Am.* **214**:6.

Lévi-Strauss, C. 1964. *Mythologique 1. Le Cru et le Cuit.* Plon, Paris.

Lindsey, P. H., and D. A. Norman. 1972. *Human Information Processing. An Introduction to Psychology.* Academic Press, Inc., New York.

Locke, J. 1665. *An Essay Concerning Human Understanding.* Edinburgh.

Lyons, J. (ed.). 1970. *New Horizons in Linguistics.* Penguin Books, Harmondsworth, Middlesex, England.

MacCormac, E. R. 1971. Meaning, variance, and metaphor. *Br. J. Philos.* **22**(2):145–159.

Mandelshtam, L. I. 1950. *Polnoye Sobranie Sochinenii* (Complete Works), vol. 5. The USSR Academy of Sciences, Moscow (in Russian).

Mandelshtam, O. E. 1921. Word and culture. In: *Al'manakh Tsekha Poetov "Drakon."* Petrograd (in Russian).

Masao Abe. 1969. "Life and Death" and "Good and Evil" in Zen. *Criterion* (Autumn), pp. 7–11.

Mathesius, V. 1942. *Reč a Sloh. Čteni o Jazyke a Poesii.* Prague.

McWilson, R. (ed.). 1963. *New Testament Apocrypha. Gospels and Related Writings,* vol. 1. Lutterworth Press, London.

Mel'chuk, I. A., and R. M. Frumkina. 1966. Cybernetics and some problems of modern linguistics. In: *Kibernetika na Sluzhbu Kommunismu,* vol. 3. Energuiya, Moscow (in Russian).

Meshaninov, I. I. 1940. Introduction to the book *Obshchee Yazykoznanie* (General Linguistics). Uchpedgiz, Moscow (in Russian).

Meyendorf, I. F. 1974. On Byzantine Hesychasm of Eastern Europe in the XIVth century. *Trudy Otdela Drevnerusskoi Literatury,* vol. 29, pp. 291–305. Pushkinskii Dom, Leningrad (in Rusian).

Meyrink, G. 1915. *Der Golem.* Wolff, Munich.

Mikhailov, A. I., A. I. Chyornyi, and R. S. Gilyarevskii. 1968. *Osnovy Informatiki* (Introduction to Information Science). Nauka, Moscow (in Russian).

Miller, G. A. 1951. Speech and language. In: S. S. Stevens (ed.), *Handbook of Experimental Psychology.* John Wiley & Sons, New York.

Mitokhin, L. 1960. James, pp. 470–471. In: *Filosofskaya Entsiklopediya,* vol. 1. Sovetskaya Entsiklopediya, Moscow (in Russian).

Moore, G. E. 1903. *Principia Ethica.* Cambridge University Press, London.

Moore, G. E. 1959. *The Conception of Reality, Philosophical Studies.* Littlefield, Adams and Co., Paterson, N.J.

Morris, C. 1946. *Signs, Language, and Behavior.* Prentice-Hall, New York.

Nabokov, V. 1967. Afterword to the Russian edition of *Lolita,* pp. 296–299. Phaedra Publishers, New York.

Nagel, E., and J. R. Newman. 1960. *Gödel's Proof.* New York University Press.

Nalimov, V. V. 1971. *Teoriya Eksperimenta* (Theory of Experiment). Nauka, Moscow (in Russian).

Nalimov, V. V. 1974. Logical foundations of applied mathematics. *Synthese* 27:211–250.

Nalimov, V. V. 1976. *Yazyk Veroyatnostnykh Predstavlenii* (The Language of Probabilistic Concepts). Nauchnyi Sovet po Kibernetike, Moscow (in Russian).

Nalimov, V. V. 1978. *Nepreryvnost' Protiv Diskretnosti v Yazyke i Myshlenii* (Language and Thinking: Discontinuity Versus Continuity) (in Russian).

Nalimov, V. V., and Z. B. Barinova. 1974. *Sketches on the History of Cybernetics. Predecessors of Cybernetics in Ancient India.* Darshana International (April).

Nalimov, V. V., and Z. M. Mul'chenko. 1969. *Naukometriya* (Scientometrics). Nauka, Moscow.

Nalimov, V. V., and Z. M. Mul'chenko. 1972. On logico-linguistic analysis of the language of science, pp. 534–554. In: *Problemy Strukturnoi Lingvistiki, 1971.* Nauka, Moscow (in Russian).

Nemirovskaya, Ye. M. 1972. The theory of presentative symbolism (to the critical analysis of the semantic conception of art by S. Langer). *Voprosy Filosofii* 7:119–127.

Nida, E. A. 1965. *Morphology, the Descriptive Analysis of Words.* University of Michigan Press, Ann Arbor.

Oldenberg, H. 1881. *Buddha, sein Leben, seine Lehre, seine Gemeinde.* Hertz, Berlin.

Panchenko, A. I. 1975. *Kontinuum i Fizika* (Continuum and Physics). Nauka, Moscow (in Russian).

Paul, G. A. 1956. G. E. Moore, Analysis, common usage, and common sense, pp. 56–69. In: A. S. Ayer (ed.), *The Revolution in Philosophy.* Macmillan, London.

Paul, H. 1937. *Prinzipien der Sprachgesichte,* 5th ed. Halle.

Pears, D. F. 1956. Logical atomism: Russell and Wittgenstein, pp. 41–55. In: *The Revolution in Philosophy.* Macmillan, London.

Phillips, D. C. 1966. The three-dimensional structure of an enzyme molecule. *Sci. Am.* **215**(5):78.

Plato. 1953. Cratylus. In: *The Dialogues of Plato,* vol. 3. Clarendon Press, Oxford.

Podgoretskii, M. I., and Ya. L. Smorodinskii. 1969. On axiomatic structure of constructing physical theories. In: *Voprosy Teorii Poznaniya. Materialy v Pomoshch Filosofskim Seminaram.* Tchapchinkova, Moscow (in Russian).

Pole, D. 1958. *The Later Philosophy of Wittgenstein.* University of London, London.

Polya, G. 1954. *Mathematics and Plausible Reasoning.* Princeton University Press, Princeton, N.J.

Pomerants, G. S. 1965. Krishnamurti and the problem of religious nihilism. In: *Ideologicheskie Techeniya v Sovremennoi Indii.* Nauka, Moscow (in Russian).

Pomerants, G. S. 1968. *Nekotorye Techeniya Vostochnogo Religuioznogo Nigilisma* (Certain Trends of Eastern Religious Nihilism). Synopsis of candidate's thesis. Institute of Asia of the USSR Academy of Sciences, Moscow.

Pomerants, G. S. 1974. Iconological thinking as a system and dialogue of semiotic systems. In: *Istoriko-Filosofskie Issledovaniya, Pamyati Akademika N. I. Konrada.* Nauka, Moscow (in Russian).

Popovich, M. V. 1966. *O Filosofskom Analize Yazyka Nauki* (On Philosophical Analysis of the Language of Science). Naukova Dumka, Kiev (in Russian).

Popper, K. R. 1962. *Conjectures and Refutations. The Growth of Scientific Knowledge.* Basic Books, New York.

Popper, K. R. 1965. *The Logic of Scientific Discovery.* Hutchinson, London.

Potebnya, A. A. 1926. Thought and language. In: *Polnoye Sobranie Sochinenii* (Complete Works), 5th ed., vol. 1. Gosudarstvennoe Izdatelstvo Ukrainy, Khar'kov.

Preobrazhenskaya, G. B., N. M. Prutkova and Yu. V. Granovsky. 1974. Analysis of statistical terms in publications on spectral analysis and analytical chemistry. *Ind. Lab. (USSR)* **40**(10):1240–1244.

Printsip Dopolnitel'nosti i Materialisticheskaya Dialektika (The Principle of Complementarity and Materialistic Dialectics). 1976. Obninsky Gorkom KPSS, Obninsk (in Russian).

Pye, M., and R. Morgan (ed.). 1973. *The Cardinal Meaning. Essays in Comparative Hermeneustics. Buddhism and Christianity.* Mouton, The Hague.

Quastler, H. 1964. *The Emergence of Biological Organization.* Oxford University Press, Oxford.

Quinton, A. M. 1966. Excerpt from "Contemporary British Philosophy." In: *Wittgenstein. The Philosophical Investigations.* Doubleday, Garden City, N.Y.

Radhakrishnan, S. 1948. *Indian Philosophy,* vol. 1 and 2. Allen and Unwin, London.

Rankine, J. 1968. The consequences of literacy. In: J. Goody and J. Wart (ed.), *Literacy in Traditional Societies.* Cambridge University Press, London.

Reich, C. A. 1970. *The Greening of America.* Random Books, New York.

Rhys-Davids, T. W. 1880. *Buddhism: Being a Sketch of the Life and Teaching of Gautama, the Buddha.* Society for Promoting Christian Knowledge, London.

Russell, B. 1921. *Analysis of Mind.* Allen and Unwin, London; Macmillan, New York.

Russell, B. 1948. *Human Knowledge. Its Scope and Limits.* Simon & Schuster, New York.

Ryle, G. 1956. Introduction, pp. 1–11. In: *The Revolution in Philosophy.* Macmillan, London.

Sankoff, D. 1969. Simulation of word-meaning stochastic processes, *Introductory Conference on Computational Linguistics,* Stockholm, September, Preprint No. 49.

Sapir, E. 1921. *Language.* Harcourt Brace Jovanovich, New York.

Sapir, E. 1933. Language, pp. 155–168. In: *Encyclopaedia of the Social Sciences,* vol. 9. Harcourt Brace Jovanovich, New York.

Schleicher, A. 1869. *Die Deutsche Sprache.* Z. Verbesserte und Vermehrte Auflage, Stutgart.

Schopenhauer, A. 1862. *Parerga und Paralipomena,* vol. 1 and 2. Berlin.

Schwartz, J. 1962. The pernicious influence of mathematics on science, pp. 356–360. In: *Logic, Methodology, and Philosophy of Science, Proceedings of the 1960 International Congress.* Stanford University Press, Palo Alto, Calif.

Schweitzer, A. 1960. *Kultur und Ethik.* C. H. Beck'sche Verlagsbuchhandlung, Munich.

Shannon, C. 1956. The bandwagon. *IRE Trans.* **IT-2**(1):3.

Shaumyan, S. K. 1971. *Filosofskie Voprosy Teoreticheskoi Lingvistiki* (Philosophical Problems of Theoretical Linguistics). Nauka, Moscow (in Russian).

Shreider, Yu. A. 1966. On definition of the basic concepts of semiotics. In: *Kibernetiku na Sluzhbu Kommunizmu,* vol. 3. Energuiya, Moscow (in Russian).

Shreider, Yu. A. 1969. Science: a source for knowledge and superstitions. *Novyi Mir* 10:207–226.

Shreider, Yu. A. 1971. *O Ponyatii "Matematicheskaya Model' Yazyka"* (On the Concept of "Mathematical Model of Language"). Znanie, Moscow (in Russian).

Shvyryov, V. S. 1966. *Neopozitivizm i Problemy Empiricheskogo Obosnovaniya Nauki* (Neopositivism and the Problem of Empirical Foundations of Science). Nauka, Moscow (in Russian).

Sinaiko, H. W. 1971. Translation by computer. *Science* **174**:1182.

Sivananda, Swami. 1967. *Sadhana; a textbook of the psychology and practice of techniques to spiritual perfection.* Divine Life Society, Sivanandanagar.

Skalička, V. 1948. Kadansky Structuralismus a "Prazska Skola." *Slovo a Slovesnost* **10**:3.

Slavnyi, V. A. 1969. Quantitative criteria of precision and sensitivity and the possibility of consideration of prior information in substance analysis. *Ind. Lab. (USSR)* **35**:7.

Smirnova, Ye. D., and P. V. Tavanets. 1967. Semantics in logic. In: *Logicheskaya Semantika i Modal'naya Logika.* Nauka, Moscow (in Russian).

Sobolev, R. 1971. Underground cinema and Hollywood. In: *Burzhuaznoye Kino Segodnya: Mify i Real'nost'.* Iskusstvo, Moscow (in Russian).

Spirin, A. S., and L. P. Gavrilova. 1971. *Ribosoma.* Nauka, Moscow (in Russian).

Stassen, M. 1973. *Heidegger's Philosophie der Sprache in "Sein und Zeit" und ihre philosophisch-theologischen Wurzeln.* Bouvier Verb (Grundmann), Bonn.

Steintahl, H. 1855. *Grammatik, Logik und Psychologie. Ihre Prinzipien und ihr Verhältnis zu einander.* F. Dummlers Verlagsbuchhaus, Berlin.

Stepanov, Yu. S. 1971. *Semiotika.* Nauka, Moscow (in Russian).

Strawson, P. W. 1956. Construction and analysis, pp. 97–110. In: *The Revolution in Philosophy.* Macmillan, London.

Tart, C. (ed.). 1963a. *Altered States of Consciousness. A Book of Readings.* John Wiley & Sons, Inc., New York.

Tart, C. 1963b. Psychedelic experiences associated with a novel hypnotic procedure, mutual hypnosis, pp. 291–308. In: C. Tart (ed.), *Altered States of Consciousness.* John Wiley & Sons, Inc., New York.

Tavanets, P. V. 1972. *Logika i Empiricheskoye Poznanie* (Logic and Empirical Cognition). Nauka, Moscow (in Russian).

Theses of the Prague Circle of Linguistics. 1929. Prague.

Tolstoy, L. N. 1905. *Mysli Mudrykh Ludei na Kazhdyi Den'* (Thoughts of Wise People for Every Day). Moscow.

Toporov, V. N. 1960. Dhammapada and Buddhist Literature. In: *Dhammapada.* IVL, Moscow (in Russian).

Toporov, V. N. 1965. Notes on Buddhist fine arts in connection with the problem of semiotics of cosmological concepts. In: *Uchyonye zapiski Tartusskogo Gosudarstvennogo universiteta. Trudy po Zvakowym Sistemam,* vyp. 181, 2, Tartu.

Upanishads. 1965. Translated by Max Müller. Patha, Varanasi, Delhi.

Vendler, Z. 1968. *Linguistics in Philosophy.* Cornell University Press, Ithaca, N.Y.

Volkonsky, S. 1913. *Vyrazitel'noye Slovo. Opyt Issledovaniya i Rukovodstva v Oblasti*

Mekhaniki, Psikhologii, Filosofii i Estetiki Rechi v Zhizni i na Stsene (An Expressive Word. A Study and Guide in Speech Mechanics, Psychology, Philosophy, and Aesthetics in Life and on the Stage). St. Petersburg.

Voloshinov, V. N. 1929. *Marksizm i Filosofiya Yazyka* (Marxism and Philosophy of Language). Leningrad.

von Wright, G. H. 1962. Remarks on the epistemology of subjective probability, pp. 330–339. In: *Logic, Methodology, and Philosophy of Science, Proceedings of the 1960 International Congress,* Stanford University Press, Palo Alto, Calif.

Vorobiev, G. G. 1971. *Informatsionnaya Kul'tura Upravlencheskogo Truda* (Informational Culture of Managerial Work). Ekonomika, Moscow (in Russian).

Wang, H. 1961. Process and existence in mathematics. In: Y. Bar-Hillel, E. I. J. Pozanski, M. D. Rabin, and A. Robinson (eds.), *Essays on the Foundations of Mathematics,* Magnes Press, Jerusalem.

Warnock, G. J. 1956. Analysis and imagination, pp. 111–126. In: *The Revolution in Philosophy.* Macmillan, London.

Webster, N. 1942. *Webster's Dictionary of Synonyms.* Merriam, Springfield, Mass.

Wells, R. 1947. De Saussure's system of linguistics. *Word* 3:1–31.

Weyl, H. 1927. *Philosophie der Mathematik und Naturwissenschaft.* Oldenbourg, Munich.

Whorf, B. L. 1956. Science and linguistics. In: *Language, Thought, and Reality.* Chapman and Hall, London.

Wiener, N. 1954. *The Human Use of Human Beings: Cybernetics and Society.* Houghton-Mifflin Co., Boston.

Willman-Grabovska, H. 1934. Evolution semantique du mot "dherma." *Rocznik Orjentalistyczny,* vol. 10.

Winkler, R. L. 1967. The quantification of judgement: some methodological suggestion. *J. Am. Stat. Assoc.* 62(320):1105.

Wittgenstein, L. 1953. *Philosophical Investigations.* Basil Blackwell, Oxford.

Wittgenstein, L. 1955. *Tractatus Logico-Philosophicus.* Routledge & Keegan Paul, London.

Yčas, M. 1969. *The Biological Code.* John Wiley & Sons, Inc., New York.

Youngblood, G. 1970. *Expanded Cinema.* Dutton, New York.

Yule, G. U., and M. G. Kendall. 1950. *An Introduction to the Theory of Statistics,* 14th ed. C. Griffin, London.

Zadeh, L. A. 1971. Quantitative fuzzy semantics. *Information Science* 3(2):159.

Zaripov, R. Kh. 1971. *Kibernetika i Muzyka* (Cybernetics and Music). Nauka, Moscow (in Russian).

Zavadskaya, Ye. B. 1970. *Vostok na Zapade* (East in the West). Nauka, Moscow (in Rusian).

Zhegin, L. F. 1970. *Yazyk Zhivopisnogo Proizvedeniya (Uslovnost' Drevnego Iskusstva)* (Language of Painting: Conventional Character of Ancient Art). Iskusstvo, Moscow.

Ziff, P. 1964. *Semantic Analysis.* Cornell University Press, Ithaca, N.Y.

Zvonkin, A. K., and L. A. Levin. 1970. Complexity of finite objects and foundation of the notions of information and randomness by means of algorithm theory. *Usp. Mat. Nauk* 25:6.

Index of Names

Index of Subjects